dispatches from the

Former
Evil Empire

foreword by Walter Cronkite

dispatches from the

Former
Evil Empire

Richard Threlkeld
former cbs news correspondent

preface by **Betsy Aaron**
former cnn news correspondent

Prometheus Books
59 John Glenn Drive
Amherst, New York 14228-2197

Published 2001 by Prometheus Books

Inquiries should be addressed to
Prometheus Books
59 John Glenn Drive
Amherst, New York 14228–2197
VOICE: 716–691–0133, ext. 207
FAX: 716–564–2711
WWW.PROMETHEUSBOOKS.COM

05 04 03 02 01   5 4 3 2 1

Library of Congress Cataloging-in-Publication Data

Threlkeld, Richard.
   Dispatches from the former evil empire / Richard Threlkeld ; foreword by Walter Cronkite ; preface by Betsy Aaron.
       p. cm.
   Includes index.
   ISBN 1–57392–904–2
   1. Russia (Federation)—Politics and government—1991- I. Cronkite, Walter. II. Aaron, Betsy. III. Title.

DK510.763 .T49 2000
947.086—dc21   00–045919

Printed in the United States of America on acid-free paper

Contents

Foreword

by Walter Cronkite

L et me tell you a story about Sad Sam. Sad Sam is not a person, it's a place. It's a block of Stalinist-style offices and apartments along the Garden Ring, one of the main thoroughfares in Moscow. That particular section of the Garden Ring has a tongue-tying Russian name which the English-speaking inhabitants of the neighborhood long ago shortened to "Sad Sam." And there have been many English-speakers and other foreigners who've made Sad Sam their home over the years. When Russia was the Soviet Union, foreigners were tolerated but suspect, and required to live and work in special foreigners' compounds like Sad Sam, where they could be carefully watched.

Sad Sam has been home to the CBS News Moscow bureau for almost half a century. When American news organizations were first allowed to open offices in Moscow after World War Two, CBS News was assigned to Sad Sam, along with the *New York Times* and others. But even before that, CBS News had a presence in Russia. Correspondent Larry LeSeur opened up our first Moscow office the hard way. He traveled with the Red Army, covering the combat and reporting it to CBS radio listeners, as Hitler's legions were driven back from Moscow's gates in 1941. For a while during the war, CBS also depended on the services of the *Times*'s Walter Kerr, later to become its distinguished drama critic.

Even as long ago as that, it was easy to see that the Soviet Union would loom large indeed in the history of the rest of this century, so over the years CBS News sent some of its very best to Moscow to report that story. Richard C. Hottelet was on hand to cover the beginnings of the Cold War and Stalin's last years. Daniel Schorr was in Moscow to report on the rise of Nikita Krushchev. Marvin Kalb was there to tell the story of Krushchev's fall. Twice, in 1947 and 1971, when the Cold War turned truly chilly, Soviet authorities closed the CBS News bureau. But by the time Mikhail Gorbachev came to power in the 1980s, CBS News was back in Sad Sam once again. Barry Petersen and Anthony Mason were there to report the demise of the Soviet Union and the triumph of Boris Yeltsin.

The fact that CBS News has put so much time, talent, money, and persistence into maintaining its window in Moscow all these decades is an indication of just how important Russia remains in world affairs. For an American journalist, Moscow has always been a wonderful story and a fascinating beat. Most of us, myself included, did our Moscow duty early in our careers.

Dick Threlkeld is an exception. He moved into Sad Sam in 1996, after nearly thirty years as a CBS News correspondent. He'd covered the Vietnam War, the Vatican from Rome, the conflicts in Central America, and the liberation of Kuwait during Desert Storm. Over the years he'd already made many trips to the then-Soviet Union and its satellites, before covering the fall of the Soviet Union and the collapse of the Iron Curtain.

Dick brought all of that experience and perspective, not to mention a lively sense of humor, to his time as CBS News's Moscow correspondent, as you'll see in the pages that follow. The tumultuous events he describes in the recent Russian past are the prologue to the Russia you are watching and reading about today.

Preface

by Betsy Aaron

D ick and I had been trying to get to Moscow since the spring of 1990, ever since the wall around Eastern Europe had cracked and shattered and had finally come tumbling down in Berlin and in Czechoslovakia. Ever since Romania revealed its "new" Communist approach to governing, a controlled form of chaos. Ever since the union of Soviet states dissolved into Russia and the rest.

We grew up in the world of the Iron Curtain. Good versus Bad guys. Us versus Them. Duck-and-cover exercises in classrooms. The threat of the Bomb. Both of us had spent time in the Soviet Union for ABC News. Dick always said we went together. We did. But he was working in Moscow and Leningrad, while I was in Siberia and Ukraine. Some "together"! We were nine time zones apart. Our KGB minders never let us forget where we were. Everything we'd been brought up to believe about the so-called Evil Empire seemed to be true, although we soon realized it was certainly not the people, just the system.

So now, in 1990, the thought of living in the seat of Communist power, even though greatly diminished, was a journalistic challenge we wanted. "Desperately" wanted might be too strong a phrase. But the opportunity to see firsthand how the world was changing, and to try to figure out what it would all mean, and all of that on someone else's dollar, was a really intense dream for both of us.

CBS News thought it might be a good idea to send us both to the

Moscow bureau. So we began Russian lessons, we rented our apartment, we sold the car, we packed up and picked up our airline tickets. And then, two weeks before takeoff, CBS News pulled the plug. Management decided that sending two correspondents to one post was too expensive. As they say in Russian, it was a "kashmar," a nightmare.

We rented another apartment for our tenant so that we'd have a place to live. We bought a car. We unpacked and got on with life again in New York. We went overseas in 1991 to cover the Gulf War. Dick was in Saudi Arabia and Kuwait. "The wife" was in Baghdad. This time he didn't have the nerve to say, although we were covering the same story, that we were "together."

And then one day in 1996, CBS asked Dick to go to Moscow. "Why not?" we said. With one proviso. I'd left CBS and needed to find work. The stories of what happened to unemployed wives in Russia was not a pretty one. Fragile marriages easily broke apart. Good marriages were put to a test not easily understood, unless you lived there. So I signed on to work in Moscow for CNN International.

Dick went over first, and found us an apartment overlooking the Russian White House. It wasn't easy. Nice apartments were at a premium. In desperation he took a two-bedroom, one- bath "palace." It cost CBS News $6,000 a month rent. At first sight, that "palace" brought tears to my eyes. No joy, just tears. It was a wreck! How were we going to turn this place into a home? Still, once you got past the sometimes dark and always dingy, dirty, and dank lobby, it had possibilities. At least that must have been what the real-estate agent told Dick. Eventually, we made it livable.

Most foreign journalists lived in compounds for foreigners. We didn't. And that meant we got to see a little more of what daily life was like for Muscovites, albeit upper-class Muscovites. On the morning after our first night in the apartment, we discovered Dick's car had been stolen. We would soon come to learn that was normal. Dick's office gave him an old car, like mine from CNN. No self-respecting Moscow car thief would be caught dead driving what we were driving.

For the next two years we tried to get a handle on what was happening in Russia, in the rebellious and not-so-rebellious republics and other parts of the former Soviet Union. Much of the time these were exercises in frustration. The Russians were fascinating and exasperating, open and devious, contradictory and maddeningly difficult all at once. Russia was a giant place with giant problems and a giant potential for both good and evil.

Russia's latter-day revolution had ended by the time we got there, and the economic and social disintegration that unfolded before us was often difficult to fit into a television piece. Important, yes, but difficult. The U.S. government was interested in Russia, of course, but average Americans, for the most part, were not.

That's when Dick began this book. It's a sort of diary of what he couldn't fit into his television reports. I think it has been a kind of therapy, an unleashing of his frustrations over being unable to explain to those average Americans why we should care about the Russian people and the place, to explain why Russia and Russians are so important to Americans and the rest of the world, and not just because of the thousands of bombs in Russia's nuclear arsenal.

The best part of this book for me is to once again discover what a wonderful journalist and what a wonderful writer he is. The stories were no surprise. After all, we talked, we argued, we edited each other's work. And yet, I see even more of what we lived through on these pages than I'd realized.

Our good marriage is even better now. And I have Russia and the Russians to thank for that. And, of course, Dick.

Introduction

I think the moment I began **to grow fond of the Russians** was the first time I saw them with their kids. It was a sunny Sunday morning in January in the mid-1980s, when Russia was still the Soviet Union. We were out taking TV news pictures in a park along the Leningrad canals.

The park was alive with children and their parents at play in the snow; sledding, skating, throwing snowballs, building snow forts, having a hilarious time. This was not the sort of behavior you'd expect from the inhabitants of an Evil Empire, I decided. President Ronald Reagan first hung that label, the Evil Empire, on the Soviet Union in a controversial speech to some Christian conservatives. At the time, Soviet officials, and some liberals in America, were outraged. But there was a good deal of evil in the Soviet system; political repression and an economic arrangement that took from the many for the enrichment of a few.

And it was an empire that stretched from just west of Tokyo all the way to Berlin, if you counted the Soviets' Eastern European bloc satellites. For almost half a century, the Evil Empire and the Free World scared the stuffing out of each other.

I stood at the Berlin Wall the day Ronald Reagan demanded, "Mr. Gorbachev, tear down this wall!" Within a matter of months, the leaders of the Evil Empire allowed the wall to be dismantled by the very inhabitants it had contained, permitted the unification of Germany, and stood aside while the empire evaporated. And finally, despite Mikhail Gorbachev's best efforts, the Soviet Union itself evaporated, Communism collapsed, and with the emergence of an energetic new reformer in Moscow, Boris Yeltsin, the transformation to a democratic, capitalist Russia began. The Americans, in short, got exactly what they'd demanded of Moscow. Not a shot was fired.

The children who were frolicking with their parents that snowy Sunday in Leningrad are now adults. And you'll pardon them if they're a bit bewildered. Leningrad is now St. Petersburg. Their old Soviet Union is now something called the Russian Federation, little more than half the size it once was.

And as I write, the decrepit remains of what once was the vaunted Soviet military is once again mired in the midst of the Caucasus, trying to keep little Chechnya from opting out. Americans can scarcely imagine waking up one morning to find everything west of Kansas City and north of Phoenix suddenly become a collection of independent countries, and the Dakotas battling the U.S. Army for their freedom.

Moreover, the great expectations those same Leningrad youngsters might have held for the promise and prosperity of free-market democracy have been dashed. The arrangement in the new system of robber-baron capitalism is the same as the old. It takes from the many for the enrichment of a few. And by any economic measure, Russians are living a far more meager existence now than in late Soviet times.

If they've opted out of politics, who can blame today's Russians? Most of their politicians are venal and corrupt former Communists and ex-Soviet bureaucrats. Their ex-president, the once-dynamic Boris Yeltsin, who spent his final years in office as a ghostlike figure, constantly bedridden, is now history. His handpicked successor is a career secret policeman.

This next generation of Russians will have to make its way in a nation that's basically broke, without a legal system worthy of the name, without a functioning judicial system or tax code, with most of the means of production in the hands of a few robber barons in cozy alliance with the Russian mafia, and who own most of the media to boot. And finally, the Russian economy's just beginning to emerge from a financial meltdown that makes the Wall Street crash in 1929 look, in comparison, like a hiccup.

In sum, it looks as if the Russians have their detractors right where they want them. Few peoples in the past millennium have had such bitter experience with hard times. Russians are survivors who've had to triumph over everything from the Black Death to Bolshevism. They're every bit as experienced as the British in "muddling through." And I've no doubt that, given time, this new experiment forced on this new generation of Russians will succeed.

I'm convinced of this because I was blessed with an extraordinary opportunity to see it all for myself. With my wife, Betsy Aaron, a correspondent for CNN, I was posted by CBS News to Moscow in 1996. For the better part of two-and-a-half years, from the runup to President Yeltsin's reelection, through the Russian economic crash of late 1998, Betsy and I were eyewitnesses to the human, everyday consequences of this new Russian revolution; often painful, sometimes poignant, but always fascinating.

Now and then I'd do some traveling, to see how things were going in far-flung parts of what used to be the Evil Empire. The boomtown that's Baku, in independent Azerbaijan. And the Cuba grimly clinging to Communism and Fidelismo.

But it was the sights and sounds of Russia that attracted me most; the foggy mornings in Vladivostok, the coal dust on the snowbanks of the Kuzbass, the brilliant lights of the fancy casinos in the evening along the Garden Ring in Moscow.

That, and the Russians themselves; funny and sad and stoic and angry and ambitious and lazy and gracious and rude all at once. They defy you to understand them. I count many of them as friends and I like to think I've become a friend of Russia, too.

This book is a product of that friendship. During my tour in Moscow, I developed the habit of putting what I was seeing and hearing every day, along with some thoughts and impressions, into my computer. Sometimes, along with some TV pictures, they wound up on one or another of the CBS News television broadcasts. Sometimes a smidgeon or two became a CBS radio spot. More often, it was just for the record. My own record. When my time in Moscow was up and I looked into my computer, what I found was what follows. It's my decidedly mixed reaction to the former Evil Empire. Like any true friend, I've tried to point out the failings I observed, along with some virtues. At heart, though, it's a valentine.

I'm most grateful to Betsy for her love, encouragement, and perceptive suggestions. I'm equally grateful to our colleague, Jonathan Sanders, for correcting me where I had gone wrong and for his photographs, so many of which complement the text. Jonathan and Mary Sanders were our friends and neighbors in Moscow. They were also our mentors. From them we learned to stop, look, and listen. Thanks also to my colleague William Gasperini for contributing his splendid photographs.

You've got to cut the Russians some slack, it seems to me. They are, after all, a much put-upon people. Put upon, at various times, by the Swedes, the Mongols, the French, the Germans (a couple of times), the Bolsheviks, and most recently, by some well-meaning economists from Harvard.

Attention must be paid to Russia, even though it's not the Evil Empire anymore. There are, by the best estimates, twenty-four thousand nuclear weapons currently stored in the Russian arsenal, more than enough to destroy most of civilization several times over. So far as we know, the Russian government is keeping them in good repair and keeping track of them. Why bother about Russia? There are twenty-four thousand reasons why.

chapter 1

The Wild East

(June 1996)

I t's a long way to Vladivostok. From Moscow it's seven time zones and about four thousand miles. It's not so far from America; about nine hours as the jet flies. And there is a jet, an MD-80, Alaska Airlines Flight 103, that makes the trip from Anchorage a couple of times a week. In Moscow, there's a perennial Russian presidential candidate, Vladimir Zhirinovsky, who promises that if he's elected, he'll make Washington give Alaska back to Russia. Never mind, Vladimir. Alaska's already back. Alaska Airlines now flies to four Siberian cities.

This flight's about half-full. There are some businessmen, Russian and American. A couple of oil workers from Texas or Oklahoma, judging by their drawl. A Russian family, expensively dressed, coming back from an Alaska holiday. And a smattering of tourists. Plus Betsy and me, off to the hustings to see how the Russian presidential campaign's going in what the Russians call their Wild East.

For Alaska Airlines, adding Russia to the schedule has been something of an adventure. The usual fuel stop is the Russian island of Anadyr, just past the Aleutians. Not anymore, says the flight attendant. Last week when they pulled in, the Russian military commander at the airport parked a tank in front of the jet and wouldn't refuel it until the crew agreed to increase his "landing fee" by five thousand dollars cash on the spot. Western academics are always writing about the advent of "new regionalism" in Russia. Maybe that's what they mean.

So now the stop is Petropavlosk on the Kamchatka peninsula, five hours from Anchorage. You can see why they call this wildly beautiful piece of the top of the world, from Japan to America's Pacific Northwest, the "Ring of Fire." Petropavlosk nestles between two snowcapped volcanoes, Koryaski and Avacha. Today, Avacha is smoking.

Before we take off, there's some business to be done. A military jeep pulls up, and a squad of men in combat gear emerges, armed with assault rifles. A couple of canvas bags come off the plane, filled with what the flight crew confides is two million dollars. The money, the guards, and the jeep disappear. Money for whom? And for what? And whatever happened to wire transfers?

Betsy chats with one of the guards, who speaks a little English. She gives him a copy of the magazine *Mirabella* she's been thumbing through since Anchorage. He gives her some military insignias from his uniform. "Is this a good time to be young in this country?" she asks. "We'll see after the election," he says carefully.

It's another three-and-a-half hours to Vladivostok. We land a couple of hours late, just at dusk. The airport is a carbon copy of most every Russian airport except Moscow's. It's mostly military. Tattered buildings with holes in the roof and holes in the windows. Grass sprouts on the runways. Old warplanes are still parked where somebody walked off and left them long ago.

The customs and immigration building is in the same state of disrepair. The immigration booths are done in the old forbidding style of the Soviet days. But instead of the hammer and sickle painted on the front, there's the handsome double eagle of pre-Bolshevik Russia. Time was when the formalities were lengthy and full of stern questions and suspicious stares. Now they are quick, courteous, and apparently efficient. Somebody has observed that Vladivostok looks like San Francisco would look if the Communists had got hold of it. It's a beautiful natural setting, a panorama of hills and islands across Golden Horn Bay. The city itself is a dump.

One summer day in 1860, while Abraham Lincoln was campaigning for president far away in America, a Russian warship sailed into this bay and claimed this place for the tsar. It was probably just as gray and foggy then as it is right now. A lot of history has transpired since.

While the Communists were taking over Moscow and Petrograd in 1918, the Western powers, scared to death of all that Bolshevik talk about world revolution, sent an expeditionary force to Vladivostok to help out the anti-Bolshevik "Whites" against the "Reds." For a couple of years, Americans and Canadians, French, English, Italian, and

Japanese boys fought Russian boys all around here. Eventually the allies gave up and went home. Then the Czech Legion, which was just trying to find a way to get back to Prague, took over the Trans-Siberian railway, rode it to Vladivostok, and proclaimed an independent non-Communist Siberian Republic. Until, in 1922, the Bolsheviks triumphed, and that was the end of the Siberian Republic. And the end of the Czech Legion, too.

In the 1930s Stalin removed, by one means or another, most of the large population of foreigners in Vladivostok and made it a way station for prisoners en route to his Siberian gulags.

In the 1940s, two-thirds of Allied Lend-Lease aid to the Soviet Union for the war against Hitler came through here. Not far from downtown, there's a memorial to the thirty thousand lives lost in Vladivostok during the fighting.

Eventually, Vladivostok became the headquarters of the Soviet Pacific Fleet and was closed not only to foreigners but even to Russians until 1992, unless they had Moscow's permission to be here. Perhaps because Vladivostok's only a few miles from China and North Korea, and the Russians have always been paranoid about both of them, you have to look pretty hard to find a Russian face here that doesn't look like its owner was sent here a long time ago from Pskov or Yaroslavl or someplace safely European. And you have to look even harder to find a smiling face.

On the evidence, it's hard to imagine why the Soviets wanted to keep Vladivostok a secret, unless they were simply embarrassed. Most of the once-mighty fleet is anchored in the harbor, mothballed or just rusting away. The government can't afford the upkeep these days.

San Francisco is all pastel and fog. Vladivostok is dirty, gray, and smoggy. If the city were for sale, it would be advertised as a fixer-upper. What public buildings and apartments there are were built after World War Two by Japanese prisoners of war. And it looks as if nobody's touched them since.

There is some desultory construction going on. The South Koreans are putting up a small office building. And they're working on what's supposed to become the city's first twenty-four-hour supermarket. The only sign that Japan is just over the horizon is the occasional Toyota Land Cruiser, packed with beefy Russian men in crewcuts and leather jackets. They don't look like they are joyriding.

Saturday night we're entertaining ourselves at the Hotel Versailles, a prerevolutionary relic above the harbor, restored to something like the original by Japanese investors and Chinese construction workers. There's a casino on the third floor but no drawers or closets in the rooms.

Vladivostock. (© Bill Gasperini)

In the bar are two tables of young Russian women smoking up a storm, and nearby, two tables of Korean businessmen and their Russian escorts, all quite drunk by now. Toward midnight, the Koreans stagger off to their rooms, and the Russians return and pick out the girls their clients have selected. The girls hustle off, except for one who missed the cut. She remains at the table, chain-smoking.

Those Koreans aren't the only ones who will wake up with a hangover. There are a million Vladivostokians, more or less, and on any Sunday afternoon, a good portion of them are falling-down drunk.

Vodka is on sale most everywhere most all the time, including an especially nasty version that comes in an eight-ounce beer can with a skull and crossbones on the label. It's called "Black Death" and after consuming a can of it, come Monday morning, I expect you'll know why.

There's certainly reason enough for people here to take to strong drink. At the Far East Shipworks, the city's biggest employer, the workers just got their first paychecks in three months. Says the manager, "Moscow's taxes are outrageous, and the navy won't pay its bills."

So Vladivostok's wage earners go unpaid, and since the city hasn't got the money to keep up public services, the buses and trams break down and the heat and lights go out from time to time.

It doesn't have to be this way. Vladivostok is sister cities with

Tacoma, Washington, and San Diego, California, among other places. Tacoma and San Diego are two harbor towns that have prospered in part because they collect customs duties on everything that gets shipped in or out. That's how they help keep things running. It's the way most every harbor town in the world has run its finances since the days of the Phoenicians.

Not in Vladivostok. The customs house is empty and falling apart. For seventy years, in the peculiar pattern of Soviet economics, all Vladivostok's money went to Moscow, and Moscow sent enough of it back to keep things going. Communism's gone, but like most Russian cities, Vladivostok is still waiting for Moscow to pay the bills, and Moscow is strapped. Apparently the powers-that-be here figure that demanding customs duties would be impolite. Also dangerous. And so the customs house stands empty.

But the local politicians sound as if they are figuring things out. The mayor, Konstantin Tolstoshein, appears to be accustomed to speaking without fear of contradiction. He's a big, rawboned fellow who looks like a construction engineer, which is what he used to be.

He wears a gold Rolex and sits behind a big desk surrounded by seven telephones. Including a red one. "That's for Yeltsin," he chuckles.

Tolstoshein was appointed mayor, replacing a predecessor who fell out of favor when he began making noises about cleaning up civic corruption. But this is the new Russia and this fall, Mayor Tolstoshein is standing for election. He has hired a political consultant from Fresno, California, to run his campaign, but refuses to be drawn out on that subject. Behind him, out the window, is the port of Vladivostok and Golden Horn Bay, with not nearly enough merchant ships at anchor. With a nod in that direction, the mayor observes, "I can see Vladivostok through my window a lot better than they can see it from Moscow." The mayor seems to have concluded that if Vladivostok is going to prosper, it will have to do so without Moscow. But how? In the new Russia, no one has explained how cities and regions are supposed to relate to one another, much less to the central government.

Can they levy their own taxes? Collect their own customs duties? Spend their money as they please? How much, if anything, must they send to Moscow? And what can they expect in return?

And even if Mayor Tolstoshein could solve those mysteries, he still has to reckon with his superior, the governor of the local region named Primorsky Krai. Governor Evgeny I. Nazdratenko presides in the "White House," the government complex just down the street. Nazdratenko took it over from his Soviet predecessors and set up shop there several years ago. He's well-manicured, sharply dressed, and sits behind an even bigger desk than the mayor's, surrounded by no less than eleven telephones. Hasn't anybody here heard about switchboards?

While he's chatting with us, secretaries and burly aides scurry in and out through doors recessed in the mahogany paneling. The governor always greets new visitors by showing them his prize possession: a framed news photo of himself with Boris Yeltsin, barricaded in the Moscow White House, right after the famous moment when Yeltsin mounted the tank to foil the 1991 coup against Mikhail Gorbachev. The message is that Evgeny I. Nazdratenko is not someone to be trifled with. The governor, as you might imagine, is a big fan of revenue sharing, by which he means Moscow needs to share a lot more of its revenue with the Primorski Krai region.

And Primorski Krai, he thinks, should be sharing a lot less of its revenue, such as it is, with Moscow. Judging from the way the governor and his office are outfitted, he's been doing a fair amount of revenue sharing himself. "All we want," he insists, "is government of the people, by the people, and for the people of Primorski Krai." But you can't escape the feeling that the people he has most in mind are Evgeny I. Nazdratenko and the cronies and relatives of same. When Betsy and I ask him about the presidential election, which at this point seems in some doubt for Yeltsin, the governor fixes us with a hard stare. "Let me ask you reporters a question," he says. "Don't you think there is far too much Western meddling with our election process, and don't you think Russia should have the option to postpone the presidential election if conditions are not right for it?"

I reply cautiously that I don't think Western democracies should expect to export their own forms of democracy to Russia, and that Russia must find its own way in this as in other matters.

"Exactly!" he shouts. "Hmmph!" says Betsy. At which point the governor leaps to his feet, rummages through a large cupboard behind his desk filled with what looks like the entire contents of the duty-free cart in the first-class section of Air France, and presents Betsy with the biggest bottle of Chanel No. 5 we've ever seen. Time to say good-bye.

Outside on the street, Betsy says, "Do you think I should have accepted this?" "Evgeny I. Nazdratenko is not someone to be trifled with," I reply. "Besides, see what you can get if you just keep your mouth shut?"

Just as we were about to write off Vladivostok as one more unhappy consequence of Communism, we found ourselves trudging up a muddy street in the north end of town, trying to deliver a box of nails. Finishing nails.

We were doing a favor for that flight attendant on Alaska Airlines who'd carried the nails from somebody in Anchorage for delivery to the Most Holy Mother of God Roman Catholic Church in Vladivostok.

That sounded interesting. We didn't know there was a Roman Catholic church in Vladivostok and neither, apparently, did anybody else, which is why it took four hours of wandering around the factory district to find it.

We didn't see the church at first. We heard it. Church bells on a Sunday morning, coming from what was left of a church steeple, attached to an ancient red-brick building that looked something like a storehouse. It wasn't until we got close and peeked behind the black fencing on the windows that we saw the stained glass. Inside they were celebrating mass; two hundred people, plus a choir of a dozen or so, accompanied by a small electric organ.

There were two celebrants, in full vestments and reciting a liturgy that was a hodgepodge of English, Latin, and Russian. The Reverend Myron Effing of Evansville, Indiana, was short, stout, and in his fifties, with the countenance of a stern cherub. Reverend Dan Maurer from Benton Harbor, Michigan, was lanky and in his late forties with a shock of dark hair that seemed always on the verge of flying out of control. Father Myron and Father Dan are members of a Roman Catholic order they founded to serve the faithful of Primorsky Krai. It's a religious order of just two. They have seven parishes now and they are the only Roman Catholic priests for thirteen hundred miles.

This church alone has a congregation of four hundred. "Mostly old and young folks," says Father Dan. "The old remember God. The young are now searching for something new, and we're trying to help them find it. As for the middle-aged, most of them haven't yet come to terms with the loss of their faith in Communism. We need some middle-aged folks. We also could use a tenor or two for the choir." Father Dan is also the choirmaster.

The older worshipers here are survivors. But then, so is the church. It was built in 1921, for the Roman Catholic bishop of Vladivostok and the fifteen thousand Polish Catholics in the area. But the Bolsheviks took over a year later. The bishop and most of the Catholics, along with the other Europeans here, wound up like the Czech Legion, or as Father Myron puts it simply, "martyred."

So the church became a government archive. They built two new floors around the nave and stuffed them with documents. In 1991, when the Soviet Union became Russia again, and religion was no longer frowned upon, Rome asked for its church back and got it. So now Father Myron and Father Dan are supervising reconstruction. The old Communist records are gone and the Most Holy Mother of God Church is starting to look like a church again. What they need most just now is finishing nails.

And so ready or not, the church is back in service. Among those attending is a tall dignified woman in the front row. She's dressed in white like her two daughters, who are here for their first communion. Her name is Olga, and every Sunday morning she bundles her daughters on board the train and rides seventy miles each way to come to church. Her husband was a helicopter pilot for a government rescue unit. Several years ago, when a nuclear reactor exploded far away in Chernobyl, in the Ukraine, Moscow called for volunteers to rescue victims. Olga's husband and his comrades were among the first on the scene. Maybe they didn't know about the radiation, or maybe they knew and didn't want to think about it; first things first. Now they're all either dead of cancer or dying of it. Olga's husband died last summer.

Next to Olga's little girls is Jadwiga Zelenskaya. Seventy-five years ago, she took her first communion in this church. She survived the Bolshevik's local pogrom, but her little brother didn't. He's among those who are remembered on a little monument to Vladivostok's martyred Polish Catholics that they've erected in a forest above the city near where, it is said, the foreigners were liquidated en masse. The monument is on a hiking trail and every so often they have to come up and repair it, because someone keeps knocking it down and spray-painting swastikas on it.

Jadwiga Zelenskaya has lived long enough to celebrate two communions; her first seventy-five years ago, and the one today. She stands erect and proud at the communion rail alongside Olga and her two little girls. As for Father Myron and Father Dan, they figure to spend the rest of their lives here. Why? "Well," says Father Dan, "we thought, if not us, who?" I'm not sure how we would have felt leaving Vladivostok if we hadn't happened upon the Most Holy Mother of God Roman Catholic Church. But I'm certainly glad that flight attendant gave us those nails.

And the presidential election? You know how that came out. Boris Yeltsin never came to Vladivostok. But he won anyway.

chapter 2

Zaraisk Votes
(June 1996)

T he town of Zaraisk lies a little bit southeast of Moscow. In June the snow and mud are finally gone and Zaraisk is surrounded by lush blue-green fields of grass, watered by a little stream, a tributary of the Oka River, that runs through the center of town.

Zaraisk is 850 years old, older than Moscow itself, and if circumstances had turned out a little bit differently, Zaraisk might have been the great big capital of Russia, and Moscow a little town on the Moscow River just a few miles to the northwest.

Even so, Zaraisk is a proud place, with its collection of churches and the old walls of its kremlin, or fort. This kremlin is not as big or elaborate as the other Kremlin, but it has a simple, rustic beauty to it.

This was a big day in Zaraisk, as in all of Russia. The Russians were voting for president in the first round of the election, and at this point nobody was quite sure whether the winner would be the incumbent, Boris Yeltsin, or his challenger, Gennady Zyuganov, the Communist.

You could say that this was the New Russia's first genuine presidential election. There had been an earlier one, in 1991, when Russia had just transformed itself from the Soviet Union to something called the Russian Republic. Boris Yeltsin was elected president of that in a landslide. But now, five years later, the new and improved Russian Federation, democratic and capitalist, after a fashion, had emerged.

Zaraisk. (© Richard Threlkeld)

It was the voters of this Russian Federation who were choosing a president this day, and because it was a tightly contested election, for the first time ever, their votes, each and every one, would truly matter. Of course for most of this century, when Zaraisk was part of the Soviet Union, their votes didn't matter. The Communists were the only ones on the ballot. Even then, though, nearly everybody who was eligible went to the polls here. Voting has always been just something everybody does in Zaraisk, along with going to church, handling the weekend chores, or attending the meetings of the neighborhood improvement association. Voting's regarded as something responsible, a civic duty, and Zaraisk strikes you as a solid, no-nonsense, responsible sort of place.

So it wasn't just the candidates and issues in this election that produced the customary crowd at the precinct we visited in Shoe Factory Cafeteria Number Two. The registrars were busy all day with Zaraisk voters dressed in their Sunday best.

Mrs. Bernishkova, the precinct warden (who also runs the cafeteria), told us that in Zaraisk, election day is regarded as one of the most important days on the calendar. Mrs. Bernishkova and her volunteers dutifully checked the voting lists, but that was just a formality. You can tell that everybody knows everybody else here anyway. "If somebody doesn't show up to vote," she said, "the neighbors always go over to check the house to make sure everybody's all right." Needless to say, voter turnout around here is close to 100 percent.

There were a couple of poll watchers on hand, along with the town cop. For the record, there were no apparent shenanigans.

Mrs. Bernishkova said they'd been using the cafeteria as a precinct polling place for about thirty years. They hadn't had a chance to do much remodeling since the old Soviet days. The customary statue of Lenin was gone, having been replaced on its pedestal by some potted plants. And they hadn't yet gotten around to painting out the old Communist hammer and sickle on the ballot box. They just turned the insignia to the wall.

The voting was secret, of course, and the ballots were paper, and it was all very much a family affair. Fathers and mothers brought their babes in arms right into the polling booth. The poll watchers and the town cop didn't seem to mind.

Mr. Lubov, who was towing his five-year-old son, said he wanted to show the boy how this thing called voting is done, "so he'll know all about it when he grows up."

Mrs. Sazonova, who parked her groceries from the market over in the corner while she went to mark her ballot, said, "If we're going to make life better for ourselves, it's up to us, and voting is part of it."

We left Zaraisk before the polls closed, after sampling some of Mrs. Bernishkova's sweet cakes, and we never did find out which candidate got the most votes here. But I know the winner in Zaraisk that day—Democracy.

chapter 3

Slavyanskaya Surprise
(November 1996)

I t certainly got our attention. A rattle of gunfire. Not just any gunfire. This was AK-47 gunfire. The unmistakable sound of a 5.45-mm Kalashnikov assault rifle.

Betsy and I had heard that sound many times before. In firefights with the North Vietnamese in the delta south of Saigon. In the battered rubble of apartments in Beirut when the Palestinians and the Maronites were having it out. In Kuwait City, when the kids fired their weapons in the air to celebrate their liberation from the Iraqis after the Gulf War. It's the sound of a string of firecrackers going off at Chinese New Year, and I can never help but flinch when I hear it.

Nor can Betsy. There we were, all dressed up for dinner and waiting just outside the bank of doors at the entrance to the Radisson Slavyanskaya Hotel in downtown Moscow. We flinched and looked at each other.

"What's going on?" I asked the doorman. He didn't flinch a bit.

"*Eto Narmalna*," he said. "Everything's normal."

"That's what I'm afraid of," I said.

The doorman had a point. Moscow's one of the few cities in the world where you can walk out of a downtown hotel, hear a burst of gunfire, and think not much of it. Gun control is only one of the New Russia's many issues currently unaddressed.

But this gunfire was close at hand, from the direction of the big Kiev railway station just down the street. Seconds later, a young lean blond man in a dark suit came running up the walkway and disappeared into the hotel. Beneath his lapel you could see the sling of a shoulder holster. A bodyguard? He looked highly agitated.

Betsy and I shrugged and went to dinner. We'd only been in Moscow a few hours and perhaps, we thought, maybe these days, in this place, this sort of thing really is *Narmalno*.

It wasn't until the next morning when we saw the papers that we discovered we'd missed a big story. That AK-47 fire was the sound of the first contract killing of an American businessman in Moscow.

The victim, Paul Tatum, was walking between his two bodyguards in a Metro underpass nearby when the assassin leaned over a parapet and from thirty meters away fired eleven bullets into Tatum in a pattern no

American businessman Paul Tatum was gunned down November 3, 1996, at a Moscow subway station. (AP Photo/Sergei Karpukhin)

bigger than a pie pan. A passerby was slightly wounded by a ricochet. The bodyguards escaped with what was described as "light shock." Tatum was pronounced dead half an hour later at a local hospital. Whoever that hit man was, he certainly knew his business.

Paul Tatum had been expecting something like this. He'd told everybody who'd listen—TV, the newspapers—that he was a marked man. There had been several threats on his life, he said, and he'd taken to wearing a bulletproof vest, which didn't help him in that Metro underpass. The gunmen got him in the back.

Tatum was typical of the pioneer American entrepreneurs who drifted into the Soviet Union just as it was disintegrating in the late 1980s. He was flashy and flamboyant, with a fast mouth and flair for self-promotion. In short, he was not so different from so many of the New Russians who've gotten rich quick by mastering the murky conversion to capitalism. Ordinary Russians call them *Byiznyessmen*, and they spit the word out like an epithet.

Tatum grew up in the Oklahoma oil country, got interested in Republican Party politics, and became a proficient fund-raiser. There was, in fact, a lot of the Oklahoma wildcatter about Tatum. He took chances—and lost. A million dollars, they said, when a bank he financed collapsed back home.

So he struck out for Moscow and begged and borrowed enough to open a company that provided business centers for hotels. And in 1990, he got a major interest in the first big Soviet-American joint venture, a $50-million hotel-business center in downtown Moscow; what became the Radisson-Slavyanskya.

Tatum and the Slavyanskaya seemed a perfect couple: brash and glitzy, both of them. The hotel is a semicircular pile of windows overlooking a bend in the Moscow River. It seems to be thumbing its nose at the Edwardian curlicues and dados on the old Kiev railway station next door.

There's a gallery of fancy clothing and jewelry shops, plus an American business center on the second floor where, despite a profusion of secretaries and desks and fax machines, it's rare to see any business conducted, at least of the sort that involves lawyers and accountants.

The lobby is usually full of beefy young men in crew cuts, with telltale bulges under their leather jackets. Those who aren't listening intently to their electronic earpieces are muttering into their cell phones. The bodies they are guarding are having dinner in the expensive steak house or gaming at the hotel casino. It's rumored that the hotel's popular with the bigwigs in the Chechen mafia, a particularly nasty element in the Russian mob scene.

There is an American-style health club, but the only ones who seem to give it a real workout are the Americans who are passing through. The other regulars are lithe young women in tight bodysuits who drape themselves languidly over the weight machines after pumping a dumbbell once or twice. They're all wearing pagers. Fat men in tracksuits and gold neck chains sit on the weight machines smoking cigarettes and ogle them. These people don't make any bones about who they are. A friend of mine from *Time* magazine swears he saw one of those health-club nymphs sporting a white T-shirt that simply said, "Mafia."

The hotel was a success. President Clinton stayed there during the Moscow summit in 1994. But Paul Tatum didn't share in the good fortune, although you'd hardly have known. He drove fancy cars, wore fancy clothes, and went to fancy nightclubs. As it turned out, that was more than he could afford. His company ran out of money, and he soon fell out with his Russian partners. The project was taken over by new owners, including the city of Moscow. Tatum was evicted from his office in the hotel and spent several years filing lawsuits from Minneapolis to Stockholm, sending protest letters to Russian officialdom, and talking to reporters. He was, in short, making a nuisance of himself.

None of Tatum's friends, and he had a lot of them in the Western business community here, could ever explain why he hadn't taken the hints and gone home. Perhaps, wildcatter that he was, he was hoping to bring in one big gusher and go home a success at last. Or maybe he was afraid there would be an indictment waiting for him as a result of his shady business dealings in the United States. We'll never know. Paul Tatum was forty-one.

As you might expect, Tatum's demise cast something of a pall on the struggling American business community here. A lot of people were wondering, "Who's next?" In Washington, the State Department expressed concern and the hope that the perpetrator would soon be brought to justice (he never was). And in a remarkable little piece of candor, the head of the American Chamber of Commerce in Russia, one Peter Charow, told me, "You have to be careful who you do business with, who you get involved with, because it could come to this."

But the concern was temporary and probably misplaced. Tatum was one of a kind, a throwback to the early days of Moscow capitalism, marked by dreams and dollars and danger and not much else.

Americans who do business in Moscow today are much more the button-down corporate types, more concerned with long-term profits than the quick killings, so to speak. Doing any kind of business in Russia today remains difficult if not downright risky. In the absence of a legitimate legal system, Russian businessmen tend to settle their disputes by simply terminating the other fellow with extreme prejudice. It certainly saves a lot of money on legal bills.

This makes foreign investment here problematic. A friend of ours, who heads up one of the biggest American accounting firms and sees the books of most of the Americans who invest here, says, "Anybody who puts money into Moscow these days is a lunatic. You know what those Russian joint ventures really are. You, the foreigner, put up your money and do the venturing, and pretty soon you're out and the Russians wind up with the joint."

Even so, Paul Tatum's murder was exceptional. Virtually all of the other victims of contract killings here are Russians, about six hundred of them every year nationwide. In Moscow, there's a contract killing every few days. Ninety percent of them, like Tatum's, go unsolved, which is not surprising. If you were an underpaid, overworked police detective, seeing all that armed muscle in the lobby of the Slavyanskaya, knowing what you know about the mafia, and what happened to Paul Tatum, how hard would YOU work to put his killer behind bars?

The fellow who invented the Moscow hit men's weapon of choice is named, not surprisingly, Mikhail Kalashnikov. He's now seventy-seven years old, and they brought him to Moscow the other day to be on hand for a fiftieth birthday party for the AK-47 at the Museum of the Russian Army.

Kalashnikov is a little fellow who was dwarfed by all the braided brass standing around him. He explained, rather shyly, that he'd invented his weapon to fulfill a promise to himself as he lay wounded in battle against the Nazis. The Germans, he thought, always seemed to have better weapons, and he was determined to change that if he survived.

The result is a killing machine with only nine moving parts that spits out bullets at a rate of six thousand per minute, according to the *Moscow Times*. It is simple, durable, and efficient, and has sold more than seventy million copies. It helped Hanoi win the Vietnam War, spread mayhem through much of the Third World the past couple of generations, and is featured on the national flag of Mozambique.

Mr. Kalashnikov never made any money from his invention. He seems content simply with the prestige of holding an official document certifying his patriotic contribution to the Motherland. So he lives on a small state pension in a two-room apartment in a town near the Urals, a thousand miles east of Moscow. He calls the AK-47s, now in their third edition, "My children."

And Mikhail Kalashnikov is still alive and kicking, which is more than can be said for Paul Tatum.

chapter 4

Merry Xmas or Else
(December 1996)

T ired of all the crass commercialism that's
infected Christmas in America? Annoyed that the Christmas
season now seems to last almost as long as a U.S. presidential campaign? Irritated by all the vulgar displays of wealth on a holiday
that's supposed to be devoted to Peace on Earth, Goodwill toward
Men?

Well, don't spend your Christmas in Moscow. Even to this jaded
American holiday shopper, the yuletide here is very weird.

To begin with, it's long. The Moscow mayor, Yuri Luzhkov, a big
fan of Christmas, has decreed that every store and shop in town has
to display some sort of Christmas decoration, or risk a fine. And he
even sends inspectors around to check. Merry Christmas or else.

And the decorations must be in place by December 1, which
means the first trees and tinsel start sprouting on Tverskaya Ulitsa,
the main shopping street, early in November. You'd think they'd
come down after December 25, but no, there's the Orthodox Christmas, the traditional Russian festival, on January 7, and in the
Russian way, they've simply decided to celebrate both. So Christmas,
Moscow-style, takes up the better part of two months.

You can't blame the Russians. They used to have a very nice,
short, simple Orthodox Christmas; a little tree, dinner with the
family, some Christmas carols, a nice church service, a little vodka
afterward, and that was it.

Then, in 1918, the Communists came along and cancelled

33

Christmas. So New Year's Day became the big holiday here. The Christmas tree became a New Year's tree, and the star on its top became red, just like the big one on the Spasskaya Tower over the Kremlin. Unlike the white star over Bethlehem, the red star stood for Soviet power and prestige. Instead of angels and little drummer boys, the decorations on the trees were little tanks and warplanes and cosmonauts.

After the Soviet Union and Communism crumbled, Russians were a little confused about what to do at Christmas. In Moscow at least, the city fathers have decided for them. They've wrapped two Christmases and New Years into one huge holiday designed to get people to spend some of what money they have.

And you have to admit, the city fathers have done a pretty snazzy job of gift wrapping Moscow itself. Long strands of red and green lights frame the main boulevards and the graceful bridges across the Moscow River. And of course, Moscow being where it is, Christmas here is almost always white.

It would be a lot nicer if that lovely Moscow Christmas card weren't so badly defaced by all the advertising. There are billboards everywhere, around the Kremlin, next to the concert halls, hard by the churches they've restored. Christmas brought to you by Coca-Cola, or Nestle's or Smirnoff's. Instead of the gifts of the Magi, there's the gifts of Maggi, a kind of chicken soup. And the billboards are all lit up in several colors that blink all night long, like the thirty-foot-wide Bayer Aspirin tablet atop my apartment house.

Moscow wants to cash in on Christmas, and from the newly rich Russians, it has certainly succeeded. The shopping mall of choice these days is the Sadko Arcade, down along the river, richly outfitted for the season in plastic fir and tinsel and a sound system playing old Frank Sinatra tapes of Christmas carols. There's Versace and Hugo Boss here, and most all the other designer shops you'd find in Paris or Milan or New York. The clothes resemble something you'd see at a factory outlet, but the prices are definitely not secondhand.

That nightgown ensemble for the missus is $1,500. A child's blue blazer for little Sergei is $700. The toy BMW convertible with the cloth top that opens and closes, just like Dad's, is $80. And then there's the four-foot-high dollhouse, completely furnished, for little Galia, that's $3,500. At that price, it's more expensive than some of the real houses I've seen in the rude villages beyond the Ural Mountains.

This orgy of gift buying is something new and decidedly American. Russians never gave each other gifts for this holiday before free enterprise came along.

But some of the old traditions do survive, with some embellishments. At the bigger stores, you are likely to run into Ded Moroz,

Red October Chocolate Factory madonna prepares New Year's gifts for Father Frost. (© 1994 Jonathan Sanders)

otherwise known as Father Frost, the favorite of every Russian child. He's like Santa Claus, with the same red suit with white trim and a long white beard. But he's tall and without the little round belly. He doesn't seem quite as jolly as Santa, either, and apparently he doesn't live at the North Pole. Perhaps, like so many other Russians, he is homeless.

Traditionally, Father Frost is usually accompanied by Snegurochka, the Snow Maiden, a kind of Sleeping Beauty character with, one presumes, thermal underwear. But the Father Frost you'll see at the Moscow malls is usually in the company of a couple of Snegurochkas in red-and-white fur-trimmed miniskirts and net stockings, made up like bar girls in a cheap casino. Betsy calls the trio "Father Frost and the Hookers."

And Father Frost himself, when we discussed things with him, makes no bones about his new role. "Our main duty," he said, while surrounded by a display of toys whose prices would make a Bill Gates gasp, "is to make mothers and fathers buy presents for the children, plus the toys, decorations, and all the other things necessary for life."

The average Muscovite, who has enough trouble making enough to buy the real necessities of life, regards all of this with a mixture of disdain and envy. The Moscow proletariat will celebrate the occasion in its own way. Some will go to services on January 7 at one of the many churches and cathedrals that have been reconstructed.

Others are keeping a celebration that's a sort of hangover from the Soviet days. They'll celebrate New Year's with a New Year's tree instead of a Christmas tree. It's odd to see the streets suddenly filled with fir trees for sale starting the day after Christmas, but a whole generation of older Russians have gotten used to doing things that way, and are loath to change.

If you've got the wherewithal, you can go over to Sadko's, a Swiss-Russian joint venture catering to foreigners and wealthy Russians, and buy a nine-foot-tall artificial tree for $4,500, decorated with silver-winged and golden-haired angels($1,290 apiece) and a little machine that spurts plastic snow over everything ($528).

Said the Sadko salesmen, "Many of our customers need three trees; one for the house, one for the apartment, and one for the *dacha.*" Most ordinary folks will pay about three dollars for a real tree and decorate it as best they can.

But for Muscovites rich or poor, the nicest thing about this holiday is that there are not only two Christmases, but two New Years. The New Year on the old Orthodox calender is January 13, and that's an official holiday, too. So from about December 21 to January 14, most everybody here just takes a vacation.

And a Happy New Year (*Snovum Godom*) to you!

chapter 5

Dark Days in the Kuzbass

(January 1997)

The Kuzbass in January is black and white. Mostly black. Snow is piled high against the clumps of dark trees, naked to the wind. Mounds of snow. Hills of it. Mountains of it.

Most of what public work there is in the Kuzbass is currently dedicated to snow removal. Or rather, snow displacement. A brisk night here is twenty below zero Fahrenheit, so there's no way the snow will melt until, say, April. So the snow crews inch their way along the roads and streets in caravans of weird, Rube Goldberg-style machines the size of earthmovers. Mechanical claws grasp the snow and shovel it onto a conveyor belt that dumps it into waiting trucks for stowing in the river or wherever there's some open space. The Russian nickname for these huge, grasping contraptions is "capitalists." Never once in the Kuzbass did I see an ordinary snowblower.

The only color you see is on the people. Red cheeks and an occasional yellow or green scarf. But most of the population is dressed like the landscape, gray and hunched against the cold.

The sun is a stranger this time of year. At ten in the morning it's still pitch-black. The sun peeks over the hills for a moment at midday and is setting by midafternoon. That's if it's not cloudy—or snowing.

The Kuzbass is just south of the 56th parallel, south of Moscow on the map. But Moscow winters are balmly compared to those of the Kuzbass, which is smack in the middle of Siberia, thousands of miles to the east, and not far from Mongolia. Beneath all that Kuzbass snow is coal, a whole mountain range of it. It is the same coal that runs

Snow removal implements. (© 1996 Jonathan Sanders)

the public furnaces that heat hundreds of Russia's cities and towns, and keeps the lights burning through the endless winter nights.

To get to the Kuzbass you must find your way to one of Moscow's several regional airports, push your way through the crowds outside the tattered terminal building (taking care to protect your personal belongings from the inevitable pickpockets), plunk your pile of rubles down in front of the clerk in the proper cubicle (credit cards are still problematic for transactions of this type), and get yourself a seat on an Aeroflot flight to the Kuzbass capital, Keremovo.

Aeroflot, the biggest airline in the world in Soviet times, remains the airline of necessity within Russia. Much of the domestic fleet still consists of transport jets that were built to carry military cargo. They've been converted to civilian use, but the plexiglass bombardier's window remains on the nose of the plane, and you can see where the passenger seats are quick-bolted, so that they can be easily removed if it becomes necessary to carry soldiers instead of paying customers. Aeroflot's domestic jets are feeling their age, and the accident rate shows it. If I were a Russian soldier, I'd almost rather take my chances in combat than climb on some of those Aeroflot transports for a trip to the front.

Aeroflot has made some concessions to capitalism, though. The flight attendant now passes out damp towels and coffee. Not so long ago, the best you could hope for was an occasional glass of cold tea from the samovar in the rear, served to everyone from the same glass. And they no longer insist that foreigners board the plane first, so they won't lose track of us, in case we might be up to no good.

Thirty years ago, I flew an SAS jet from Bangkok to Copenhagen. SAS was the only western airline allowed to overfly the then-Soviet Union. It stopped to refuel in Tashkent, a big city in Soviet Central Asia, twice a week. When we foreigners got off the plane to hike to the transit lounge, there was a huge crowd behind the runway fences. I mean huge: thousands of people, whole families. I wondered what the occasion was.

"Oh, it's always like this when the SAS plane comes in," said a fellow traveler. He'd made this trip before. "They just come out to see the foreigners. It's something to do, a sort of entertainment." Well, the folks from Tashkent watched us get off the plane, and an hour later, they watched us get back on. Then they went home. These days, though, the foreigners are allowed to crowd on the plane with everybody else. I suppose that's progress. But progress is not what you will find when you finally get to the Kuzbass after a full day of flying five hundred miles an hour, halfway across Russia. Quite the contrary.

The Kuzbass is Russia's Appalachia. Watching the miners come up in their cars from the dark, dank coalshafts at shift's end, covered with coal dust, switching off their headlamps, you could imagine yourself outside Scranton or Wheeling. More like the Scranton or Wheeling of forty years ago. The equipment is old and patched together. The mineshafts are disintegrating and in constant danger of collapse.

The mines are still owned by the government. The miners get their salaries from the government. But the government doesn't have enough money. So the mines go unrepaired. And the coalminers go unpaid.

How do you live without a salary through a Kuzbass winter? Alexei, who's just come out of his elevator cage, tips back his miner's hat, smiles as he considers the question, his teeth white against his grimy lips, and answers. "What do we live on? Promises. Promises."

On the road outside the mine, Tolstoy would feel right at home. Horsedrawn troikas weave their way among the wheezing Ladas and Zhigilis, the Russian Fords and Chevys. Along the roadside, Nikolai has set up a little table in the snow, to sell what is left of his summer potatoes. "I'm here because I've nothing else to eat," he says. "They haven't paid my pension in five months."

Across the way, Vera is selling what appears to be all that's left of her toilette, a silver hairbrush, plus some dolls she played with as a child. But they are things that nobody's got the money to buy. "How can people live this way?" she asks. "How can I live this way?"

Inside the mine office, there's a long line of miners, waiting patiently. Eight years after the end of Communism, Russians in the hinterlands still spend a lot of time in line, waiting patiently. At the head of this line is Jacov. The woman at the window has just handed him two sausages and a large piece of fatback. The mine has managed to trade some of its coal for some meat from the butcher. So the miners are getting paid in coldcuts instead of cash. Jacov displays his wages with contempt. "And they deduct this from the money they still owe me!" he says.

Even so, Jacov is luckier than most. He lives in a snug little house nearby that was built by his father. There's a tiny garden plot behind it where he raises cabbages and potatoes in the Kuzbass's brief summer, to store in his root cellar when the snow comes.

In the kitchen, his wife, Zoya, is cooking up the cabbages. She used to be a teacher, but had to quit when her salary stopped coming. Now she's a cleaning woman for the family of one of the local government officials, and she's bitter about it.

"You should be bringing money home instead of sausage," she barks at Jacov. "You can't even make ends meet!"

Jacov's too broken, too defeated, to answer her. He stares at the snow outside his window, tears in his eyes.

Jacov and the other miners have been on strike four months, in the forlorn hope of pressuring Moscow to pay up. There is just enough work going on in the mines to keep the machinery from breaking down, and to keep the miners warm.

Outside Primary School Number 16, the kids are playing in the snow. That's what they do all day now. The school is closed. The teachers are on strike because the government hasn't paid their salaries either.

One of the teachers, Miss Elizaveta, happens by. She reminds me of Miss Smith or Mrs. Brown or Miss Conibear, who taught me the ABCs and how much is four times four when I was these kids' age. "The children in my third grade said they'd try to get us money so we can keep teaching," she says. "It was sweet."

Miss Elizaveta and the teachers and so many of the unpaid people you meet here are well-dressed, well-groomed, and what the Russians would call *kultorny*, or cultured. They are what in Soviet times would have passed for middle class. They're not accustomed to poverty, and they are doing their best to keep up appearances. But it's hard. By the most conservative estimates, living standards for average Russians have dropped 40 percent in the last five years.

The economists could tell Miss Elizaveta what the trouble is, although not how to fix it. Russia is not a former Communist economy gone capitalist. It remains stuck in an economic twilight zone; half Communist, half capitalist. Most all the potentially profitable enterprises from the Soviet days have now been privatized, now owned by multimillionaire robber barons who, in many cases, simply expropriated them. Those industries that don't make a profit and never will, like coal mines, remain state property because nobody wants them. But they employ millions of Russians who need the jobs and the salaries to live.

The government can't pay the salaries of the people in Kuzbass, for example, because it can't get enough money from taxes. The companies that make a profit don't want to pay taxes if they can avoid it, and usually, by bribing the tax man or his boss or his boss, they can avoid it. And the companies that are losing money can't afford to pay taxes. So months go by in places like this, and instead of rubles, the people get paid in sausages.

But they can still watch television, which has been privatized to a fault, and is full of commercials hawking the same consumer goods they are selling in Berlin and Paris, for about the same prices. The trouble is, Russians are making, on average, only about 20 percent of what people make in Berlin and Paris.

Not all Russians, of course. The other day a Paris newspaper claimed that the Russian prime minister, Victor Chernomyrdin, had managed to raise his net worth, during the four years he's been in office, from $28 million to $5 billion. Not a bad return, if true.

The prime minister used to be head of Gazprom, Russia's natural-gas monopoly that is said to control one-third of the gas reserves in the entire world. He called the newspaper report "tactless" and claimed his monthly salary is only $709. A few weeks later, they gave the prime minister a raise. He now gets $1,400 a month.

Meantime in the Kuzbass, Vera and Nikolai and Jakov and the others are still waiting for their monthly salaries, which are seven months past due. President Boris Yeltsin has promised that everyone will be paid in full by the middle of 1997. You can pardon the miners here if they don't believe him. When Yeltsin took power in 1991, the coal miners, Russia's biggest organized labor force, were among the first to back him. The trouble was, nobody needed all that Russian coal anymore. So, under pressure to make the coal industry competitive, he tried to make it lean and mean by closing 80 percent of Russia's two hundred fifty mines and laying off almost a million miners. Even that radical surgery didn't work. As for the miners, they were supposed to get more than $2 billion in pensions, wages, and subsidies from the Russian government and the World Bank, to help tide them over. But in the Russian fashion, most of that money has simply disappeared.

In the old Soviet days, the workers used to say, "We pretend to work and the government pretends to pay us." Now, out here, they've lost even that pretense. In the Kuzbass, they've lost everything but their dignity.

chapter 6

Live Free
or Die
(January 1997)

Da-Ug is standing in the snow near his shed, where his horse is munching breakfast. It is his last horse. Da-Ug is telling a story, a story you sense he has told many times before.

"It was a warm day last summer. I was in my field back there with my mare and her colt. I heard some rumbling and at the edge of my field, a few hundred meters from me, some tanks emerged. They were Russian tanks, of course. We don't have tanks. There were six of them and they parked in a semicircle. Then, one by one, the tanks began firing their cannon. At me. There was no one else around. I waved at them to stop, but they kept firing, one shell after another. I jumped into a ditch. A moment later, one of the shells killed my mare. The colt didn't know what to do. The little animal ran to her mother's body, then ran around in circles, frightened by the explosions. But the tanks kept firing. After a while I realized they were using us for target practice. They kept shooting at the colt as she ran, and finally they killed the colt, too. I guess they figured they'd got me as well, because after awhile the tanks went away. I could hear the soldiers laughing."

Da-Ug is short and wiry, with a wisp of white beard, and dressed in the baggy trousers and round black sheep's wool cap that mark him for a Chechen. An old man with a head full of memories, most especially the memory of that one summer afternoon. He ought to have been a grandfather by now, but events have precluded that.

He lives in the ruins of his farmhouse along a muddy track that eventually winds up into the peaks of the Caucasus which on this day are perfectly outlined in snowy white against a bright blue January sky. This might be Switzerland except the landscape is such a shambles. Da-Ug's family is smaller than it used to be. Now it's just his wife, Zina, and their teenaged son. Two other sons are buried with a dozen other young men from the village, in the little cemetery nearby.

Da-Ug is clearly perplexed. "How could they do this to us, those Russian soldiers?" he asks, more to himself. "I was one of them. I fought for Russia in the Great Patriotic War against the Fascists. When Stalin moved us away, we didn't complain. We knew that they would bring us home someday, and they did. And we remained loyal citizens. I wore my uniform on Red Army Day. When his turn came, my eldest son fought with his Russian comrades in Afghanistan, and served with distinction. We were brothers with the Russians, compatriots. How could they do this to us?"

Why the Russians did what they did here in Chechnya now, six months after the fighting has stopped, seems as mysterious and inexplicable as why the Americans did what they did in Southeast Asia a generation ago. It must have seemed to somebody a good idea at the time, but in the end, in both cases, the perpetrators also became victims.

Da-Ug's tragedy, like that of Chechnya itself, is part geography and part history. His farmhouse is in the village of Yahndee, an hour's drive from Grozny, the Chechen capital. For more than a year, Yahndee was on the front line of the war for Chechen independence. It changed hands a dozen times. Now it looks like hell. Hardly a wall is left standing. There's no more than a handful of families here now. Everybody else has gone for good. Once upon a time, there were a million Chechens in Chechnya. Now there are only half that many.

And you're careful where you walk. A neighbor, Sa-Id, comes down the track holding a Russian mine. "It's four kilograms of dynamite," he says. "I've defused twenty-six of these myself. The Russians left them in our houses. 'You'll keep on being killed for another twenty years!' they said. And that's what's happened. Seven people here have already had their legs blown off. Seven!"

Chechnya is about half the size of Belgium, in what the Russians call the North Caucasus. It is landlocked and bordered by ill will. On one side are the Georgians and Ingushetians, ancient enemies. Azerbaijanis on the other side. No friends there. The rugged Caucasus peaks lie to the south. Everywhere else there's Russia.

Chechnya's been part of Russia for 140 years, since the tsar's divisions finally conquered it in a brutal war that took half a century. But though the Chechens were always "in" Russia, and later the

Soviet Union, they were never "of" it. They're Muslims and they always spoke their own language, when they could.

Though Da-Ug and a lot of other Chechens fought with the Red Army when Hitler invaded, Stalin convinced himself the Chechens were Nazi collaborators, even though the German army never even got this far. In 1944, he moved the whole population to the steppes of Central Asia. There they stayed till 1957, when Nikita Krushchev allowed them to come home. It was all a mistake, Krushchev said.

In 1991, when the Soviet Union was coming apart, Chechnya, under its firebrand leader, Jokar Dudayev, a former Soviet air force general, joined the exodus and declared independence. Moscow, which had other things on its mind at the time, put up only token resistance.

But by 1994, Chechnya had become a haven for smugglers, drug dealers, and bandits, and a big headache for Moscow. The Chechen mafia was partly responsible for the new Moscow crime wave. The hard-line cronies who surrounded Boris Yeltsin convinced him, in a series of meetings said to be liberally lubricated with vodka, that it was time to bring Chechnya back into the fold, by force if need be. The then-defense minister, Pavel Grachev, boasted that the whole thing could be done, "In two hours with a single paratroop regiment."

Just before Christmas that year, forty-thousand Russians troops invaded Chechnya. It was a disaster for Moscow and an apocalypse for Chechnya. Russian troops shelled and carpet bombed Grozny and for a time, captured it and much of the Chechen plain. But Chechen guerrillas, and that included almost every able-bodied Chechen man, proved themselves superior fighters. One of Da-Ug's sons died fighting for Yahndee. The eldest boy, the veteran of Afghanistan, died in the battle for the presidential palace in Grozny.

The Russians managed to kill Dudayev and perhaps eighty-thousand other Chechens, most of them civilians, in twenty months of fighting. Casualties also included hundreds of Russian citizens, trapped here in the fighting with no place to go. More than four thousand Russian troops, most of them ill-trained recruits, also died.

By late summer of 1996, with Chechen forces back in control of Grozny, Moscow at last made peace. It agreed to withdraw what troops were left in Chechnya and finessed the question of Chechen independence by agreeing to leave it open for five years.

So now, once again, the Chechens have Chechnya to themselves and are deciding what to do with it, deciding democratically in what is, according to the international observers here, a fairly free and democratic election campaign to choose a president and a parliament. Among Chechens, independence isn't an issue, it's a fact.

In front of the destroyed presidential palace in Grozny, Chechen Republic. (© 1996 Jonathan Sanders)

There are thirteen candidates for president, and freedom from Moscow is the first item on the platform of every one of them.

For political reporters like Betsy and me, campaign coverage Chechen-style is a lot different than following American politicians on the hustings. For one thing, it's dangerous. The Chechen countryside is alive with bandits and kidnappers who'd like nothing better than snatching a foreigner in hopes of a fat ransom. It's essential to make friends with one faction or another. Each faction has its own militia, which provides safe housing in a neighborhood it controls. The only way to get from one campaign event to another is with an escort: a battered jeep filled with the toughest-looking fellows you can imagine, bristling with automatic rifles and grenade launchers.

Betsy and her CNN crew are protected by one faction, and our CBS News crew are under the wing of another. Campaign coverage ends at dusk, since you don't dare go driving around Grozny at night, so the last thing I do before sunset is to go over and check out Betsy's safe house, to make sure she's made it safely through another day. Some nights we have time to share our dinner of C rations.

The campaigning is something out of Lincoln-Douglas. No TV commercials (there's hardly a working electric socket left in the whole country), no photo-ops or position papers. One of the few candidates who actually goes out and meets people is Shamil Basayev, a thirty-two-year-old former computer salesman who led a bloody hostage-taking expedition on a Russian town during the war. In an effort to show the voters he's not just some young hothead, he sets up shop at a table in the center of a village and surrounds himself with village elders, complete with long white beards and shepherd's canes. At least you assume they are village elders, until you see the same fellows at every village rally. Rent-an-Elder.

In fact, Shamil is a young hothead. A Shamil rally is an hour of Baseyev speaking nonstop about Chechen freedom and Russian atrocities, answers to a couple of questions from the crowd that turn into more harangues, and then a quick exit to his black BMW, and away.

An interview with Baseyev, if it happens, is surreal. His campaign headquarters is in one of the few relatively undamaged buildings near what was downtown Grozny, behind an iron fence manned by a platoon of combat-fatigued bodyguards who look like they stepped out of a Sylvester Stallone movie; AK-47s, bandoliers of ammunition slung over shoulders, even a rocket-propelled grenade launcher or two.

Baseyev himself sweeps in long after midnight, and holds court in an anteroom, seeing petitioners and hangers-on like a baron in some medieval castle. Courtiers scurry in and out carrying huge stacks of rubles. Is Shamil giving or receiving, or both? It's a reminder that there's a lot that is still very feudal about Chechnya, a country full of warring clans, which helps explain all that firepower that surrounds The Candidate.

He'll entertain a couple of questions. "Why do you suppose the Russians call you a terrorist?"

"The Russians are the terrorists and murderers," he says. "For two years they kept our whole nation hostage . . . and we had to defend ourselves, and we will continue to do so. It's like the old Russian proverb, 'Hit someone before you start getting hit.'"

"Aren't you too young to be a president?"

"Thirty-two is the perfect age," he answers. "I haven't had time to go downhill and dry up like the leaders in Russia."

"How will you deal with the Russians?"

"I'll simply issue a decree confirming Chechnya's independence and make sure that Russia compensates us for the damage it has done."

Shamil Baseyev is the most visible of the presidential pretenders.

But the likely winner of this election is hardly ever seen in public and gives no interviews. He's Aslan Maskhadov, who was head of the rebel armed forces. If Baseyev is Chechnya's Patrick Henry (some would say he's closer to Billy the Kid), Maskhadov is its George Washington; mature, dignified, and somebody the Russians think they can do business with, eventually. As it turned out, Maskhadov would win in a walk.

But win what? Grozny, once a graceful city of four hundred thousand, is in ruins. In the central square, there's no longer any evidence of the presidential palace, the parliament building, the main hotel, or the national museum. The city center is a pile of rubble.

Chechnya's main industry was oil. But what oil wells there were are capped and the Grozny refinery is a tangle of shattered pipes. Baseyev and the other hotheads insist Russia needs to pay for all this damage, but having been bloodied and humiliated by a "bunch of Blackasses," as the Russians are fond of calling the Chechens, the prospect of Russia paying Chechnya even a single ruble in remunerations seems preposterous.

And yet, even now, six months after the fighting has stopped and in the dead of a Caucasus winter, Chechens are starting to put Chechnya back together with the same energy and initiative they used to whip the Russians.

There's traffic on the streets now, fueled by home-brewed gasoline that's sold in bottles from street vendors. Take twelve tons of oil, put it in a tank, heat it up for thirty-six hours, and you wind up with seven tons of diesel fuel, three tons of gasoline, and a little kerosene left over. Just don't be anywhere near the cookstove if anything goes wrong.

Grozny's telephone system was completely destroyed, but there's a Chechen entrepreneur who has set up a cell-phone network, and if you know how to dial, you can get a better line to New York from Grozny than from Moscow.

The central market's back in business in a ramshackle sort of way, and the produce that used to go to Moscow is now for sale here at home. In a side street just past the butcher stalls, there's a thriving market in pistols, submachine guns, and grenades.

Over at City Hospital Number One, once the best in the country, the administrator, Dr. Musa, is supervising reconstruction. Russian tanks pulled up one day during the fighting and deliberately pulverized the place. Now it is being rebuilt with mostly volunteer labor and bricks from Grozny's rubble. There are a lot of spare bricks in Grozny.

"As you can see," says Dr. Musa, "the quality of the repair work isn't great. It's being done by us doctors. But we've got some of the patients' rooms restored and we're working on the operating room. What we need now is equipment."

Dr. Musa saw the casualties that came through this hospital, and saved the lives of some of them. As you might imagine, that experience has tempered his feelings about Chechen liberty.

"The price of independence was too high," he says. "You see for yourself the colossal destruction and how many more people have been crippled, both physically and morally. But it's done now and we won't leave Chechnya. We'll rebuild things. Someday we'll have the best hospital in Chechnya, again!"

No doubt the Chechens and the Russians would love to be rid of each other. But despite their nasty mutual history, they seem condemned by geography to coexist, at the very least. Chechnya can't get along without Russia. There's already talk of building a trans-Caucasus pipeline across Chechnya, carrying oil from the Caspian Sea to the Mediterranean. That would do wonders for the Chechen economy and net a pretty penny for Moscow investors.

And Russia needs a peaceful, stable, and prosperous Chechnya on its southern flank, which is why the Romanov tsars went to all that trouble to annex Chechnya in the first place. If that comes about, what difference does it make whether this place flies a Russian flag and is called Chechnya, or flies its own flag and calls itself Ikcheria?

At the moment, no Russian politician in his right mind would countenance Chechen independence. But Russia may have learned its lesson in Chechnya about the folly of trying to strong-arm parts of the old empire that want to be left to themselves. Time may not heal all wounds, but time and necessity may heal this one.

And Chechens will have to find out, now that they've got a new president and a new parliament, whether they can govern themselves with compromise instead of Kalashnikovs. The outlook for that, at best, is uncertain. There is every possibility that the Chechen warlords will soon turn upon themselves and convert victory to anarchy.

Was this all worth it, for Chechen independence? There's no doubt in the mind of Da-Ug and Zina, standing there in the snow, with the graves of their sons just down the road. "The price of our freedom was too great for me," says Zina, "but for our nation, yes, it was certainly worth it. We lost our sons, but you can't have a war without victims."

The question is pointless of course. The war was yesterday. And tomorrow? Chechens are Muslims. The Muslims say, "Inshallah." If God wills it. Peace and freedom for Chechnya? Inshallah.

(Postscript: Aslan Maskhadov won the presidential election, but he was unable to stop the Chechens from squandering their freedom. Chechnya swiftly lapsed into anarchy. There were more kidnappings, more assassinations, many of them involving Russian nationals, and the Chechen mafia in Moscow grew and prospered. Meanwhile, the Russian military fumed in the wake of its defeat in Grozny, and waited for vengeance. That moment came in 1999, with a series of apartment-house bombings in Moscow that caused heavy casualties. The bombers were never caught, and some critics suggested it may have been the work of Russia's own security services. But the then-prime minister, Vladimer Putin, himself a former security agent, blamed Chechen terrorists and unleashed the Russian army on Chechnya for a second time. What little was left of Grozny was obliterated, and thousands more Chechen civilians were killed and wounded. Grozny was reoccupied by Russian troops. The Chechen rebels fled into the mountains to resume the guerrilla war at which they'd proved so adept. Putin used his "victory" in Chechnya to launch his presidential campaign. He won easily.)

chapter 7

Bad Medicine
(February 1997)

Her name was Tanya and she was four years old and she had a hole in her heart. We found her in the waiting room of St. George's Hospital in St. Petersburg, a cavernous building left over from the Soviet period that still and all remains one of the best hospitals in the city.

Nature had given and Nature had taken away in the case of Tanya Korbenikov. She was a strikingly beautiful child, with huge dark eyes and a creamy complexion that seemed to belong in a Botticelli painting. But she'd been born with a heart defect. Her little body wasn't getting enough blood because her heart couldn't work properly, so she was small for her age and listless. In the village where Tanya had come from, there wasn't even a doctor, much less a heart specialist. And the Russian doctors that might have helped her were hundreds of miles away in Moscow, and the Korbenikovs had neither the money nor the connections to get her help there. So Tanya's hole in the heart had gone untreated since birth.

Now Tanya and her mother were in the waiting room because somebody had promised to do something about Tanya. Mrs. Korbenikov was fidgeting anxiously, and Tanya was playing with the pages in a magazine and looking about, excited by all the hospital commotion.

Tanya's help came in the form of Dr. Leo Lopez of New York City, a heart surgeon who, attended by a couple of orderlies, showed up with a hospital gurney and asked Tanya if she'd like a ride. She would. And with a pat on her mother's hand, Dr. Lopez and Tanya were off to the surgical ready room.

Dr. Lopez is part of an eight-person American surgical team from Mt. Sinai Hospital in New York. They come to St. George's for a few days every year, loaded down with a couple of tons of medical and surgical supplies, to patch up as many faulty hearts in the children of Russia as they can. The supplies and expenses are paid for by a charity called "Healing the Children." The doctors and nurses do this for free. "When we heard the American doctors were coming," said Tanya's mother, "we jumped at the chance. And we prayed."

This visit was organized by Dr. Anthony Rossi, another heart surgeon, who has been healing children all over the world on missions like this. But he confesses to a sad fascination every time he visits St. Petersburg.

"We always had the opinion of Russia as a great world power, yet having done this in so many other Third World countries, in Africa, in Central America, you find the conditions here are depressingly similar."

You only have to look around to see what he means. The hospital is mostly empty of patients and equipment. Russia doesn't have enough money to keep its massive healthcare system going. And what little money there is goes to hospitals according to the number of beds, whether there's anybody in the beds or not, no matter if they're occupied by heart patients or kids with the measles. The result is that some hospitals are awash in money they can barely spend, and others like St. George's get short shrift.

The Mt. Sinai team has to bring along almost its entire operating room. St. George's is short of even basic things like catheters and thermometers. In the corner of one room is an old iron lung, for polio victims, like the ones I remember from the 1950s. Polio has been eradicated in the West. There are still cases of it in Russia.

It's not as though Russian doctors don't have the know-how. They do. But they're overworked and sorely underpaid, when they get paid at all. Two hundred dollars a month is about average for a heart surgeon here. He, or she, has to make the rest of a living by taking bribes from patients who are rich enough to pay for treatment. Most of them aren't.

Tanya and the other children on Mt. Sinai's waiting list are from poorer families or orphanages; the chosen few from thousands of Russian children with heart defects that have gone without treatment of any kind. Without surgery, most of them will live a short, painful, sedentary existence.

There's pain in the eyes of the chief surgeon at St. George's, Dr.

Boris Bondarenko, when he tells you of the kids he and his doctors have been unable to help, for lack of equipment and resources. Bondarenko has a confident, kindly face that puts you in mind of Lionel Barrymore playing Dr. Gillespie in the early *Dr. Kildare* movies; the sort of doctor to whom you'd feel comfortable entrusting your health.

"I am sure the American doctors here will teach us some things, and will leave us with some of their supplies, and we are very grateful. And I also know they will learn something from us Russian doctors," he says with a wry smile. "How to survive in a difficult situation."

This year, the government cut the meager budget for Dr. Bondarenko's heart clinic by 70 percent. "As you can see," he says, "the paint is peeling from the walls and ceilings. I suppose I should be embarrassed, but I'd rather spend the money on bandages than on paint."

Medical care used to be one of Soviet Russia's proudest accomplishments. It was one of the things you were guaranteed as a Soviet citizen, along with a lifetime job of some sort, a place to live, of some sort, and cheap prices for bread and vodka and other basics. You might have to wait in a line for an eternity to get treated for what ailed you, but you eventually got your treatment. And it was for free, paid for out of the national budget. Soviet Russia pioneered socialized medicine.

Free medical care remains the right of every Russian citizen, guaranteed in the constitution. But that's just on paper. Since 1993, Russians have been legally entitled to national health insurance, paid through regional insurance funds. But that system never really got started, and in actual fact, the public health service has essentially ceased to exist. Russia spends less than $100 per person on health care. That's about one-fiftieth of what America spends.

You can buy private health insurance here, if you can afford it, at astronomical rates. Or you can dish out your life savings as a bribe to some doctor or clinic to get the treatment you or your loved ones need. Never mind catastrophic health coverage, getting really sick in Russia is already a catastrophe.

And Russians are making themselves very sick indeed. Alcohol, tobacco, a fatty diet, lack of exercise, and air and water pollution are killing off Russian men and women at a truly alarming rate. Consider: Seventy percent of Russian men and at least a third of Russian women smoke cigarettes. Surveys indicate that the average Russian male consumes three gallons of vodka a year, much of it cheap rotgut that can kill you instantly. Vodka consumption is more than twice what it was when Mikhail Gorbachev launched a brief and much-ridiculed antialcohol campaign in the 1980s. In fact, medical experts say, Gorbachev's edict probably saved a million Russian lives. But you can deduct from that the casualties among the millions of young, newly liberated Russian women who've joined the Virginia Slims generation and are smoking themselves to death. And that catalogue of health horrors doesn't even include the officially under-reported scourge of AIDS, which within a couple of years is likely to infect eight hundred thousand Russians.

Moreover, preventive medicine has virtually ceased to exist. With the result that, in some areas, there are epidemics of tuberculosis, which is not only curable, but has been nearly eradicated in much of the West.

The mortality rate for Russians is now about fifteen per one thousand people. That's almost twice the rate in the United States and puts Russia in league with places like Cambodia and Afghanistan. Before the collapse of the Soviet Union, a Russian man could expect to live to age sixty-four. The current life expectancy for Russian men is fifty-seven, and for women seventy-three. That means that barely half of the sixteen-year-old boys in Russia today can expect to reach the retirement age of sixty. That's much worse than in tsarist times, a century ago.

What is of equal concern is that, because of Russia's continuing economic depression, the birth rate has dropped dramatically.

The consequence: Almost alone among the nations of the world, the Russian population is shrinking, by about half a million people every year. Predictions are that if present trends continue, in the next three decades the population will have dropped from 148 million to 123 million; predominantly old, sick people who will need lots of expensive medical care. Even today, more than one-fourth of Russia's regions now have more old-age pensioners than children.

And too many of those children aren't getting the medical attention they need. Heart surgeons know that if you can operate on a baby with a heart problem right away, the chances of a successful surgery are monumentally higher. The older the child becomes, the more the child's heart and body change, the less the surgeons can do to help.

Among the other mothers with children in the waiting room of St. George's Hospital that day was Lyuba Karachalova. She'd been trying in vain for over a year to get help for her two-year-old daughter, Katya, who sat silently by her side.

Said Mrs. Karachalova, "The doctors in my city told me, 'You are young, you will have another child.' They had already buried my Katya."

Heaven knows how her mother managed to get Katya here, but it probably was in vain. The American surgeons could have repaired Katya's heart when she was born. Now it may be too complicated and dangerous, says Dr. Rossi. "The saddest part is when you see someone that if you'd seen them two years earlier, you could have offered them a normal life."

Tanya Korbenikov, at least, will now most likely have a normal life. In a two-hour operation, Dr. Lopez closed the hole in her heart. By the time she was in the recovery room, you could see the change. Her face was already flushed with new blood pumping from a newly efficient heart. "It's a new beginning for the whole family," smiled Dr. Lopez. "They're now living with a child who doesn't have a disease."

Long life, Tanya Korbenikov. And please, take care of yourself.

chapter 8

The Reindeer People

(February 1997)

W e are, all of us, prisoners of the pictures in our heads. It's the way we remember our history; our own, and the history we share with everybody else. Those shared pictures in our heads might include the last desperate wave from Richard Nixon at the top of the helicopter steps on the White House lawn as he prepared to chopper into exile, or the salute that little John-John Kennedy gave as his father's funeral cortege passed by, days after that president's assassination.

Among the pictures trapped in my own head is one that's more than a quarter-century old. A dusty street outside a trading post on the Navajo reservation near Window Rock, Arizona. It's 9 o'clock in the morning and a Navajo man, already drunk on cheap beer, is staggering up to the trading-post steps. He never makes it. He collapses in the dust, where he'll sleep it off all morning. Above him, flying proudly in the breeze over the building, is an American flag.

It's a picture of failure. The failure of a century-old attempt to take what was left of the Native Americans we'd crowded off their land, confine them to reservations on the meanest part of the land that was left, make them into something resembling the rest of us, and do it all on the cheap. The Sioux, the Cheyenne, the Apache, all of them. First we stole their land, then we robbed them of themselves.

When the taking was done, there were more Navajo left than any of the rest. Their reservation is the biggest, sprawling over four states. The land itself is mostly worthless, although at sunrise or sunset the rouge and purple landscape is a priceless feast for the eyes.

There's no industry or commerce to speak off, and virtually full unemployment.

The Navajo have been on the dole for most of this century. More than half the adult males are arrested at least once a year for getting drunk in public, after squandering their relief checks on overpriced booze at the trading posts. The kids are sent off to boarding school, where they must learn to urinate in open communal lavatories, despite the tribal teachings that a person's toilette is the most private of undertakings. The Bureau of Indian Affairs school I visited had the children busily working away at posters to celebrate St. Patrick's Day. They'd never seen a real shamrock and never would. Every spring, when the snow melted, they'd usually find the bodies of a few children who just walked off into the snow one winter night, to go home, and never made it. The Navajo and the other Native Americans had not come to a pretty pass on the reservations.

But now there's another picture I have in my head. It's the 1990s. And it's a picture of a herd of reindeer, hundreds of them, pounding through the snowdrifts and the scrub pines and white birch in northern Siberia, two hundred miles south of the Arctic Circle. They're wild animals, and the men who are shouting at them, driving them, herding them, seem just as wild, and unafraid of those antlers and sharp hooves that could impale or crush them in an instant.

This is an ancient exercise, one that hasn't changed very much in a couple of thousand years. Herders, on foot, equipped only with a stick, a lasso, and a loud voice, corralling these brawny animals, their antlers taller than any of the herders, into a roped enclosure. Each of the men is clad in a bright blue tunic over his "malitsa," a fur cloak fashioned from the pelts of eight reindeer.

The men are Nenets, and they've lived with and off these animals for almost as long as there have been reindeer on this Yamal peninsula sticking into the Arctic Ocean. The Nenets are Native Russians, just as the Navajo are Native Americans. There are perhaps twenty-five hundred Nenet families here, who move a thousand miles with the seasons and the reindeer; north along the seacoast in winter when the February temperature can drop to fifty below zero Fahrenheit, and south in the summer, where the reindeer pick through the wet snow to feed on the lichens beneath.

Two hundred years ago, when the Sioux and Cheyenne were chasing the buffalo across the American plains, the Nenets were following their reindeer just this way. Like the Plains Indians, to whom some researchers believe they're related, the Nenets live in a kind of

Nenets men lassoing reindeer. (© Bill Gasperini)

tepee. They call it a *choom*, and it's a conical home thirty feet in diameter, made of sixty reindeer pelts strung up on wooden poles. The Nenets can set up a whole village of chooms in less than an hour. Inside, by the heat of a small woodstove, the whole Nenet family spends the long winter nights; eating, sleeping, arguing, laughing, loving, and making love.

The only evidence of modern times is a few porcelain teacups, a small radio, and a gasoline generator. Even the deer harnesses are made from reindeer bone, and the ivory from tusks of prehistoric mammoths entombed in the ice. For dinner it's reindeer meat or fish washed down with reindeer milk and the blood from freshly butchered calves. The Nenets wouldn't know a vegetable if they saw one.

The reindeer set the rhythm of their lives and when the herd moves the chooms come down and, with everything else, are packed aboard the Nenets wooden sleighs; troikas of sorts, each drawn by three reindeer.

This resemblance to the life the Plains Indians once lived in America, before they were cooped up on the reservations, strikes every outsider who comes here. Like Bryan Alexander, an author and naturalist, who has lived with the Nenets and studied them.

"My first impression," he says, "was that I'd arrived on the American prairie of hundreds of years ago."

The Nenets' "reservation," though, is where it always was; on this patch of Arctic tundra entirely circumscribed by the migration of the reindeer. Russian governments, tsarist and Communist, never bothered to try to shove the Nenets someplace else, because nobody wanted this frigid part of Siberia. The Nenets were lucky. Unlike the Native Americans, the Nenets were already living in a part of the country that nobody else coveted.

Not that the government left the Nenets entirely alone. The Soviets enmeshed them in the usual red tape and made them part of the state farm system, at least on paper. But it was a mixed blessing. They could get money for welfare and pensions, like any Soviet citizen, and barter their reindeer pelts and the fish they caught at any of a couple of dozen state exchange stores for whatever they needed. Soviet helicopters airlifted food and supplies in the dead of winter. The children were sent to boarding school for a few years, but they came home every summer to tend the herd. And though many of the thirty thousand Nenets in Russia moved away to the big cities, those that remained with the reindeer could still live their lives as their ancestors had. Nobody got rich, but nobody starved. Even today, most of the younger men in this tribe have served their required two-year hitch in the Russian army. A few saw combat in Chechnya and Afghanistan. But all of them have returned to their families, and the reindeer.

And the Nenets here say they wouldn't trade their get-up-and-go way of life for anything. "This is Maxim," said Maxim's mother, Irina. She is hugging a two-year-old so bundled up against the cold he looks like a large laundry parcel. "He'll be a reindeer herder when he grows up, I hope, although I wouldn't mind if he wanted to go to college. But we'll need him here when he's a man. Besides, the men have it good here. The women do all the work. We light the fires, make the tea, and then get our men out of bed."

Her husband, Yasha, nods. "I don't think life is that hard for us Nenets. I like the freedom, we're at one with nature all the time. Whenever we go to the town, we can't stay long there. Bricks are oppressive to us."

But life is very likely going to get harder for the Nenets, a lot harder. Now that the Soviet system has collapsed and the new Russian government is strapped for money, the social safety net has all but disappeared for the Nenets, as it has for tens of millions of other Russians. The trading posts have been abandoned, the helicopters have stopped coming, and welfare and pension payments are months in arrears.

Anatoly Vanuito, the head of this tribe, is worried. "We're not used to this new way of life. In the past we had money to go to the shops and buy things. Now we don't receive any cash. They say we must sell our reindeer pelts and meat. But we're not salesmen. The Nenets are a hardworking people, but we wouldn't make good businessmen."

The Nenets have always had one advantage over most other Russians, who live in the cities. The Nenets could still live off their reindeer. The question is for how long?

Because suddenly, the Nenets' home has become something of value for somebody else: Russia's huge private gas company, GAZPROM, which has discovered that the Yamal peninsula sits atop one of the largest natural-gas deposits in the world. So GAZPROM is building a natural-gas pipeline, and it hopes to have it in operation by 2005. And with the pipeline comes civilization; roads and traffic and towns and townspeople and trouble, trouble for the reindeer, trouble for the Nenets.

Trucks are already chewing up the fragile tundra, and exhaust soot is killing the lichens that feed the reindeer. Gas workers are shooting the reindeer, dynamiting the fish, and polluting the ocean. And it shows. The reindeer are getting smaller and more prone to disease. The fish are harder to come by now.

Says Chief Vanuito, "If the number of fish continues to fall and the reindeer get sick, it's the end for us. That's it. Our main source of food is fish and reindeer meat."

Bryan Alexander, the naturalist, is worried, too. "The problem is when your whole culture revolves around reindeer herding, if reindeer herding stops, then inevitably, there goes the culture. There go the Nenets. The gas company will be here, who knows, maybe twenty years, thirty years, tapping the gas deposit. Then the gas will be gone and they'll leave. But the big question is, what will they leave behind them and what kind of life will the Nenets have once all the money goes?"

Chief Vanuito and Bryan Alexander could ask the Shoshone and the Pawnee and the Blackfeet all about that.

Two hundred years ago, the Indians and the buffalo had the run of what is now North Dakota, just like the Nenets have had the run of the Yamal Peninsula. That was before they killed off the buffalo and moved the Indians away. I read the other day that so many people have left North Dakota in recent years, there's now some talk of turning it back into a territory. All of a sudden there's room again in North Dakota for the buffalo and Indians. Now they tell us.

chapter 9

Tsar Boris
(March 1997)

Russia doesn't have a Jefferson or a Franklin or a Washington, but Vladimir I, Prince of Kiev, in what is now the Ukraine, is probably as close to a Founding Father as you'll find. He's the one who adopted the Eastern Orthodox religion for his subjects, after carefully considering Roman Catholicism, Judaism, and Islam. Russian history is vague about whether the Muslim strictures against vodka consumption played a part in his rejection of that faith.

Vladimir I died in 1015 after ruling the Russia that was then for almost forty years. He left twelve sons by various mothers and a real succession problem. So when he died, his courtiers managed to keep it a secret for several weeks while they tried to arrange a peaceful transition. Unsuccessfully, as it happened.

Ever since Vladimir, Russians have been (a) subject to more or less one-man rule (or one-woman rule, in the case of Catherine the Great), and (b) extremely circumspect about the health of their leader.

A current case in point is Boris Nikolaivitch Yeltsin, or "Tsar Boris," as his critics call him. There's no president of anywhere that's important who is more powerful than Russian President Yeltsin, at least on paper. Imagine if Bill Clinton could fire most anybody in government he wanted, dissolve Congress, and rule by decree. Boris Yeltsin can do all of that and more. It's a consequence of the new constitution Yeltsin rammed through the electorate a couple of years ago, with the hearty approval and advice of Western politicians and academics. Now some of the academics, at least, are having second thoughts.

"When Communism collapsed, we thought it would be a great idea for the new governments of these newly democratic countries to have very strong chief executives, so they'd be immune to some of the electoral consequences of making the hard decisions necessary for the transition to market economies," one of those Western academics and advice-givers told me over lunch one day.

"We figured that the parliaments wouldn't be as important, so electing them could wait. In hindsight, we should have advised just the opposite. If parliamentary elections had been held right away, the new parliaments would have been packed with reformers. But the parliaments weren't elected until after the economic pain had set in, and people voted their resentment. So they are full of old Communists and others dead-set against reform. Meantime, the new leaders, with all their constitutional muscles, are acting just as autocratically as their Communist predecessors, and ordinary citizens feel just as estranged and disconnected from their leaders as before. Instead of taking initiatives, they just wait for the president to do something, just like they used to wait for the tsar or the local commissar to do something. It's discouraging."

And suppose something should happen to the all-powerful captain of one of these jury-rigged ships of state, with its fractious parliament and poverty-stricken, estranged electorate, seething with rage at the consequences of capitalism? What then?

That was the *kashmar*, the nightmare, as the Russians say, that troubled Western governments in the last half of 1996, whenever they contemplated Russia. Boris Yeltsin was the keystone of the new Russia. He had a personal relationship with Bill Clinton. Boris and Bill. He was best buddies with the German chancellor, Helmut Kohl. Boris and Helmut. And now Boris Yeltsin was suddenly desperately ill.

What was worse, the same constitution that had made Yeltsin so all-powerful was maddeningly vague on the subject of succession. Russia has no vice president. If Yeltsin were to die or become incapacitated, the prime minister, Victor Chernomyrdin, a colorless Yeltsin loyalist, would run the government for three months. Then there would have to be a new election for president, and the result of that would most likely be a real *kashmar*.

Boris Yeltsin had only himself to blame. He'd overindulged on food and wine and vodka for too many years. At age sixty-five, he was sixty pounds overweight and had a history of heart trouble going back at least a decade.

In 1995, a couple of days after downing a remarkable quantity of white wine at a luncheon in his honor at Hyde Park, New York, hosted by President Clinton, Yeltsin was rushed to a Kremlin hospital after suffering his first heart attack.

Nonetheless, by the following spring, Yeltsin was out on the Russian hustings, glad-handing and doing his version of the two-step onstage with local rock bands at his campaign rallies, as the Russian presidential elections approached. Yeltsin managed a narrow victory in the first round of voting, but then dropped from view. For the remainder of the campaign, he was a candidate in absentia, but thanks to some neat political maneuvering by his advisors and friendly TV coverage from the Russian media, which was owned and controlled by Yeltsin backers, he won the final round comfortably, and was elected to a second term.

What Russians didn't know was that between the rounds of voting, Yeltsin had suffered a second heart attack, and that they'd elected a chronically ill man, virtually incapacitated by heart disease. For months, Yeltsin's last heart attack was kept a secret to all except his family and a few advisors. The courtiers of Vladimir I would have been proud.

But by late that summer, it was obvious something was wrong with Tsar Boris. He could barely walk, much less talk, at his inauguration ceremony. He was spending all of his time at his country residence. And in the parliament, his critics were demanding that Yeltsin step down.

In the end, the doctors saved his life and preserved, at least for a time, the Russian Experiment. A team of eight Russian heart specialists, headed by Dr. Renat Akchurin, performed quintuple-bypass surgery on Yeltsin's heart at Moscow's cardiology center early in November. The operation took eight hours and Dr. Akchurin, who'd performed hundreds of other such bypass surgeries, said, "I tried to put out of my mind that this was the president of Russia and just thought of him as a patient."

Dr. Akchurin was counseled by Dr. Michael DeBakey of Houston, who pioneered heart-transplant surgery a generation ago. The morning after the surgery, following a visit to Yeltsin's bedside, Dr. DeBakey, who is eighty-eight years old now, radiated optimism.

"He's doing fine, really," DeBakey told me. "As a matter of fact, if you wanted to script it, you couldn't do better." But could this Boris Yeltsin, this florid-faced, obese man, so obviously crippled by pain, the one we'd seen in his rare TV appearances of late, ever really recover? Would the new Boris, even if he survived, ever again resemble the old Boris?

"Sure," said Dr. DeBakey. "If he takes care of himself, he can live a healthy life for the next twenty years. I think you're going to see a vigorous, vital person again. All the rest of his body is in good shape. Now that he's got a good heart, the body should function perfectly normally. And I would predict he'll be able to return to his office and carry out his duties in a perfectly normal fashion."

We put that on TV, but I never said what I was thinking; that at the very least, Dr. DeBakey was guilty of practicing hyperbole, and at worst perhaps that eighty-eight-year-old brain of his was going a bit spongy.

My view of all this seemed to be confirmed in the weeks that followed. Yeltsin emerged from the hospital, and by Christmas pronounced himself "prepared for battle." He'd lost sixty pounds, his suits hung on him like sackcloth, his voice was barely audible, and he was obviously still in some agony. He looked, in short, just like somebody recovering from major surgery.

By early January, Yeltsin was back in the hospital with pneumonia, and his principal adversary, Alexendar Lebed, was saying Yeltsin ought to resign for the good of Russia. "There's simply a power vacuum in this country," said Lebed, "it's rudderless." Most of the media, domestic and foreign, were saying more or less what I was saying, "It's now questionable whether Boris Yeltsin will ever be healthy enough to lead Russia to recovery."

So much for the wisdom of politicians and journalists. The other day Boris Yeltsin went out in public to deliver his most important speech in six months; his state-of-the-nation address to the parliament. It had been less than two months since his bout with pneumonia. He stood tall and confident. Yeltsin was full of vim and vigor and moral outrage, railing against crime, corruption, and tax deadbeats, and promising that tax reform, military reform, and law and order will be his first priorities for the next three years. Tsar Boris was back, looking like a man who's got another twenty years of life left, and meaning to make the most of it.

Looks like I owe Dr. Michael DeBakey an apology. But I want to spend a few more months observing the patient before apologizing. I'm a pessimist at heart.

chapter 10

NATO Nightmare
(March 1997)

"I t's quiet up here," says Lt. Col. Hugo Ostreng. "It's always quiet up here. The hardest thing I have to do is to convince my soldiers that they must always be prepared for the impossible."

Lieutenant Colonel Ostreng commands a couple of hundred Norwegian army troopers whose mission it is to guard several hundred square miles of Norway's border along the Pasvik River in Lapland, two hundred miles above the Arctic Circle. He and his predecessors have spent much of the last half-century on watch here.

Just now, he's squinting through the eyepiece of a three-foot-long pair of binoculars in a watchtower that resembles the fire towers the U.S. Forest Service keeps to watch for brushfires in the Sierras. But this isn't the Sierras. The snow is waist-high outside and the only greenery is the occasional stand of scrub pines that dot the tundra.

And Hugo Ostreng is not worried about forest fires. His official concern is what he's looking at on the opposite bank of the Pasvik: Russia. It's just as barren and snowy over there as it is over here, and the only clear and present danger to Norway seems to come from what he's peering at; the pollution from the ore smelters in Nikel, which drifts across from Russia now and then, carrying heaven-knows-what nasty chemicals.

Day and night the Norwegians patrol the border on skis and snowmobiles, carefully staying on their side of the ice. The Pavlik's usually nothing but ice. The weather here, the locals say, is "ten months of snow and two months of bad skiing." The Russian border guards have their own patrols, and like the Norwegians are under strict instructions; when they encounter the other fellows, they salute correctly and keep moving.

Hardly a shot has ever been fired in anger here, and there has been nothing in the way of what you'd call border "incidents."

The squad leader in this watchtower, Cpl. Petter Hagen, who looks like he just stepped out of a surfboard commercial(and in fact spent a year attending San Diego State) admits, "Sometimes when it's foggy and nothing happens, it gets boring to sit up here in the tower, but I think we do feel we do an important job."

Like all eligible Norwegian men over eighteen, Corporal Hagen has to spend a year on active military duty. As soldiering goes, this is pretty good duty. Except nothing ever happens. Well, one time.

That was on a misty morning in 1956, which, as it happened, was the day Moscow ordered the invasion of Hungary. When the mist cleared, the Norwegians looked up to discover that the riverbank on the Russian side was lined with Soviet tanks, their muzzles pointed at Norway. A show of force, apparently, in case the Norwegians were going to get any ideas. The Norwegians had one idea.

"We called our commanders, and they called the Soviet commanders," says Hugo Ostreng. "We asked the Soviets if they'd mind turning their gun turrets around in the opposite direction. After a while they did, and finally the tanks themselves turned around and went home."

The border here was closed for a long time, but after the Soviet Union became Russia, it was opened up. Now there's a bustling new customs-immigration building at Kirkenes, Norway, which services busloads of Russian merchants who come over from Murmansk on weekends to sell trinkets to the Norwegians in Kirkenes's town square. It's all perfectly legal.

And there's no illegal immigration to speak of. No Norwegian in his right mind would want to sneak into Russia. And any Russian who'd want to leave certainly wouldn't want to come all the way to Lapland when these days he can save up and buy a plane ticket to Vienna or Prague.

So Lieutenant Colonel Ostreng and his soldiers are the Maytag repairmen of this little piece of Lapland. Things are so friendly nowadays that they sometimes get together with the Russian border guards for cross-country ski competitions. Off duty of course.

Which is something of a curiosity, because this is the one single place where the North Atlantic Treaty Organization actually touches Russia. Norway is one of the sixteen NATO countries and has been since NATO's inception almost fifty years ago. Although the Norwegian parliament decided early on not to let NATO troops from any other countries anywhere near this border, the fact is that all the time there was a Soviet Union and a Warsaw Pact, the Communists and the West were eyeball-to-eyeball right here.

The Soviet Union is now Russia, and the Warsaw Pact has disintegrated into a collection of independent, more or less democratic nations. Many of them are begging to get into NATO just in case the Russians ever again start getting ideas.

You could argue that it was precisely because there *is* a NATO that things have been so quiet along the Pasvik River all these years, not to mention along the rest of the border with the West. That's Mutual Deterrence. And in that sense, NATO has been one of the most successful and enduring military alliances in history; a brotherhood of like-minded democracies each pledged to defend the others in the event of an attack, and to share defense strategies and intelligence.

Up here in the clear cold air of Lapland is a good place to reflect upon what's happening to NATO these days. And from where I'm standing, it doesn't seem so good.

NATO was organized, you'll remember, to protect Western Europe, Canada, and the United States from the Soviet Union and its satellite nations in the Warsaw Pact. So now the Soviet Union has become Russia, tacitly democratic and capitalist. The Warsaw Pact is history, and the Cold War is over. So what's happening to NATO? It's *expanding.* It appears that by next summer, Hungary, Poland, and the Czech Republic, three veterans of the Warsaw Pact, will be the newest members of NATO, for reasons that have less to do with defense than with politics and economics.

Here's President Bill Clinton (quoted by the Associated Press), stumping through Detroit last October, in the final days of his reelection campaign, intent on wringing every last vote out of the Polish-American, Bohemian-American, and Hungarian-American communities in the Midwest:

> Today, I want to state America's goal: By 1999, NATO's fiftieth anniversary and ten years after the fall of the Berlin Wall, the first group of countries we invite to join should be full-fledged members of NATO. (Applause)

After which Mr. Clinton went over to the Polish Village Café and dined on kielbasa. His opponent, Bob Dole, seemed just as anxious to get out the ethnic vote for the Republicans. The same day, in Frankenmuth, Michigan, Dole accused the president of foot-dragging: "The time to begin [NATO] expansion for Hungary, Poland, and the Czech Republic is now."

A year previously, Mr. Clinton and his aides had quietly decided to press for NATO expansion, adopting an idea originally suggested by the Germans. Washington figured that since NATO is the most prominent official vehicle of American influence in Europe, a bigger NATO would be an even better one, but the politics of Campaign '96 also loomed large. So now Bill Clinton is a second-term president and ever since, the White House has been trying to figure out how to deal with the consequences of this impetuousness.

The nations of Western Europe, which owe their peace and prosperity to NATO, have supported the American initiative to bring in some new members. (The Germans have been most vociferous in their support, mainly because they'd rather have the Poles, instead of themselves, on NATO's eastern border with Russia.) Why have the Europeans, who are a lot closer to Russia, let America take the lead in this matter? Aren't they worried that their mutual defense club will be compromised?

Not as worried as they are about the economic threat from Eastern Europe's farms and factories. Though they don't like to talk about it, the original members of the NATO club, now part of the European Union, are hoping they can keep the Poles and Czechs and Hungarians happy with a NATO membership, and keep them out of the EU. That way, they reason, they won't have to worry about competing with cheaper products and cheaper labor from behind what used to be the Iron Curtain. In the words of Michael Mandelbaum of Johns Hopkins University, "We are going to extend the NATO nuclear umbrella to the Eastern Europeans so that the Western Europeans won't have to buy their tomatoes" (quoted in the *Washington Post*).

Mandelbaum is one of a number of Western academics who have real misgivings about a bigger NATO. Not least of whom is the granddaddy of Russian experts, George Kennan, who thinks that, "Expanding NATO would be the most fateful error of American policy in the entire post–Cold War era."

Hyperbole? Not necessarily. Kennan is most concerned about what it will do to Russia's still shaky experiment with capitalist democracy. Will it weaken Boris Yeltsin's hand? Will it help the nationalist hardliners who've never been comfortable with either capitalism or democracy? Will it put a stop to progress on arms control? In short, will making NATO bigger to protect the West from a return of the Soviet bogeyman become a self-fulfilling prophecy? Answer: very likely.

Washington has been trying to prevent that by putting the best face on things; giving Russia a consultative role in NATO (although not a seat at the NATO table), signing a security charter with Moscow full of assurances about future deployment of nuclear weapons closer to Russia, and even outright bribery, reportedly promising the Russians tens of billions of dollars in credits and investments in return for not protesting too much. Finally, Russia has been awarded a consultative role in the G-7 group of industrialized nations.

The fact is, there isn't anything much the Russians *can* do about NATO expansion except protest, which they've done long and loudly. Russians have long memories; they know that most of the calamities that have been visited on them have come from the West. And no matter the assurances and goodies from the West, NATO expansion (even if it doesn't eventually include the Baltic nations, which are also on the NATO waiting list) will leave the largest nation on Earth sitting on NATO's eastern flank, feeling left out and bitter about it.

But leave aside what all this may or may not do to Russia. What will it do to NATO? What's always been so important about NATO is its nuts and bolts; the network of standardized airfields, standardized weapons, and logistical facilities with which it faced the Warsaw Pact. That and the demonstrated willingness to react promptly and in concert to a threat against any member nation.

Even as late as the 1970s, when West Germany no longer seemed under constant threat from the East, the summers always featured a big NATO exercise, when U.S. Army troops would hold joint maneuvers with the West Germans and other NATO forces. I can still remember the columns of American tanks in "Operation Reforger," tearing across the green fields near Munich, practicing in case the real thing ever became necessary. The local farmers, of course, were more than happy to watch their farmland being turned into tank tracks; they were getting generously compensated for all the NATO damage. Like the corn farmers back in my home state of Iowa, who used to get paid by the government for not planting corn, it was a no-lose proposition.

"Reforger" was more than practice. It was NATO's way of showing the Russians, and the member nations themselves, that NATO was more than just a charter; it was a military alliance fully prepared to back up its promises with action.

Are Poland, Hungary, and the Czech Republic ready for that kind of role? Not now, certainly, and not for a very long time. Most NATO officials think it will take at least a decade to get the military forces of those three countries in shape to participate in full-scale NATO maneuvers. As one NATO officer has remarked, "It could take Poland twenty years to be as compatible with NATO as Greece is now."

And if, heaven forbid, the Poles or Czechs or Hungarians are attacked by Russia or another non-NATO member, which NATO countries will come to their aid? Will American boys be sent to die in defense of Lublin or Bialystok? Will French boys? Or German or British boys? Don't bet on it.

Or will NATO's taxpayers be willing to foot the bill for enlargement? Depending on whether you talk to the White House or the Congressional Budget Office, the total bill for NATO expansion will run between $35 billion and $61 billion. That's over and above the $474 billion that the sixteen NATO nations are already spending on defense every year.

All of this to defend against Russia, which presently has a gross domestic product of just $284 billion, a military establishment that has been cut by a third, ground troops who haven't been paid in three months, infantry soldiers who are reduced to scrounging for food, and an air force that didn't purchase a single new combat plane last year.

It seems clear enough up here on a bright March day in Norway's north; NATO expansion is going to be a bad thing, accomplished for all the worst reasons. Instead of a security alliance that helped win the Cold War, NATO is in danger of turning into another debating society like the old League of Nations. If you want to insure peace and prosperity in Eastern Europe, bring it into the common market of the European Union. If you want to make Russia safe for democracy and make a friend and ally east of the Elbe, include Russia in a new Congress of Vienna, where all the nations that are part of NATO, and those which are not, formally guarantee all present European frontiers and vow to refrain from forceful aggression against one another.

A new and bigger NATO is the last thing the world needs with which to confront the twenty-first century. I keep thinking about an afternoon in the summer of 1984, at the Democratic Convention in San Francisco. I was sitting with the late Morris Udall—the congressman from Arizona, and by far the most entertaining of the various candidates for president. The Democrats had nominated poor Walter Mondale to run against the incumbent, Ronald Reagan. And even at that point, most everybody, including Mondale I think, realized it was a lost cause. "You know," Udall remarked, "the trouble with politicians is that they are just like the generals; they are always fighting the last war."

Mo, wait until you hear what the politicians are doing to NATO!

chapter 11

Vladimir and Nicholas
(April 1997)

I t's official. Vladimir Ilyich Lenin is in great shape and should last for at least several hundred more years. That's the verdict of the embalmers who have just finished fixing up Lenin's mummy, a periodic process, to make him presentable. While they were at it, the authorities also fixed up Lenin's mausoleum in Red Square and now Lenin is again available for viewing, although only a small crowd of schoolkids and tourists were there to see him at the reopening.

Lenin, whose real name was Vladimir Ilyich Ulyanov, died of a stroke in 1924, seven years after engineering the Bolshevik revolution. And you know the rest of that story. Communists didn't believe in saints—religion was the opiate of the people, that sort of thing. But if Communism had ever had a saint, Lenin would have been it.

It has been almost a decade now since Communism fell out of favor here, and Russians are having a hard time dealing with Lenin's place. Not just his place in history, but around town in Moscow.

A gigantic statue of Lenin remains on Leninskiy Prospect, one of those huge Moscow boulevards built wide enough to accommodate a platoon of army tanks, should they ever be needed (which they were once or twice a few years ago). Now he faces a panorama of brightly lit billboards advertising cigarettes, underwear, soda pop, and electronic gadgetry, all produced somewhere else than in Russia. Lenin's arm is raised in what you imagine is outrage.

A while ago, they changed the name of Russia's second city, from

A statue of Lenin is found in the square of most every town and village . . . even today. (© George French)

Lenin's Tomb. (© George French)

Leningrad back to St. Petersburg. But another of those vast Moscow boulevards, Leningradsky Prospect, remains just that. It is, incidentally, the way to Sheremetyevo, the international airport. I wonder sometimes if perhaps Lenin has his arm raised to try to hail a taxi for Sheremetyevo.

Anyway, we have it now on authority that Lenin is aging splendidly. The problem is, what to do with him? Last month President Boris Yeltsin, who until recently, with all his heart troubles, seemed in far worse condition than Lenin's last remains, took to wondering publicly whether it might be about time to remove Lenin's mummy from Red Square.

There are historians who insist it was Lenin's dying wish to be buried quietly next to his mother in St. Petersburg. Instead, Stalin ordered him mummified and put on display. It wasn't so long ago that no self-respecting Soviet couple would think of getting married without visiting Lenin's tomb on the wedding day. Now he's a white elephant.

Even so, Lenin's probably resting more peacefully than his ideological mentor Karl Marx, who is buried in a tomb in Highgate Cemetery in London. They say that Marx rests on the bottom, underneath, respectively, his wife, his daughter, and his housekeeper, each of whom made his life miserable.

But Lenin's heirs, the Communists who dominate the Duma, the lower house of Russia's parliament, are not about to take President Yeltsin's musings about Lenin's proper place lying down, so to speak. One of the deputies rose to shout "Hands off Vladimir Ilyich," and threatened violence if anybody tried to cart Lenin away. The Duma has now passed a resolution condemning the idea as "vandalism."

While the Lenin question is still up in the air here, the matter of what do about the other principal in the drama of 1917 seems to have been pretty well decided. Namely, Nicholas II, the last of the tsars. Tsar Nicholas, you'll recall, was arrested shortly after the revolution broke out, and the following year, murdered with most of the rest of the last of the Romanovs.

There's also a statue of Tsar Nicholas in Moscow, the only one in Russia. Or rather there *was* one, because at this writing it's scattered in little pieces where it once stood, in a barren field overlooking an old power station on the northeast outskirts.

The other night, person or persons unknown attached a pound of TNT to it and blew the tsar to smithereens.

The statue was commissioned last year to commemorate the one-hundredth anniversary of the tsar's coronation, but plans to put it in downtown Moscow never quite got off the ground, and the consequence was a nasty argument between the Russian Communists and the Russian monarchists.

The authorities have made no arrests and seem frankly flummoxed as to who's responsible. There was one theory that it was the work of critics of the sculptor Vyacheslav Klykov, who has been campaigning for a restoration of the monarchy. People in the neighborhood thought it was some of the local farmers who complained that the statue was taking up part of their potato patches. Some thought it might even have been some Moscow city officials, who were never that excited about finding a spot for the tsar in the first place.

A couple of days later, something called the "Workers and Peasants Red Army," an outfit previously unheard from, claimed responsibility. It said the statue was destroyed as an "act of reprisal against those who intend to commit a sacrilege against the national shrine, the V. I. Lenin Mausoleum." In other words, let Lenin be. The authorities insist they are not taking the claim seriously.

No question, though, that whoever blasted the tsar did a professional job: wiring, car battery, trigger device, the whole package. Normally, this sort of summary method of dispatch is reserved for living people.

Bombing is a favorite mob method of terminating troublemakers here. Just the other morning an explosion jarred Betsy and me out of our morning fog while we were having coffee in the kitchen. Down the street, a neighbor, one of those Moscow "businessmen" whose "business" it is wise not to inquire about, was crossing the threshold of his apartment just as somebody triggered a bomb in a nearby drainpipe. The result was that our neighbor wound up in roughly the same condition as the tsar's statue.

Then again, you don't always have to be breathing to be a bomb target here. A while back somebody snuck a bomb into the grave of a Chechen war veteran who was being buried (he'd been the victim of, what else? a bomb attack) and blew him up again, along with eleven of the mourners. That's overkill.

But don't feel too sorry for the tsar. The sculptor has vowed to replace his statue. And meantime, the Russian Orthodox Church, which has made a big comeback after seventy-odd years of Communist suppression, has announced its intention to rebury the tsar (the genuine article) and his family in the Romanovs' imperial vault next summer in St. Petersburg.

And further, the church intends to canonize Nicholas and his family. An ecclesiastical commission has spent the past five years doing the necessary research for making somebody a saint, and the Romanovs have passed the test. They won't be included under the "martyr" category, but they qualify as so-called passion sufferers, those who, according to the church examiners, are to be revered for the humble Christian way in which they faced their execution. Although it's not quite clear, given the circumstances of their arrest and detention, how the Romanovs could have done otherwise.

In the meantime, Russia's church and state will presumably have to settle a nasty little issue that's bedeviled the matter of the tsar's demise almost since it took place.

A couple of years ago, the Holy Synod of the Russian Orthodox Church submitted a series of questions about the Romanov murders, including one which inquired whether Nicholas and his family were victims, not of the Bolsheviks, but of Jews and Masons, who sacrificed them in a ritual murder.

A government commission has been established to examine this question and report its findings in due course. Russia may be the only place on Earth where this scurrilous charge would even be given a hearing. But the church hierarchy is responding to its Wacky Wing, the nationalist-monarchist reactionaries, who have been peddling this sort of anti-Semitic bilge since before the Russian Revolution. They refuse to believe either the historians or the DNA evidence that the bones exhumed from an unmarked grave in Yekaterinburg in 1991 are in fact those of the royal family. No, it's all simply a deception to hide a vast international conspiracy, say the diehards.

It's the same sort of bloody-mindedness that launched any number of pogroms against the Jews when the tsars were still around, and it's obvious that a big broad streak of anti-Semitism exists here even after seventy years of Communism and almost a decade of quasi-democracy.

No wonder when you go to Israel these days, half the signs seem to be in Russian. The minute Communism collapsed here and the barriers were lifted, tens of thousands of Russian Jews picked up and went to Israel. They knew where they were not wanted. In retrospect, it seems as though they have done the right thing.

No doubt that government commission will eventually blame the Romanovs' demise on the Bolsheviks, which will doubtless fail to convince the diehards among the Russian proletariat, who will continue to think dark thoughts about Jews, Masons, Protestants, Blacks, Chinese, and anybody else who isn't them.

Thus in the eighty years since 1917, Russia's come full circle. Vladimir Ilyich Lenin, the brilliant, benevolent father of the Russian proletariat, as the communists portrayed him, has been reduced to so much excess baggage taking up valuable commercial space in Moscow's downtown. And Tsar Nicholas, the bloody tyrant whose demise made Russia safe for Communism, as the Bolsheviks saw it, will now become a saint.

In fact, the evidence indicates, Lenin was certainly brilliant, but to put it kindly, wasn't a very nice man. And Tsar Nicholas was no bloody tyrant, but a rather timid, henpecked husband who wasn't up to playing autocrat, much less running Russia.

To an outsider, it's revealing that you won't find many Russians who take the middle view. Russians like going to extremes. You're either a Lenin-lover or a tsarist.

This penchant for all or nothing may explain why, almost a decade after the Soviet Union ceased to exist, the Russians still haven't come up with a new national anthem. There is a tune they play here at occasions of state. It's a stirring melody by Michael Ivanovich Glinka, the nineteenth-century Russian composer, whose best-known work is the opera *A Life for the Tsar*, just so you know where his sympathies lay. But nobody's yet come up with words to accompany the music.

So there's America with a national anthem that's got great lyrics and a tune that is, for most of us, virtually unsingable. And here's Russia with a great tune and no words for it. Perhaps somewhere beyond the Urals there's a Russian Francis Scott Key waiting for the proper muse.

In any case, the debate over doing something or not about the Bolshevik and the tsar is at least a diversion from some more pressing, and depressing, concerns of ordinary Muscovites, like the prospect of a steady paycheck, or how to cope with sky-high prices, and a government that doesn't do much of anything because it's almost broke.

Will Lenin move out of the Kremlin? Will Tsar Nicholas become St. Nicholas even though, as every child knows at Christmas, there already is one? The Russians have a saying: "In Russia today, the only thing more unpredictable than the future, is the past."

chapter 12

Buy Russian!
(April 1997)

J ust like the president of another country with which I'm familiar, Boris Yeltsin, the president of Russia, has a weekly radio address devoted to little homilies about the issues of the day.

A couple of weeks ago, the Yeltsin topic was buying Russian. In a grandfatherly sort of way (he is a grandfather), he scolded Russians for their penchant for buying things from other countries when, he insisted, there are perfectly good Russian versions for sale right here at home.

That news prompted a call from one of my editors back in New York, wondering whether there was a funny story in all that.

"Everybody knows the Russians can't make anything that works right, much less that anybody, including Russians, would want to buy," he said. "Can't we do a piece about how silly he's being about all this?"

I replied that I didn't think Yeltsin was being any sillier than the wife of a former American president who some years ago tried to get a handle on the country's drug problem by urging young people to "just say no."

"Russia does make a lot of shoddy consumer goods," I said, "but when Russians put their minds and resources to it, they can make stuff as good as we do, sometimes better."

"Name one thing."

"Well, let's see. Nuclear bombs. Missiles. The AK-47 assault rifle.

Their new jet fighters are said to be every bit as good as ours. Their space-launch rockets are among the best in the world. And the chicken and vegetables you get here at the market stalls are better than anything I remember at the supermarkets at home."

"Oh, never mind," said my editor. I hung up with him, convinced that he'd already written me off as just another in a long line of foreign correspondents who'd already "gone native"; become an advocate for the people of whatever overseas capital they happened to live in. Humph, might as well be talking to a Muscovite, I could hear him thinking to himself.

Had I "gone native"? I searched my soul and declared myself innocent. I'd been living in Moscow for only six months. And like any "ex-pat," somebody from someplace else who's living here for a while and will go home someday, I'd found a lot of fault with this place: the traffic; the filthy air; the creaky, oppressive bureaucracy; the rude, brusque way Russians often behave with strangers (not to mention each other); the dearth of smiles.

But Russians, I had discovered, are also a clever, inventive, industrious, and extremely well educated people who've managed to play the best hand they can with what history has dealt them over the past several centuries, from serfdom to Soviet.

And these days, like Rodney Dangerfield, they get no respect. In the last few years, Russia has lost a big war in Afghanistan, a nasty little one in Chechnya, and lost one hundred million of its Soviet citizens who've been absorbed into a long list of newly independent nations, parts of what used to comprise the Soviet empire. Russia's presently the sick man of Europe, and so it's not surprising that, just now, Russians aren't feeling very good about themselves.

Except, of course, for some of the "Novy Russky," the New Russians, who've managed to find a way to profit from the pell-mell rush into capitalism. They're the ones who race around in fancy cars and pay top dollar for the new Turkish-built apartment houses that are going up all over Moscow. And they're the butt of all the Novy Russky jokes. (Example: two Novy Russky kids are playing in a sandbox and one says to the other, "Sasha, stop using your cell phone to shovel sand into your sand pail. You'll break it and then your dad will replace it with nothing put a pager, like any ordinary kid!")

They're the ones who can afford to buy all those new foreign-made goodies, and presumably were President Yeltsin's target audience. And the reason they buy new Volvos and BMWs and interface with their Japanese and American computers is that they are better than the domestic models. In that the Novy Russky are just like Americans.

Those ordinary Russians who listened to their president on the radio must have done so with wry amusement. When they can afford a car, it's usually a Moskvytch or one of the other Russian runabouts; basic transportation, to be kind. It's still commonplace for Russians to take their new Russian car from the assembly line straight over to their local mechanic, to install all the missing parts, reconnect all the misconnected widgets, and get it in running condition.

Russia doesn't make good cars or computers or other consumer products because under the old Soviet system, it wasn't necessary. It was not a supply-and-demand economy; it was demand and supply, and the demand was not from consumers but from some guys way up in some big offices somewhere. And Russian factories still haven't got the hang of making things people want to buy, and making them better and cheaper than somebody somewhere else.

I would have conceded, had my New York editor thought to observe, that most of the things Russia still does make well are not what most Russians could or would want to own: guns and tanks and missiles, etc. Long after the end of the Cold War, Russia remains one of the most prolific and proficient weapons makers on Earth. For more than half a century, when it came to design, production, and quality control of the tools of war, the industry here was every bit as adept as Detroit was with automobiles. While we were obsessed with Keeping Up With the Russians, they were trying to Keep Up With the Americans. By the late 1980s, perhaps a third of the entire Soviet economy was devoted to defense spending. Nobody knows exactly. But it was in no small part that drain on the Soviet system that doomed it. Back in 1972, while he was running for president of the United States, I recall George McGovern warning about the consequences of the continued massive spending on defense by both countries. If it didn't stop, he said, America and the Soviet Union would find themselves "fellow travelers on the road to ruin." The Soviets were simply ruined first.

So here's Russia today, caught in the twilight zone between capitalism and Communism, where the rich only want to buy things that don't have a made in Russia label, and everybody else can't afford to buy much of anything. And their president is reduced to whining about it on the radio. I can hear my editor snickering right now: "Can't those Russians do anything right?"

Oh yes. Take the Moscow Metro. You can take the Moscow Metro to any of 161 stations over 162 miles of track, for only twenty-five cents. Nine million Muscovites take it every working day. It's the busiest subway in the world.

It's certainly the most beautiful. It was begun in the 1930s,

A woman sweeps the stairs as commuters walk through Komsomolskaya subway station, in Moscow. Chandeliers, intricate mosaics, bronze statues, and marble columns give Moscow's subway an air of elegance in sharp contrast to the above-ground view that tends toward the dreary. (AP Photo/Peter Dejong)

during the Depression in the West. When in America the government was setting the unemployed to work on public buildings and dams and highways, in Moscow they were building the Metro.

Communist youth brigades and students worked side by side with the sandhogs and labor gangs. The kids were volunteers. Some of the others were not. But they kept at it, even during World War II, when the German army was at Moscow's front door.

They're still building it today. The Moscow Metro will probably always be a work in progress. As it is, though, it remains the closest thing that Communism ever had to a cathedral. The central stations, most often seen by visitors, are galleries of Socialist realism: statuary, frescoes, chandeliers. Lenin is everywhere. Lenin in bas-relief, Lenin in stained glass. It remains a monument to the hopes and dreams of a Soviet utopia. Heroic Red soldiers and sailors stand guard, preserved in stone. Happy peasants dance on the ceilings, captured in colorful tile. The dream is gone now, but the artifacts remain, perfectly preserved, at every Moscow Metro station. It's like a museum, really. A place for contemplation in quiet moments. A place to meet. A place to talk. And it's high on the list of every tourist group. The Metro never ceases to elicit a chorus of "oohs" and "aahs" from veterans of the subway systems in say, New York or Tokyo.

Like a museum, the Metro is almost hygienically clean. The platforms are done in marble, eleven kinds of it, and they are scrubbed several times every day, along with the statues and everything else. No graffiti, either. No self-respecting Muscovite would think of using spray paint on the Metro. "*Nyekultorno!*" "Uncultured!" they'd say.

It's relatively safe because there are plenty of transit policemen; a cop on every corner. And though the Metro is big and bustling, it's not necessarily impersonal. There are lots of uniformed women, station agents, to help people through the turnstiles and give them directions. People like Faina Alexandrovna, a stout, motherly woman who tends the turnstile at the Metro stop near my apartment. Faina manages to keep smiling ten hours a day while the huddled masses flow past her. She's been doing this same thing for thirty years, and she actually seems to like it. "The Metro is an amazing place!" she says.

It *is* amazing. And efficient, too. There's a train arriving at your station every seventy seconds, on average. And though some of the cars are forty years old, there's a big shop at the end of the line where they keep them fixed up like new. The ride is so smooth you can read a book. In fact, as you'll notice, most Muscovites don't read the sports scores or the stock market on their Metro. They read books. Can't those Russians do anything right? They do the Moscow Metro right.

After I hung up with my New York editor, I thought to myself, I should have told him about the Moscow Metro! In one of those imaginary lectures I always give to New York editors after I've finished talking with them on the phone, I remarked sternly, "Listen! I'm no Russian apologist, but don't sell the Russians short! They whipped Napoleon, they whipped Hitler, they were first in space, and in Moscow, the trains still run on time!"

chapter 13

Second in Space
(May 1997)

I
t was a chilly October morning and the last few
leaves were still gripping the maple trees on the campus of Ripon
College in central Wisconsin. It was 7 A.M. and I turned on the radio in
my dormitory room as always, so I could listen to the CBS World News
Roundup and just have time for a shower before my 8 A.M. Byzantine history class over in Lane Library with Dr. Webster. It was 1957.

The big news on the radio that morning was about a sound. A
beep. The Soviet Union had just launched something called a satellite; the *Sputnik*, they'd named it. It was in orbit around Earth, right
overhead. And you could hear it making "beeps" at regular intervals
if you could tune into the right radio frequency. I was dumbfounded.
How could the Communists do something like that, something
America couldn't?

A month later, the Soviets launched another *Sputnik*. This one
had a live dog, Laika, aboard it. Two years later, they sent an unmanned probe to the moon. And by 1961, they put the first human
being in space, Yuri Gagarin. It took me and the rest of America a
long time to get over the shock. And though I wasn't all that vocal
about it (central Wisconsin, the stomping ground of the late Senator
Joe McCarthy, was about as anti-Communist as you could get), I
admired what the Soviets and their cosmonaut had done. Little did I
realize what they'd started with *Sputnik*. The other day, somebody
figured out that there are now 8,658 man-made objects orbiting
Earth, most of them space junk.

Yuri Gagarin is immortalized in a huge shiny metal monument, riding a column of energy on Leninskiy Prospect, one of the big Moscow thoroughfares, where tens of thousands of people welcomed him back to Earth thirty-six years ago. But these days his expression looks more pained than determined.

The Russians dropped from first in space to a distant second a long time ago, of course. Now that Washington and Moscow are cooperating in space, it's become a source of deep embarrassment, even to ordinary Russians, that their country's space effort has become so feeble that Moscow's having terrible troubles even holding up its end.

Item: The Russians' $300 million Mars 1996 probe, designed to drop equipment on the Martian surface, never even got into Earth orbit. A booster malfunction caused it to crash into the ocean last November.

Item: A week later, Moscow officials had to admit that Russia's last two spy satellites had finally fallen from orbit, leaving the country without any satellite reconnaissance.

Item: In the first few months of this year, the world's only space station, the Russians' MIR, was plagued by a fire, a leak in the cooling system, a glitch in the carbon dioxide filters, a balky gyroscope, and a failure in the crew's oxygen equipment. When docking with a cargo unit failed, crew members couldn't even unload their own waste. The MIR was designed to last for five years. It's now been in use for eleven, and it's showing its age.

The reasons for all this are obvious enough: Russia no longer has the wherewithal to afford a big space program, not to mention much of anything else that requires government money. Funding for the space effort is now only about 20 percent of the more than three billion dollars the old Soviet Union was spending annually on space as recently as 1989.

So Russia is staying in space on a shoestring, and it shows. At the cosmonaut training facility in Star City, at the edge of Moscow, there's no longer enough money to pay people to paint the walls or do the gardening or pick up the trash. Rich tourists pay a thousand dollars each to sample weightlessness training. Nearby, at Russia's mission control, the equipment is mostly all-American, modeled on mission control at Houston. The rest of it is Soviet vintage.

Things are even worse at the Baikonur Cosmodrome, Russia's Cape Canaveral. It was built when Baikonur was still in the Soviet Union. Now it's in the independent republic of Kazakhstan. On an early spring day, clouds of dust from the Kazakh steppe blow over the deserted and rusting launch gantries. Parked in an old hanger, its windows cracked and its paint peeling, is one of Russia's space shuttles, the *Buran*. Russia is out of the space-shuttle business now. Well, not quite. Another *Buran* has been turned into a theme exhibit in Gorky Park, Moscow's biggest amusement park.

Russian space scientists, who now can earn, at best, $200 a month when they get paid, have moved out in droves. Kazakh settlers have moved in, and a shantytown has sprouted around the launch buildings.

Alexei Ivanovich, one of the launch-pad supervisors, will take you around the control room. But he needs a flashlight because the power is off. The electricity is now supplied by the local Kazakh power company, and Moscow hasn't paid the light bill lately. The launch computers are at least a decade old. The telephones look as if they'd bring a pretty penny at a tag sale.

"We should have carried out a major renovation of the launch pad," says Alexei, "but we don't have the money, so we're forced to do the minimum to keep things running. Just look at the periscopes we use to watch the launches. They've been taken from submarines!"

His comrades are just as despondent. "In 1966, orders were flooding in and there was lots of work," says Yuri. "Now everything's collapsing. We haven't been paid in three months. And we're old men now. We wouldn't be able to get jobs anywhere else in Russia, so we're stuck here, among the Kazakhs!"

The Cosmodrome commander, General Alexei Shumilin, shrugs his shoulders. "I've been here since 1959. Life here was so much better then, people's attitude, hope for the future. Now we're not receiving even the small minimum financing which we are assigned in the new state budget."

As he wanders among the *Burans* and the *Energiyas*, the huge space-rocket boosters, each the size of a small building and now gathering dust, Shumilin looks as if he wants to weep. "So much work was put into these great machines by the whole of the Soviet Union, then Russia. It's a shame; it's very upsetting to see this all going to hell."

Well, purgatory perhaps. It's not hopeless. Russia still has a nucleus of scientists and technicians who can turn out quality space hardware. They launch *Proton* booster rockets from Baikonur, charging $50 million a shot to launch commercial satellites. The *Protons* remain among the most powerful and dependable rockets in the world.

At Star City, they charge seven million dollars a seat for astronauts to train and live aboard the *MIR* space station. The Americans are the best customers. The United States has been sending astronauts to live on *MIR* more or less continuously, and has already paid the Russians more than $400 million for the privilege, if that's the word.

Jerry Linenger, the latest U.S. astronaut to return from the *MIR*, lived there with his five cosmonaut colleagues for almost three months. He found it, well, interesting. As reported by the Associated Press and Reuters, while in training with the Russians at Star City, he said, the equipment was akin to that of the old U.S. Mercury program of the 1960s. And one night on board the MIR he was reading when the fire alarm rang in one of the modules. An air canister had caught fire and the fire extinguishers were no match for it. What was worse, the fire was blocking the only path to the Soyuz space capsule, the crew's only means of escape to Earth. The fire burned itself out, but the crew spent much of the time thereafter wearing gas masks.

Thanks to a visit from the U.S. space shuttle Atlantis, the MIR has been repaired and Linenger is now home and has been replaced on board the MIR with Astronaut Micheal Foale (wonder what Linenger and Foale whispered to each other when they traded places?).

Washington and Moscow still insist the MIR is still a safe place to live, despite its problems, and have agreed to maintain the visiting astronaut program for at least another year, to prepare both astronauts and cosmonauts for life aboard the International Space Station, the next step in humankind's march to the heavens.

The ISS was first proposed by President Ronald Reagan thirteen years ago, and by now it's well off the drawing boards. It will involve at least fifteen nations, weigh 450 tons, stretch longer than a football field, contain seven laboratories and a dormitory, and become home to a crew of six, all orbiting 250 miles overhead. It will cost at least $60 billion, about three-fourths of it to be paid for by the United States.

The ISS was to be in orbit and receiving its first guests late in 1998. Now that's been put off until at least early 2000. Why? The Russians again. A lack of funds forced them to virtually stop work on the module they are building, with American dollars, at the Krunichev Space Center near Moscow. Their cargo module must be launched before anything else, so even though work has started again, thanks to some timely loans from Russian banks, and Moscow's accountants wringing a few more rubles out of elsewhere in the budget, the module still can't be launched until at least 1999, two years late. And just in case the Russians can't make that, NASA is spending an extra $200 million developing a substitute American module.

Outside the Baikonur Cosmodrome in the wilds of Kazakhstan, among the statues of Sergei Koralyov, the father of Soviet space science, and the memorial to the cosmonaut trainees who died in pursuit of the Soviet Union's path to the stars, is a huge portrait of Yuri Gagarin (who else?) in mosaic. He seems to be flying. And he's smiling. I wonder why.

chapter 14

Kremlin Fiction

(June 1997)

E verybody knows most Russians are woefully underpaid. A good doctor here gets only the equivalent of $150 a week. But it's comforting to know, at least, the people who are running Russia aren't much better off. Or so they say.

As part of his new anticorruption drive, President Yeltsin has just ordered all government officials to reveal their annual incomes. Yeltsin himself claims he made only the equivalent of $42,000 last year. Of course, he was sick a lot of the time.

Poor Victor Chernomyrdin, the prime minister, earned only $8,000, he says. Mr. Chernomyrdin owns a big stake in the biggest natural-gas company in the world, but maybe the company had a bad year.

The deputy prime minister, Alfred Kokh, says he would have gone broke except for a $100,000 book advance he got from a publisher in Switzerland. The book is about accounting practices. Kokh's staff concedes the book may never be published, but you know how it is with authors.

Yeltsin's deputy in charge of reform, Boris Nemtsov, says he made just $16,000 last year. And him with a family to support.

And finally, Boris Berezovsky, head of the Security Council, even revealed his net worth. Just $38,000, he says. *Forbes* magazine just listed Berezovsky as one of the world's richest persons. Forbes says he is worth $3 billion. But then you can't believe everything you read.

There were a lot of hoots and guffaws in the Russian press when

Russian President Boris Yeltsin (right) hugs Russian
Prime Minister Viktor Chernomyrdin outside the Russian
government building in Moscow, April 9, 1997. Yeltsin
presented Chernomyrdin with fifty-nine roses, to mark
Chernomyrdin's fifty-ninth birthday. (AP Photo/str)

the figures came out. But then, nobody in his right mind in Russia tells you how much he really makes. You want the tax man to find out? And besides, who's going to go over to the Kremlin and check?

But let's give Russia's rulers the benefit of the doubt. They jotted all this down in Russian rubles. It presently takes about 5,800 rubles to make a U.S. dollar. So 35 million rubles, say, is about 6,000 dollars. Maybe Boris Yeltsin and those other guys all got confused filling out the forms, and just put rubles down when they meant dollars.

chapter 15

Gone Fishing
(July 1997)

T wo hundred ten years ago, in 1787, when the United States was still just a baby among nations and Russia no more than an adolescent, the Russian empress, Catherine the Great, decided to take a trip out to the southern hustings to see the latest acquisitions to her empire.

As legend has it, Prince Grigory Potemkin, her escort and one of her favorites, wanted to impress the empress with the wealth of her empire. So Potemkin took some rubles from the treasury and constructed some facades of villages, here and there, rather like Hollywood sets. That way, Potemkin reasoned, Catherine wouldn't be disappointed while she was traveling about, as long as she didn't get too close to these "Potemkin Villages," as they came to be called. The villages are long gone, but the phrase lives on as a way of describing a particular sort of artifice or illusion. The Russians call this "potemkinizing," *pokazukha*, for show.

Something like that is going on this summer with Boris Yeltsin. Call it the "Potemkin Fishing Hole." The president is taking the last two months of summer off, for a working vacation in the Karelia Lakes region of the north. Russia's Minnesota, if you will. Two months may seem like a long time for a presidential vacation, but in Russia, most everybody who can takes off most of the last two months of summer, judging by the drop off in Moscow traffic and the understaffed offices.

This vacation must have been long planned because two years

ago, a couple of hundred Turkish workmen (all the most reliable construction crews in Russia these days seem to be Turks) began building a huge, two-story summer retreat for Yeltsin at Shuya on Lake Ukshe. This summer, construction crews resurfaced the bridges and roads from the airport to Lake Ukshe and repainted all the buildings along the route.

To ensure that Yeltsin would have good weather (they'd had a lot of rain in Lake Ukshe in the spring), a squadron of light planes was flown in to seed any approaching rain clouds to try to make sure it would rain somewhere else.

By all accounts, Yeltsin, who is a fisherman, is having a wonderful time. His wife, Naina, says that her husband often comes home with twenty or thirty fish he's caught. "I think the water is very good here," she says.

Well, it's not just the water, Mrs. Yeltsin. A local fisheries official says they brought in an extra ten thousand fish to stock the lake. "We were told by the authorities to make sure Yeltsin had a good time," he said. Every morning, Yeltsin's bodyguards go out to dig up worms for bait. None of that fly-fishing nonsense for Boris Yeltsin. He's a worm-and-bobber man.

All you get to see of Yeltsin these days is some snippets of him on TV, traipsing around with rod and reel or talking with the local farmers, but even so, to those who remember the doddering heart patient with his eyes glazed over from eight months ago, the transformation is remarkable.

At age sixty-six, he's fifty pounds lighter than before and is, by all accounts, drinking only in moderation, which is something of a first.

He's confident enough now to leave Moscow for two months without worrying about some coup d'etat while he's gone, and has even started making jokes about the derisory term Russians have for him (under their breath), "Tsar Boris." That nickname used to infuriate Yeltsin, but the other day Interfax, the Russian news service, reported that he remarked about Karelia, "No Russian leader has come here on holiday since Peter I. Now Boris I has been here."

While he couldn't keep up in a footrace with Bill Clinton, Yeltsin is visibly in better shape than his other presidential comrade, the portly Helmut Kohl of Germany, and everyone here now expects Boris I to finish out his presidential term, which ends in the year 2000, a reasonably healthy man.

What's more, he's a changed man. There really seems to be a new Yeltsin. The old Boris was a money-player, a crisis guy, who always seemed bored with the day-to-day business of governing. For a long time, that was okay in Russia, where the business of government was hardly ever boring. A war in the Caucasus one day, shelling the Russian White House the next. And Boris Yeltsin was Joe Montana, the fellow you went to in the last couple of minutes in the fourth quarter when you were six points down. Not a bread-and-butter man like Dan Marino or Jim Kelly.

Lately, though, Russia is blessedly fresh out of crises, at least the ones that have people shooting at each other or bashing heads in the street. And Yeltsin has accommodated, or perhaps is using this more peaceful moment to resume his role as Boris the Reformer.

The man who brought Russia privatization and price reform in 1992 has now promised to start revising the tax code, and to make some sense of commercial and customs regulations, so crucial for attracting Western investment. He has announced big cuts and bigger revisions in Russia's defense establishment, and acquiesced in the expansion of NATO, while fashioning a Russian role in NATO policy making.

Yeltsin still faces problems with the lower house of parliament, or Duma, which is controlled by a Communist majority, but he's managed to co-opt the Communists rather the way Bill Clinton has co-opted the Republicans in Washington.

This summer, the Russian government paid back some of its arrears, $3.2 billion, to millions of pensioners, and promises to restore most of the back wages it owes to millions more workers by the end of the year. It managed this in part with money it finally dunned out of Gazprom, the energy monopoly that, like most Russians, hadn't paid its share of taxes in years.

Yeltsin achieved all this by becoming a sort of CEO of Russia, and leaving the details to his two young, dynamic deputy prime ministers, Anatoly Chubais and Boris Nemtsov, who've been treading on the toes of some of Russia's biggest movers and shakers in the process of carrying out their reforms, all of it apparently with the blessings of Boris I.

So far so good. The ruble now seems to be a reasonably sound currency, inflation is just over double-digit but manageable, and after eight years, during which the Russian economy plummeted and economic output dropped 40 percent (compared with a 30 percent drop in the United States during the worst of the Great Depression), the country's economy may actually start growing again by the end of the year.

Has this all been just Boris Yeltsin, or what? Some of it may be Chechnya. As one of the wiser observers in Russia, Sergei Kovalev, has pointed out, there have been three moments in Russian history when the loss of a war has led to a blooming of liberal reforms.

Russia lost the Crimean War in the 1850s, and what followed was the freeing of the serfs. Russia lost the war with the Japanese in 1905, which led to new limits on the tsar's authority, the creation of a kind of parliament, and new civil liberties, although, alas, not enough to prevent a bloody revolution. When Russia lost the war in Afghanistan in the 1980s, it wasn't long before the Soviet Union and Communism crumbled.

Boris Yeltsin, the old Boris Yeltsin, stumbled into the morass of Chechnya in the early 1990s. Russia lost that war, too, last year. Chechnya is now independent in fact, if not officially.

But the other casualties were the Russian bureaucracies that authored that war, the ministries of defense, of state security, and so forth; the all-powerful and secret governments within the government that had existed for most of this century. They've been damaged, perhaps irreparably, and that has opened doors for change, for real political freedom, and for economic reforms that seemed impossible before.

All of which has created an opportunity for Yeltsin to use the consequences of his mistakes in Chechnya to correct so much of what's been wrong in Russia, if he has the time and the will.

Whatever the reason, this has been the best summer for Russia in quite a while. And if it takes dumping a few thousand more perch in Lake Ukshe to keep Boris I happy, well, as they say here, *pozhalista.* Please, go right ahead.

Old Russia overtaken by the new. (© 1997 Jonathan Sanders)

chapter 16

The Kopeck
Is Back
(August 1997)

M el Brooks, the comedian, used to complain that when he was a writer for the old TV comedy program *Your Show of Shows* (along with Woody Allen and a lot of other geniuses), some of his best brainstorms for comedy skits were ignored.

His favorite unprogrammed idea, Brooks allowed, was about "This Bulgarian guy, see," who is accosted by a couple of Romanian spies while he is in Bucharest one day, who seek to enlist him to spy for the Romanians. "No chance," says the Bulgarian, "I am a patriot." "We'll give you one million zlotys," say the Romanians. The Bulgarian mulls that over and finally agrees. So he gets the million zlotys in a big suitcase and takes the train to Sofia to start spying. He gets off the train at Sofia, goes to the nearest newsstand, and buys a paper. "How much is this?" he asks. Replies the vendor, "One million zlotys."

Zlotys are actually the Polish standard of currency, but in those years, when all those countries were behind the Iron Curtain and suffering the economic consequences, *zloty* became a word for anything that was worthless.

In the nineties, since the fall of the Soviet Union and Communism, the Russian *kopeck* has replaced the *zloty* in this regard. The kopeck is worth one-hundredth of a Russian ruble.

I haven't seen a kopeck here in Moscow in a long time, mainly because they really have been worth next to nothing. But it wasn't always so. Rubles used to be worth more than a dollar, at least under the old Soviet rate of exchange, even if the world's financial markets giggled at that. When you visited here in Soviet times, you had to exchange a certain amount of dollars for rubles at the official rate, and make sure you spent them here, because no bank outside the Iron Curtain would touch them.

Since 1990, though, when the Russian government finally had to confront the fact that the country was an economic basket case, the ruble has floated free on the currency markets, where a standard of currency's value is one index of the amount of confidence the rest of the world has in the economy of the country in question. It says something that the Russian ruble is now worth only about 5,800 to the dollar. So figure out what a kopeck is really worth, if your calculator has enough zeroes.

But all that is changing come January 1, 1998. The government is going to lop off the last three zeroes. The new rubles will be in one-ruble notes instead of 1,000 rubles. Prices, theoretically, will also be reduced by a factor of one thousand. So instead of using two one-thousand-ruble notes to take the Moscow metro, for example, riders will pay with a pair of one-ruble coins.

For any visitors interested in the new rate of exchange, the new ruble will be worth about seventeen U.S. cents at the going rate, or about fourteen to the dollar, just like the French franc. And a kopeck, of course, will be worth one one-hundredth of that seventeen cents.

True, that's still not much, but the same Metro ride that once upon a time cost five kopecks, right now would cost, well, you'd need a big bucket of kopecks to get on the Metro, if they'd even let you.

All of the new money, kopecks and rubles, and all the old rubles with all the zeroes, will be valid until the year 2002, so nobody needs to dash to the bank. And that alone is a remarkable step forward.

During the Communist years, the Soviet leadership played some games with the ruble that would have embarrassed a Swiss gnome. Every time they changed rubles, since the government set all the prices, the ruble would lose most of its value, and only those fortunate few who were well connected made a killing, while the proletariat lost its collective shirt.

Even in the post-Communist era, it took the government a while to get it right. In 1993, when inflation was a ruinous 2,600 percent, the Kremlin ordered another of these currency exchanges, but gave Russians only three days to turn in their old bills. Naturally, there was a panic. The next year, the ruble's value took a 25 percent plunge in a single day, after the central bank refused to intervene to support it. No wonder so many Russians don't believe in banks.

It may be that this sudden seizure of fiscal responsibility is an indication that times really are changing in Russia. This spring, the government finally proposed a tax overhaul that would make it much more attractive for both Russian and foreign investors. The current tax system is so antiquated and full of caprice that the government is collecting less than half of what it is probably owed from both businesses and individuals. The parliament still has to approve it, but it's a beginning. [*Editor's note: That particular tax-reform legislation was never approved.*]

The Moscow stock market (yes, there really is a stock market in Moscow now) is up 160 percent since the first of the year. Inflation is now down to 15 percent and dropping. And the government is actually predicting a modest growth in the economy next year. The Kremlin is always overly optimistic about these things, but for the first time, some foreign economists think that optimism may be well placed.

As a result, Russia is reaping some rewards. The International Monetary Fund and the World Bank are contributing more than $16 billion to help Russia back on its feet in the coming years.

And this summer in Denver, the so-called Paris Club of leading industrialized nations welcomed Russia as a new member. Among other things, that will help Russia collect at least some of the $120 billion owed it from developing nations that received aid from Moscow during the Soviet era.

The details were worked out between officials of the seven member nations and the Russians in the inner sanctum of the Federal Reserve Bank of New York, about as capitalist as you can get. And when it was done, Lawrence Summers, the U.S. Deputy Treasury Secretary, observed, "In a real sense, this agreement represents the financial end of the Cold War" (Associated Press, July 1997).

It's a long way from the paneled boardrooms of the Federal Reserve Bank to the alley behind my Moscow apartment, where every morning I see my Russian neighbors shyly going through the trash cans, searching for bottles to sell, and perhaps some food to eat. They're well-groomed, neatly dressed people, for the most part. No doubt they are on their way to work somewhere and they're ashamed to see me, so I try to stay discreetly out of sight.

It's a reminder that the vast majority of Russian citizens still get paid only a pittance, and in millions of cases rarely get paid on time. Outside of Moscow, most of Russia remains in the grip of a terrible economic depression which is now almost a decade old. Three out of four Russians will tell you that their living standards have significantly declined in the past few years, and no more than half believe the new government can, or will, do anything to improve things for them.

So Europe's invalid is by no means healthy yet. But perhaps, just perhaps, he's on the mend. And I'm going to rummage through my dresser drawers tonight, looking for kopecks. I'm sure there are still a few of them in there somewhere. I wonder if they're still any good?

chapter 17

ЖИЗНЪ

(August 1997)

I t's pronounced "ZHEE-zun," and in the Russian Cyrillic script it's spelled with a weird-looking "X," followed by a backward "N," a "3," an "H," and a strange little "b." It means "life." Most of this book is about life as experienced by the citizens of the former Evil Empire. But it's worth mentioning life as experienced by Betsy and me, and our colleagues in the Western media, as we went about our work and play. Moscow was our home, too, after all.

It was a life of privilege, to be sure. I imagine it was rather like the lifestyles of the *nomenklatura*, the upper-level bureaucrats and their families who ran the old Soviet Union. For example, Betsy and I lived in a floor-through apartment on the sixth floor of a building near the Russian White House, the office complex for the Russian cabinet and parliamentary leadership. We had a nice view of the Moscow River and there was a little park behind our building for walks and talks. The apartment took a lot of remodeling, but our employers paid for that. We put up with the ancient elevator and its moods. At least we had an elevator, sometimes. And if the foyer and stairwell looked like, and smelled like, a slum, we knew that was customary even in the most expensive apartment complexes. Russian apartment-dwellers still hadn't discovered co-op boards and condominium associations. They'd not yet shaken the old Soviet habit of expecting the government to so something about the public areas of their buildings. Their attitude was, "Let George do it!" Of course neither "George" nor the government ever did. Betsy always said we had a three-bathroom apartment: one in the apartment, one in the foyer, and one in the elevator. But we did have two bedrooms, not to mention a living room and a dining room, an abundance of floor space for two people that the average Russian family would have considered astonishing, not to mention severely selfish on our part.

Despite the concern of friends back in America, some of whom were in the habit of sending us jars of peanut butter and tins of sardines, we ate regularly and well. There was a big supermarket just down the road where you could buy some version of the victuals you needed: Bavarian hams, Norwegian salmon, Tyson's chickens, at outrageous prices. A typical week's grocery bill for the two of us might come to five hundred dollars, more than a month's income for many Russians. We were grateful our employers were paying for most of it.

This was a time when Moscow's upper crust, and we were part of it, was getting its food and clothing and other necessities shipped in from the West, so supermarket shopping wasn't all that different from home. Except that the market was owned by Germans, so when you gave them your credit card, they had to compute it from U.S. dollars to German marks to Russian rubles to complete the transaction.

To save a little money, and to find the best fruits and vegetables, we'd frequent the neighborhood markets, or *reenoks*. It's where most Russians do their shopping, and much of their socializing. You have to bargain for what you want, and I don't think we were ever very good at it, for whenever we showed up at our favorite greengrocer's stall, he acted as if he'd just won the state lottery.

It had been only a decade since the Soviet era, when foreigners were confined to special compounds where the authorities could monitor them, and the only way to get things like toilet tissue and a few beefsteaks was to airfreight it all in from Helsinki, Finland. Now you could live and shop and dine anywhere you liked. We saved the fancy restaurants for special occasions, partly because they were so expensive (even by New York City and Tokyo standards), and partly because the food wasn't nearly on a par with either New York or Tokyo. And then there were the customers. If the restaurant was pricey enough, there would almost always be a big noisy table of fellows wearing a lot of gold, with a clutch of bodyguards standing around. And everybody had a cell phone and talked on it all through dinner, when it wasn't ringing.

So mostly we dined at home with friends: colleagues in the Western media, or businessmen, or academics, or some of the folks we'd met at the nearby U.S. embassy where we'd exercise every morning, or English-speaking Russians we'd met on one assignment or another.

Paulina Pavlovna, goat-cheese seller in Ryzhkii, Ryonk.
(© 1996 Jonathan Sanders)

So it was also a sheltered life we led. We didn't spend nearly enough time with all those Russians who weren't privileged and didn't speak English, and we were poorer for it and so was our reporting. Our Russian was never good enough to carry on a real conversation, and the nature of our work, seeking information, seemed to require we spend more time with the powers-that-be than the powerless. Even so, we envied those many Western journalists we knew who'd taken the time and effort to make themselves proficient in the language. Betsy and I had to depend on our own interpreters, well-meaning and professional ones, to be sure, but the questions and answers were always once removed.

I often thought back a generation to the years I'd lived in Saigon during the Vietnam War, trying to tell that story to the American people. Vietnamese is an extraordinarily difficult language for Westerners to learn. I didn't speak it, and neither did most of my fellow journalists. As a result, the only Vietnamese we talked to in conversation, without the help of an interpreter, were those who spoke English. In Vietnam that meant that they were probably ex-Northerners, not Southerners, and were probably Roman Catholics in a nation that was almost exclusively Buddhist. That was quite a barrier for anyone trying to get into the hearts and minds of most South Vietnamese.

What was worse, hardly any American diplomats spoke Vietnamese either. They were up against the same language barriers as we were. I've always thought that language problem played a big part in how Americans got Vietnam wrong. In Russia, I felt the same way about our own language barrier, Betsy's and mine, and I worried.

That said, we did spend a lot of our time with everyday folks, not only because that was our job, but because we generally found them a good deal more interesting to chat with than most of the English-speaking Russian movers and shakers with whom we dealt. And Westerners chatting at all with ordinary Russians was quite a change. When I'd visited Russia during the Soviet period, it was difficult to have any sort of a talk with the man or woman on the street, and almost impossible if you were accompanied by a television camera. Government escorts made sure you talked to only the interviewees they'd lined up and carefully coached. Anybody was smart enough to know that if you were seen talking to a foreign news reporter, you could expect a prompt visit from the security services.

One of the most important freedoms in this post–Soviet Russia, I soon discovered, was the freedom from fear, at least the fear of being arrested for speaking out of turn. People no longer ran the other way when they saw a foreign TV camera. They gathered around to find out what was going on. They'd actually wait in line for their chance to say something on camera. And it was almost always a diatribe against the Yeltsin administration or politicians in general. One of the most bitter antigovernment tirades I recall came from a security agent who'd been retired from the KGB when the Soviet state collapsed. He'd been reduced to living on a small pension and felt that after all his years of patriotic service spying on his neighbors, he deserved better.

Eventually, what you'd hear from people on Pushkin Street in Moscow began to sound like what you'd hear from people on Main Street back home. Russia's wall of silence had been shattered, and Western journalists were no longer feared, but often sought out by passersby as messengers to the West: "You tell people back in America to get rid of NATO; we're supposed to be friends!" And sometimes, just like back home, people tended to blame the messenger. When the West punished Belgrade for its atrocities in the civil war with Bosnia, outraged Russians organized protest demonstrations in Moscow in support of Russia's old friend and ally, Serbia. If you were a Western reporter, you tried to keep your distance from protests like that, for fear of taking a beating.

In Moscow's swiftly changing times, there was always more than enough news to go around. It was an editorial feast, and each of the dozens of foreign journalists had ample opportunity to pursue a lead, usually without stepping on the toes of his colleagues. But even though the system had changed, the Kremlin remained as opaque as ever. In Washington they say the ship of state leaks from the top, meaning that news leaks usually start at the presidential level. Not in Moscow. As it had always been under the tsars and the Soviet commissars, the Kremlin remained virtually leakproof, and so much of the "news" that emanated from the Yeltsin administration consisted of little more than rumors and crystalgazing.

That made news reporting especially difficult for people like Betsy, who worked for a twenty-four-hour news network. She'd be gone from early in the morning until long after dark (when it was still late morning in New York and Washington), doing interviews, churning out two or three stories a day, and talking live with the CNN anchors, often with not much more than rumors and crystalgazing to go on.

My job was easier, but perhaps more frustrating. My network had only one major newscast a day, which was forced to compress the news of America and the world into twenty-two minutes. Apart from occasional radio reports and a little live conversation on the network's morning information show, that didn't leave much opportunity for me to tell our TV audience anything from my Moscow outpost. Considering the competition from others' news stories in America and overseas, I'm surprised we got as many stories on the air from Moscow as we did. So, unlike Betsy's, my stories were fewer and further between, and it was rare indeed for both of us to show up at the same story at the same time.

And even then, we wouldn't see much of each other. When we were both suddenly dispatched to Krasnoyarsk to cover the rescue of a balloonist whose attempt at a round-the-world voyage had wound up in a cornfield, I was able to do my interview with him and go right home to the comforts of Moscow. Betsy had to spend three days slogging through the Krasnoyarsk rain and mud to get a shot of the balloon on CNN. If you need an example of the difference between an all-news network and a sometimes-news network, that's it!

The fact that we were not in daily head-to-head competition for news helped our relationship, I think, by removing one source of domestic discord. We edited each other's writing, gave each other editorial advice, and shared our sources and our secrets, but only in the privacy of our bedroom. We've always followed a simple rule about revealing our exclusives to each other: Look but don't touch! News is part of the pillow talk between journalists who are husband and wife, and it needs to remain on the pillow.

Our Moscow bedroom windows faced out on the Russian White House. In the winter months, it's dark for most of the night and day, and in the darkness, I'd often look out from our bed at the great tower looming above the White House. It was illuminated so that you could see it, all night, all over Moscow. And fluttering atop the tower was a huge flag of the Russian republic. Like the United States flag, it's colored red, white, and blue. In another time in Moscow, I'd looked out over the Kremlin to see nothing but a forest of huge red flags with the hammer and sickle on them. They were all gone now, replaced by the red, white, and blue. It reminded me that things had truly changed here, and whatever this new Russia is to become, it will never again be what it was.

chapter 18

Unorthodox Church

(September 1997)

T he first thing you should know about a
Russian Orthodox church service is that it is always standing
room only.

There are no pews inside the churches because worshipers are
expected to stand throughout the proceedings, which sometimes last
as long as three hours. There are usually some benches along the
walls for the infirm or elderly to sit upon, but you'd better appear
barely ambulatory if you expect to claim them. The very old women,
in fact, spend much of the service traveling about on their knees. In
short, this is a no-nonsense Christianity in which form and substance are virtually indistinguishable.

For an Episcopalian like myself, Russian Orthodoxy takes some
getting used to. The calendar is different, for one thing. Russian
Christmas comes after our New Year, and Russians always seem to be
taking days off in memory of St. Something-or-Other, even though
most Russians have rarely been inside a church of any sort. And
much of the service itself is heard rather than seen, taking place
behind a huge gold and gilt screen (how elaborate depends on the
means of the parishioners) from where the priests emerge every so
often to attend to the visible part of things.

Which is not to say that the service itself is not beautiful. You
don't have to be an Orthodox churchgoer to be genuinely moved by
the powerful effects of the gold and silver icons gleaming in the can-
dlelight, the priests in their long beards and splendid vestments, the

haunting voices of the choir, and the rapture in the faces of the congregation.

For half a millennium after Constantinople, the Orthodox capital, fell to the Turks in 1453, the Russian Orthodox Church had a monopoly on matters spiritual here. It was the national religion, the religion of the tsars, and ruled by the patriarch of Moscow. Eventually, in the eighteenth century, Peter the Great decided to take over the church, the way he'd taken over everything else in Russia, and ruled through a synod, with a lay person in charge. The patriarch was reduced to merely passing along the tsar's wishes.

The result was that until early in this century, the Russian Orthodox Church was an arm of the Russian state. Priests commonly passed along what they were told in the sanctum of the confessional to the tsar's secret police. The patriarch blessed the tsar's armies before every battle. As the Romanovs went, so went the church.

And with the aid of the tsars, the church never had to worry much about competing for converts with the Lutherans, Roman Catholics, Jews, and others who were alternately tolerated as long as they stayed properly confined, or brutally persecuted. The great schisms the church suffered through were always within the confines of what it meant to be Russian Orthodox. Bloody battles of faith were fought not over the relative merits of Jesus of Nazareth versus Muhammed or Abraham, but whether a true Orthodox believer ought to cross himself with two fingers or three.

All that came crumbling down with the Romanovs in 1917. Churches and cathedrals were looted and burned; priests and bishops, monks and nuns were murdered; the seminaries and religious schools shut tight. Communism was the new religion.

The Moscow patriarchy was revived, but it was a shadow church, composed of complaisant clergy trotted out to show foreigners that the new Soviet man and woman were still free to worship God if they so chose (although woe betide them if they tried to make a conspicuous habit of it).

In 1941, under threat of a Nazi invasion, Stalin allowed some of the churches and seminaries to reopen, in hopes of using the church to rekindle Russian patriotism. But even then, the clergy who ran the church were still Soviet-era yes-men, serving the state and the secret police the way they'd served the tsars.

When Communism itself came crumbling down a few years ago, nobody was more surprised than the leaders of the Russian Orthodox Church. Suddenly, it was okay to go to church again. And millions of Russians did. And millions more, who'd never been to church, especially young people, flocked to the services. Russians were trying to

Christ the Savior Cathedral, Moscow. (© Bill Gasperini)

rediscover themselves and unearth the heritage that seventy years of Socialism had done its best to bury.

One problem was that there weren't enough churches anymore. Of the seventy thousand that existed before the revolution, only about six thousand remained. So Russia has gone on a church-rebuilding binge. The number is now up to nearly twenty thousand and in Moscow, there's a run on gilt to resurface the deteriorating onion domes of churches under reconstruction.

The centerpiece is the vast, new Cathedral of Christ the Savior, hard by the Kremlin. It's just been finished and it cost $350 million to build from scratch. Stalin had it torn down in 1931, in order to build a Soviet-style Empire State Building, but the ground proved to be too soft for such a skyscraper. Instead, he installed a huge heated swimming pool. Even now opinion among Muscovites is divided among those who are grateful that, whatever the cost, the cathedral is back where it belongs, and those who lament that now they've gone and put up this ghastly gold-domed building and ruined a perfectly good public swimming pool.

A lot of this religious reconstruction has been government-financed with the conspicuous blessings of the post-Soviet politicians, who are just as eager to cash in on the religious vote here as are the politicians in America. President Yeltsin never misses a moment to be seen in public with the church hierarchy whenever there's a religious excuse for it. And from the scenes on the TV news at night, you'd think the mayor of Moscow, Yuri Luzhkov, spends all his time in church.

In fact, there's some evidence to indicate that Russia's Orthodox revival is neither as universal nor as fervent as advertised. Church attendance appears to be dropping off from the glory days of the late 1980s, and while perhaps half of all Russians call themselves Orthodox, fewer than twenty million attend church regularly.

If so, the Russian Orthodox church has only itself to blame. Those millions of Russians who first flocked to the churches when worshiping God became permissible again, had hoped and prayed that the church might at last take the lead in restoring the old Russian values of honesty, industry, self-sacrifice, and charity that it had represented for a thousand years. In that they have been disappointed.

In a faith in which form and substance are so intertwined, it's worth noting the form in which the head of the church, Moscow Patriarch Aleksei II, gets to work every day. He travels in a shiny new bullet-proof Mercedes, tailed everywhere by a Ford Explorer full of well-armed bodyguards, just the way most of the big businessmen in the New Russia get around. And why not? Aleksei II is a very big businessman indeed. The businesses of cigarettes and booze, among other things.

In 1996, the Yeltsin government granted the patriarchate the right to import fifty thousand tons of tobacco duty-free, and pocket the profits. The press eventually got wind of the deal and Aleksei spent much of the summer in damage control, but not before the church had imported eight billion cigarettes for sale in Russia and cost the government at least $40 million in lost revenues.

Last autumn, according to one Moscow newspaper, the church was able to import 100 million bottles of wine from Germany, tax-free. That would supply an eternity of communions.

The patriarchate's biggest investment, however, has been in oil. It holds a 20 percent stake in something called the International Economic Partnership, which, through much of the 1990s, exported more than $2 billion worth of oil and oil products.

Where does all that money go? Into the banks. The church's banks. It owns all or part of three of them, including the Christ the Savior Cathedral Bank.

In return, the church hierarchy has reverted to the old habit of putting itself at the service of the state, no matter how questionable the cause. The patriarchate never blinked when Russia's chief arms-export agency contributed $235,000 to Christ the Savior Cathedral's reconstruction. Orthodox priests are routinely called in to bless the latest tanks as they roll off the assembly lines. And a year ago, the patriarchate even went so far as to bestow a blessing on Russia's nuclear arsenal.

All during the ghastly fiasco that was Moscow's war against Chechen independence, when young Russian conscripts were dying by the hundreds for a manifestly lost cause, the church stood four-square behind the Kremlin. The patriarch posed with the then-defense minister to underscore the sacredness of patriotic military duty. And when Russian artillery demolished the Russian Orthodox Church of Michael the Archangel in Grozny, the Chechen capital, the senior priest of that church, Father Pyotr Netsvetayev, pleaded with Patriarch Aleksei to call for a end to the war. Aleksei was silent.

But what the Russian Orthodox leadership seems to want most is to regain the sort of religious monopoly it enjoyed under the tsars and, in a fashion, under the Communists. One of the consequences of the new post-Soviet era is that it has had to compete for worshipers with other faiths.

The patriarchate has never quite recovered from an incident during the *perestroika* days of the late 1980s, when a Seventh-Day Adventist missionary baptized three hundred former Orthodox believers in a service at Nizhny Novgorod. Said the alarmed patriarch, "Our people are being bought by foreigners."

Nonetheless, the government went ahead in 1990 with a historic law establishing freedom of religion in Russia. Period. No exceptions.

For seven years, the Russian Orthodox Church has been fighting that law, and this month it finally got what it wanted. President Yeltsin has signed a new law on religion, putting strict limits on freedom of worship for those faiths which weren't registered under the old Communist regime. If enforced, it will mean that the Pentecostals and Mormons, to name a couple, won't be able to own property or open religious schools, or proselytize, or publish literature, or invite missionaries here.

The law was signed over the objections of Washington and the Vatican, but it was great politics for Yeltsin. In a final irony, the law was drawn up and passed by a huge majority in the Communist-dominated Duma.

Perhaps now the Moscow patriarch is satisfied. The church has gotten rich once again, and it has essentially gotten rid of the competition. But most Russians today would be hard put to answer, if you asked them, what the Russian Orthodox Church stands for, apart from a big investment portfolio, or why the church needs a law to stifle the competition when it ought to be confident enough that it can prevail against non-Russian faiths simply by the power of its ideas. Simply put, the church seems frightened.

Maybe it has forgotten what it says in the Bible, in Joshua 1:9: "Be not afraid, neither be thou dismayed, for the Lord Thy God is with thee." No doubt he is, but in the case of the Russian Orthodox Church in the 1990s, he must be a tolerant God indeed.

chapter 19

Duma Follies

(October 1997)

I remember Georgi. He's a mental souvenir of my first experience with representative government in what was then the Soviet Union, more than a decade ago.

Georgi was a Georgian, the foreman of a workers' crew building a new subway in the Georgian capital, Tbilisi. In those years, Georgia was still part of the Soviet Union. He was a bull of a man, in his early fifties, who still looked as if he could have built that subway all by himself.

More important for my purposes, Georgi was one of hundreds of delegates from all over the Soviet Union who were to attend the upcoming Communist Party Congress in Moscow. These congresses were occasional events, scheduled whenever the leaders in Moscow felt like it, usually when they were about to embark on one new five-year plan or another. Sometimes years and years would go by between congresses.

So the fact that there was going to be a congress was news of sorts, even in faraway America, and my job was to profile some of the delegates; people like Georgi.

The videotape crew and I whiled away a pleasant late afternoon in Georgi's apartment, helping ourselves to a mountain of Georgian *hatchipuri* (a meat and vegetable stew) and other delicacies prepared by Georgi's wife. Like the Russians, Georgians are wonderful hosts. And while the tape was rolling, Georgi answered our questions with the customary platitudes about the triumph of Socialism, the bright future of Soviet society, and so forth.

Then we turned the camera off. And unbidden and apparently out of long habit, Georgi's wife appeared with a full ram's horn of

Georgian vodka, at least a quart. I was afraid we'd have to drink all of it and stumble our way out into the street. Not to worry. It was for Georgi and he downed it in one draught.

"Now we can talk!" he said. "You want to know whether I and the other delegates are going to decide anything at the congress? You and I both know, everything has already been decided in the Kremlin. They tell us how to vote and we vote, unanimously."

So why go? "Because I've been chosen for my service to the party over the years," he replied. "It's a reward. I've never been to Moscow and now I'll spend a couple of weeks having a good time at the Rossiya Hotel, seeing the sights, and finding out if the Russian vodka's any better than ours, though I doubt it. And maybe while I'm at it, I can convince a couple of the bigwigs to pay more attention to us folks here in the Caucusus Mountains. What's wrong with that?"

A few weeks later, I watched Georgi and the others in Moscow, in congress assembled, all dressed up with their chests full of medals and ribbons, voting on one resolution after another. Every one was approved. Unanimously. It went on for days, and Georgi looked particularly pleased.

Georgi came clearly to mind this week while the new and presumably improved Russian government was grappling with this new and unruly beast known as Democracy. The lower house of the Russian parliament, the Duma, was in the full flower of debate and nobody looked the least bit happy.

There was a motion on the floor to vote no confidence in the government, and no one was sure how it was going to come out, least of all President Boris Yeltsin and his aides, who have replaced the old Soviet commissars in the Kremlin.

Of course as a practical matter the majority of the Duma delegates, Communists, Nationalists, and a smattering of Liberals, have had no confidence in the Yeltsin government since the day they were elected. They're furious that the new budget and tax code drawn up by Yeltsin's economic reformers either goes too far or doesn't go far enough. But actually voting their convictions was quite another matter.

Under Russia's new constitution (and pay attention now, this gets complicated) a no-confidence vote by the Duma has no legal effect unless it's followed by a second vote within ninety days. Then the prime minister has to resign and the president has to dismiss the Duma, and hold new Duma elections.

So here was the Kremlin's irresistible force up against the Duma's immovable object. There is an upper house of the parliament, the Federation Council, composed mostly of regional governors and other movers and shakers, rather like the British House of

Alexander Solzhenitsyn addressing the State Duma. (© Bill Gasperini)

Lords, except younger, richer, and more powerful. As if, say, the CEOs for the Fortune 500 all sat in the U.S. Senate. But the Federation Council usually votes the way Yeltsin wants, so we can dismiss the council for purposes of this narrative. There, wasn't that easy?

So you can see why, given the choice between Roman Catholicism, Islam, and Orthodoxy, the early Russian tsars chose the Greek way. The politicking in Moscow this week was absolutely Byzantine.

Right off, the prime minister, Victor Chernomyrdin, upped the ante by vowing that if the Duma voted no confidence in him even once, he'd be so insulted he'd resign anyway. So what's wrong with that?

Well, the Duma delegates actually like Chernomyrdin. He's an ex-Communist, a billionaire natural-gas magnate, and the one member of Yeltsin's entourage who favors the go-slow approach on matters of reform. Chernomyrdin is a pol.

The Duma opposition was afraid that if Chernomyrdin went, Yeltsin would appoint in his place one of those young economic hotheads he's got with him, like Anatoly Chubais or Boris Nemtsov. And Yeltsin knew it. And the Duma knew he knew it.

So why not just vote no confidence, let the government fall, and have new elections? It happens in Italy all the time. The Italians have the no-confidence franchise. I can recall years ago, when the Italian government fell for the twentieth or thirtieth time, David Brinkley, the newscaster, leading off the item by remarking, "In Italy, where every young boy can dream of becoming president and often does. . . ." So why not do as the Romans do?

No government in post–Soviet Russia has ever fallen over a no-confidence vote, and with good reason. Just like Georgi in Tbilisi, the status of the Duma delegates affords them certain perks. But the perks amount to a lot more than just a nice room in the Rossiya Hotel. They get fancy cars that whizz them up and down the traffic-clogged Moscow boulevards in nothing flat. They get nice Moscow offices and nice Moscow apartments and pretty Moscow secretaries and a big expense account. And if rumor is to be believed, a lot of them get rich by voting the convictions of the big businessmen and foreign governments who are buddies with them. And unlike Georgi in Tbilisi, these rewards are theirs for years. Unless there's an election.

What worried the Duma delegates—and the public opinion polls gave them good reason to worry—was that if the government fell and there were new elections, they'd be booted out and replaced by more radical folks (such is the measure of discontent out in the Russian hustings) and lose all of the above. And President Yeltsin knew it. And the Duma knew he knew it.

Even so, as the debate droned on into the evening, and the pols scurried about counting votes, the outcome was by no means certain. Not even in the Kremlin. Toward the end, Yeltsin himself phoned the Duma's speaker, Gennadi Seleznyov, to plead, "I don't want confrontations and early elections. . . . Don't put me in a difficult position." Seleznyov read the president's remarks to the delegates.

Yeltsin needn't have worried. To get a simple majority for their no-confidence vote, the Communists needed the votes of the followers of the leader of the tiny bloc of democrats, Grigory Yavlinsky. They'd patched together a kind of instant coalition. But Gennadi Zyuganov, the veteran Communist leader, and Yavlinksy are like matter and anti-matter. Imagine then-mayor Richard J. Daley of Chicago sitting down for a friendly chat with the then-young radical Tom Hayden during the disorders attending the Democratic Convention in Chicago in 1968.

The Zyuganov-Yavlinsky marriage lasted about three hours. Yavlinsky betrayed the Communists by offering his very own no-confidence vote, splitting the delegates and denying the Communists their majority. So the Duma finally voted to delay the whole thing for another week, during which the Yeltsin forces and the Duma opposition will try to iron things out behind closed doors. It's not over yet, but I'd put my money on a face-saving compromise.

Politicians are politicians. Everywhere. And the one thing every elected official most detests is—elections.

chapter 20

GAIIIIII!

(October 1997)

B ack when Russia was still the **Soviet Union and the Com-**
munists were running things, Muscovites used to tell the story of
the motorist who is cruising down the boulevard and suddenly hits a
man-sized pothole so hard that he snaps the car's front axle.

And while he's standing there cursing, the traffic cop comes over
to take a look.

"Officer, this is a disgrace!" says the motorist. "Where's the red
flag to mark this terrible traffic hazard?"

"You must be a foreigner," says the cop.

"That's right," the motorist replies. "So what?"

"So what's the first thing you see when you leave the international airport?"

"A big red flag," says the motorist.

"Well," says the cop, "that's it."

Driving around Moscow these days is even more of an adventure
than it was then. Just eight years ago, there were nine hundred thousand vehicles in the whole city, for a population of close to ten million. A lot of the cars were big, black, chauffeur-driven Zil limou-
sines for exclusive use of the bureaucrats. The man in the street
could expect to wait years to buy a little runabout, and pay a couple
of years' wages for it, too.

Now, cars are available, somewhat more affordable, and the badge
of Moscow's middle class, or middle-class wanna-bes. There were 2.5
million cars here at last count, with another three hundred thousand

Moscow traffic. (© 1996 Jonathan Sanders)

more every year. The city ran out of space for them a long time ago. The result is that most Muscovites spend most of their commute time in their cars, standing stock-still with the engine running, sometimes for hours, with the predictable effect on the city's atmosphere.

You can either wait on one of the broad, eight-lane boulevards originally built for the Communist commissars to have a stately route to get from place to place, and which are now chock-full of long lines of cars and trucks waiting, sometimes for ten full minutes, for a light to change, or you can spin off and try a detour on one of the narrow old side streets and wait in line for half an hour while a guy with a flat tire on his Volga, which is blocking the whole street, tries to borrow a jack from somebody.

Happily, the Russians have not yet adopted the practice, so popular in Third World capitals from Cairo to Calcutta, of using the horn for no particular reason. In the Middle East, you get the feeling that motorists must think the horn is somehow attached to the gas pedal, and the car won't go unless you honk. The sound is deafening and incessant.

Not so in Moscow. Not yet, anyway. Russian motorists are more inclined to wait quietly while inching their way across town, the way Russians used to wait in line for bread or vodka not so long ago.

But their patience deserts them once they're moving. For a people who spent so many generations doing just what they were told, it's hard to exaggerate the thrill of getting into your own car and going anywhere you want, any way you want. When they're behind the wheel, Russians are momentarily at liberty, and they flaunt it. They drive at breakneck speed, treat the painted traffic lanes with disdain, and tailgate as a matter of course. I've seen Italians do the same thing, but Italians, in my experience, are the world's best at pushing the envelope in traffic. The Russian motorists, on the other hand, have a lot to learn, especially those who speed about pumped up with a liter of vodka on a Saturday night. Moscow traffic is just a bunch of accidents waiting to happen. And they do happen. There are a couple of dozen serious traffic accidents here every day, and eight hundred traffic deaths a year on average.

One reason for all the chaos is that Russians haven't had a lot of practice driving cars. Most of them couldn't afford a family car before 1990, so the average Russian has got, at best, only a few years' experience fighting traffic. Oh, they all must have driver's licenses. There are two ways to get one. You can go to driving school one night a week for several months and then take a test which makes a college physics exam look simple by comparison. Or you can just go down to the motor vehicle department, plunk down the ruble equivalent of $500, and get one right away. And it's good forever.

Still, it's ironic that Russians drive so carelessly when they care so much about the cars they drive. Russian men will talk on end-lessly about them—the gas mileage, the horsepower, the quirks; as if the car was some cherished pet or offspring. (Motoring is still mostly a Guy Thing in Russia. Women are free to drive, but it's not some-thing that's encouraged.) Despite Russia's economic woes, automobiles are relatively affordable for Russia's middle class. A little Zhigili runabout, for example, costs the equivalent of five thousand dollars. Gasoline is cheaper than in most places in the United States: about $1.20 a gallon.

Since everybody in Russia either has a car now or wants to get one someday, the automobile has spawned a whole lexicon of Russian humor. Car jokes can tell you a lot about what Russia once was, and is now.

I remember in the last days of the old Soviet Union, when everybody seemed to spend most of the time waiting in line for something or other, the favorite joke was about the fellow who finally saved enough money to buy himself a new Lada runabout, and went over to the People's Lada Dealer to put in his order. The clerk took his name and his money and told him he could expect delivery on June 18, 2007.

"Will that be the morning or afternoon?" asked the buyer.

"What do you care?" sneered the salesman. "That's twenty-two years from now."

"I know," said the buyer. "But the plumber is coming that morning!"

Nowadays, in the new capitalist Russia, the rich, rude Novy Russky in their fancy new limos are the butt of the car jokes. Like the one about President Yeltsin being driven to work, as usual, from his country *dacha* on a Monday morning. He's feeling out of sorts and finally orders his driver to pull over. Yeltsin gets out of the car, says to the driver, "Nobody ever lets me drive to work, so get out of the front seat, and let me drive for once!"

Over the protests of his driver, Yeltsin gets behind the wheel of his limo, shoves the driver in the passenger seat, barrels off into traffic, and predictably runs right into the back end of a big Mercedes limo carrying a couple of tycoons.

While Yeltsin's slumped behind the wheel of his own limo, dazed, the tycoons in the other car yell at their driver to get out and beat up whoever it is that ran into them.

The driver gets out, takes a look at the other limo, returns to the tycoons and says, "I think we better get out of here. I don't know who the hell that is riding in the other limo, but he's got Boris Yeltsin for his driver!"

Russians may joke about it, but the care and feeding of the family auto here is very serious business. Every Russian motorist is serenely confident he's at least as adept at repairs as Mr. Goodwrench. A lot of them probably are. There are so many rusting hulks of ancient motor vehicles chugging down Moscow streets, and so few motorists who can afford to take them to a real mechanic, most Russian car owners have gotten to be pretty good at getting under the hood.

If only Moscow's traffic engineers were as adept. For one thing, they don't have as much mechanical help as they need. There are fewer red lights here than in Washington, D.C., a city one-tenth Moscow's size. Another reason traffic in Moscow doesn't run better is that what traffic control system there is appears to have been designed by Beavis and Butthead. One-way streets suddenly transform themselves into one-way-the-opposite-way streets with no warning. Or traffic signs (all in Russian, of course) which are written in the double-negative. ("No turns between 9 A.M. and 7 P.M. except for vehicles that are not trucks!")

The local axiom is that in Moscow, you have to drive all the way to St. Petersburg before you are allowed to make a left turn. And as for pedestrians, it's everyone for himself.

No taxi driver in his right mind would want to try to make a living driving around this purgatory (which may be why, it is my impression, that most of the New York City taxi drivers these days seem to be Russian émigrés). And in fact, you don't see many yellow cabs on Moscow streets. But you do see lots of pedestrians with their arms out, trying to hail a ride. And they never wait for long. Within seconds, they've got a lift. Not in a taxi, but from some ordinary motorist who pulls over, negotiates a price, and takes them wherever they're going. In Moscow, everybody's a taxi driver. Here, you forget whatever you were ever told about picking up hitchhikers.

And then there's parking, which is, at best, haphazard. Usually it's the sidewalk. But lately, on the busier downtown thoroughfares, the city administration has been trying to get things civilized. They installed two hundred brand-new parking meters on Tverskaya Boulevard (Moscow's Fifth Avenue, which runs down to the Kremlin), but irate motorists simply poured water into them so they froze up all winter. And nobody would think of paying a parking ticket in this city.

So they've privatized the parking on some public streets. A couple of hundred stretches of the busiest part of town have been leased out to private enterprise. Now when you find an ordinary parking place on the street, as you're locking up, somebody with a makeshift uniform and an official-looking badge walks up and takes the equivalent of a couple of dollars from you and gives you a little slip of paper. You give that back to him, usually with some more money, when you return to your car. And you better do what he says. If not, there's another company that will tow your car away and you'll be lucky if you ever see it again.

In any case, you'll be lucky enough just to keep your car for as long as you want it. Car theft is big business in Moscow. More than eighteen thousand cars are stolen in this city every year. The car-alarm business must be almost as big. Even the twenty-year-old clunkers all seem to have an alarm of some sort. And when the sun goes down, the alarms all seem to go off at once. Whatever serenity may be found in the absence of honking horns is lost in the screeches and buzzes and whistles of thousands of antitheft devices, gamely trying to do their job. I call it the Moscow Symphony, and it's long-playing.

In fact, art now imitates life in Moscow in the auto-theft business. The hottest new TV game show here is something called *Perekhvat* ("Interception"). It's played with a studio audience, a smarmy host and play-by-play announcer, plus a battalion of thirty squad cars and a helicopter manned by off-duty policemen.

The rules are fairly simple. Contestants "steal" a designated car armed with an antitheft tracking device, and the cops try to track them down through the streets of Moscow. If you can evade them for thirty-five minutes, you win a new car. The escape attempts have been exotic, to say the least, and mostly unsuccessful; pull the car over some railroad tracks so the cops can't follow, hide the car in a mountain of garbage, drive it as far underground as you can to foil the tracking signal, even put it on a barge in the Moscow River. One of the few winners was a little old grandmother who moonlights as a taxi driver, and knew Moscow's back streets even better than her police pursuers.

A word of warning to folks back home. They're trying to bring *Perekhvat* to America. So if you find, as here in Moscow, there's never a traffic cop when you need one, it may be because they've been up all night getting themselves on TV.

If the authorities are not so successful in making the streets safe from car thieves, they're certainly diligent about enforcing the rules of the road, at least when they set their minds to it. The enforcers are seven thousand smartly dressed inspectors from the State Automobile Inspectorate, known by the acronym, GAI. (It's pronounced "guy-EEE" and when it's applied to the inspectors, it's a noun both singular and plural.) They are each armed with a two-foot-long black and white traffic baton, known locally as a *"pozhalista* stick." *Pozhalista* in Russian means "please." Please indeed.

It's up to the GAI to regulate traffic, man the stop lights, investigate traffic accidents, and make sure all those two-and-a-half million drivers are abiding by the rules of the road, such as they are.

The problem is that a GAI gets paid only about $150 a month. That's a problem for the GAI and for motorists, too, because the temptation to solicit a bribe is overwhelming. And there are lots of ways a GAI can get you. He can stop you, and often does, for a document check. If there's one letter in one word missing in the mess of papers you have to show him, you get a big ticket. Or he can check your car. In addition to the usual stuff that needs to be working—lights, brakes, etc.—you better also be carrying a medical kit and fire extinguisher.

Sometimes even having everything in order does you no good. A friend of mine, a bureau chief here for an American newspaper, was stopped by the GAI the other night for a "document check," and produced all the required paperwork, duly stamped.

"But you don't have a certified document from the local head of your office giving you permission to drive this car," said the officer.

"But I *am* the local head of my office," replied my friend.

"In that case," said the GAI, "you should have written a certified letter to yourself, giving you permission to drive this car!"

On the other hand, you can simply give the GAI the equivalent of a few dollars, just for being a nice fellow. Most people do. I got stopped on my way home from work one night by a very cordial GAI (they are customarily very polite if unprovoked and always greet their next victim with a smart salute). He decided, he said, that I was driving as if I were drunk. I said, no, that's the way I always drive. Nonetheless, he said, I would need to come to his patrol car to take a breathalyzer test, and if I failed, I'd have to spend the night in the drunk tank.

Since I was stone-cold sober, I decided to risk it, rather than pony up some rubles. In all the drunk-driving checks he'd ever made, it seemed apparent, money had always changed hands before it got to getting in the patrol car, because the poor GAI hadn't the least notion how to work the Breathalyzer gear.

"Are you *sure* you want to take this test?" He was almost pleading by now. I assured him I was determined, and having done a story or two on Breathalyzers, I showed him how the equipment worked and promptly tested myself. "Did you pass?" he asked.

"Yes," I replied, "but just barely." Home free, but next time I think I'll pay off and not push my luck.

Until the city of Moscow finds the money to pay its GAI a living wage, perhaps that's the charitable thing to do. Every Muscovite knows the story of the motorist who gets stopped by the GAI and pleads with him, "Officer, I wasn't breaking any law!"

"I'm aware, sir, that you committed no traffic violation," replies the officer. "But why should my wife and five children have to wait all night for you to break some silly little law?"

chapter 21

Sort of A-OK

(October 1997)

A lot of years ago when I was still a whipper-
snapper newspaper wire-service stringer in the Midwest, I
recall seeing a little item on the sports wire, quoting a high-school
coach in southern Indiana somewhere, whose swimming team had
lost each and every one of its meets that season. His record was a perfect 0-and-17.

"Well," he said, "at least nobody drowned!"

It's tempting to regard that as a sort of commentary on the saga
of the Russian space station *MIR* the past four months. For *MIR* has
been a victim twice over: of plain bad luck, and of a very bad press.

The good news about *MIR* is that as of this writing, it is still cir-
cling 150 miles above Earth just as it has been doing faithfully for the
last eleven years. Most systems are operating and there's a full complement of crew: two Russian cosmonauts and an American astronaut, living and working on board in a fairly normal fashion. And
at least nobody's died.

The bad news is that just about everything that could go wrong
up there, short of a fatal accident, has gone wrong. And it has all
been reported in excruciating, sensational detail by the world's
media, Perils-of-Pauline style, as if, as a colleague of mine, Michael
Specter of the *New York Times*, observed, *MIR* were some kind of
"cosmic gag."

The U.S. Congress, which has been footing the $100 million-a-
year bill for keeping an American astronaut on board, doesn't think

A crewmember aboard the space shuttle *Atlantis* used the electronic still camera to capture this view of the approaching *MIR* space station during rendezvous and pre-docking operations. (NASA)

it's funny. All summer long, congressmen hectored NASA officials for assurances about *MIR*'s safety. It has been the 1990s equivalent of the dialogue from one of those old World War II air force movies: "You can't send the kid up in a crate like that!"

NASA officials, to their credit, have been uniformly reassuring, and no matter the criticism, have continued to routinely replace Americans on the space station. They plan to complete the training schedule with at least one more before the program winds up in 1998.

No question, though, the Congress has had some cause for concern, to wit:

- Last June 25, an unmanned cargo ship full of space garbage crashed into *MIR*, the worst accident in outer space ever. It pierced the hull and depressurized one of the station's six modules, or compartments, making it uninhabitable, destroyed or damaged several of the solar panels that supply electrical power to the station, and consequently shut down about half the power supply.

- The next month, *MIR* lost almost all its remaining power when the crew accidentally disconnected a cable that operates the solar panels, and it took a tension-filled day to fix that.
- In August, the oxygen generators broke down for the umpteenth time, and so did the main computer system, which automatically positions the solar panels to the sun. Computer failures on *MIR* have become almost routine.

And now, with hindsight, we know there were some real human problems on board, prompted by the mechanical ones, as revealed the other day by Michael Foale, the resident American astronaut, as reported by the Associated Press and Reuters.

Foale said he was most concerned about the physical and emotional health of his colleague, the Russian Cosmonaut Commander Vasily Tsibliyev, who was at the controls when the cargo ship crashed into *MIR* during a docking test.

"What Vasily felt would happen," said Foale, "was that it would be simplest for organizations that did not want to accept responsibility just to blame him, and he believed that in the past, in Russia's history, this has occurred. So we tried very hard to convince him that he should not be judged so harshly."

In fact, as Tsibliyev well knew, Russian mission control is somewhat less forgiving toward its space persons than is NASA. They've disciplined cosmonauts in the past for perceived mistakes by docking their pay and writing them off future missions.

Space work has always been treated in a more proletarian fashion in Russia than in the United States. It's like an ordinary job, with bonuses and penalties for performance or lack of it. There's even a schedule of extra-work fees so that, for example, if a cosmonaut has to dock an incoming spacecraft manually, rather than use the automatic system, he can earn an extra couple of hundred dollars. Russian mission controllers suspect that more than once over the years, a cosmonaut has told them he needs to dock manually, not because he really needed to, but because he might have needed a new fur coat for his missus.

That certainly wasn't the case with Tsibliyev, a veteran cosmonaut. Foale insisted that the commander simply didn't have enough navigation information at his disposal to prevent the crash, and in fact, Tsibliyev's quick reactions may well have saved *MIR* from complete destruction.

Nonetheless, the stress prompted Tsibliyev to develop an irregular heartbeat and that forced mission controllers to scratch him from a scheduled space walk inside the damaged module. His pride was involved.

Said Foale, "He felt that was a blow to him in terms of his leadership. In fact, I think they (Foale's Russian crewmates) were heroic. They stuck through."

As it turned out, some of Tsibliyev's concerns about coming back to Earth were justified. When the crew was finally replaced, the commander returned to a barrage of personal criticism. Even President Boris Yeltsin was involved in the finger-pointing. A Russian investigation of the collision later laid only partial blame on the crew, but the consequences to Tsibliyev's career are not likely to be happy ones.

As for Astronaut Foale, he takes the long view of his time on board *MIR*. "To be honest, while we were up there, much worse things were going on back on Earth; strikes and problems and such. We could tell jokes and laugh. We talked about which actor should play each spaceman in the inevitable movie about *MIR*. I want to be played by Arnold Schwarzenegger. We were, after all, being fed. We had a home to go to. Things weren't so bad for us."

Well, now there's a brand-new crew of Russians and an American aboard *MIR*, doing a version of what the Russians would call "Remont"—remodeling their home to restore it to full working order.

And Foale's cinema fantasy may come true sooner than he imagines. A Russian film director, Yuri Kara, has budgeted $25 million to make a real movie about *MIR*, and shoot it right on location. It's tentatively titled *Space Flight Has a Price*, and Kara dreams of sending a couple of Hollywood stars up to *MIR*, along with a real cosmonaut to run the ship and do the filming. The director, no fool he, would direct the whole thing from the safety of Russian mission control.

Kara has already fleshed out the plot: It's 1999, the *MIR*'s mission is up, and Moscow is preparing to bring the last cosmonaut home. But the cosmonaut decides he wants to keep the *MIR* in space and ride it out till he and it burn up in the atmosphere. "He wants to become a space monk, and *MIR* would be his monastery," says Kara. So the Russians decide to send up another cosmonaut, a woman of course, to lure him home, assuming the cosmonaut has not yet taken his monastic vows. Kara says the movie will have a happy ending.

Kara tried to get Emma Thompson for the female lead, even buttonholing her at the Cannes Film Festival. But she turned him down. So did Tom Hanks. Which is probably just as well. The Russian cast he has assembled is already taking cosmonaut training, which is a little like army boot camp, only worse. That's even before they have to learn their lines and blast off into space.

But the moviemakers may find they have some competition. Ironically, the same international news media who've been chronicling *MIR*'s crises all year apparently now think it's safe enough to get on board themselves. CNN has been negotiating with the Russians about putting one of its correspondents on *MIR* for a few days, to do some live broadcasts from space.

Russian space officials can be pardoned if they're a little skeptical about that idea. Back in 1990, they accepted $12 million from the Tokyo Broadcasting System (TBS) to send a Japanese TV news reporter up to *MIR* with the same idea. But the reporter, a young woman who'd spent a year training near Moscow for the trip, came down with appendicitis at the last moment and couldn't go. So TBS convinced the Russians to allow a replacement; a male TV news reporter who never expected to have to make the trip, wasn't at all enthusiastic about it, and worse, was an out-of-shape chain-smoker. He spent eight days on *MIR* sick, or sick at heart, most of the time. And the rest of the crew spent much of their time preventing him from lighting up some of the cigarettes he'd smuggled aboard, the result of which, in *MIR*'s mostly oxygen atmosphere, would have been to turn the *MIR*'s interior into an instant Roman candle. Spacewise and TVwise, the whole enterprise was a disaster.

Well, maybe TV news is finally ready for *MIR*. We'll see. As for me, I'm waiting for *MIR: The Movie.*

chapter 22

Yuri the Great
(November 1997)

F or a kid who wanted to **grow up to be a jour-**
nalist, as I did, you couldn't do better than grow up around
Chicago. It was then, forty years ago, and remains, pound for pound,
one of the best news towns in the world. Chicagoans are at least as
addicted to politics as the folks in Washington, D.C. Except that in
Chicago, the gossip revolves around who is up and who is down in
the Cook County building or over at city hall. Somebody forgot to tell
Chicago that Washington is supposed to be the center of the political
universe.

And any aspiring journalist couldn't do better than wind up, as
I did, at Northwestern University's Medill School of Journalism, just
across the Chicago city line in Evanston. Because Chicago was the
place where you could practice. You could actually walk right in to
the county building or the state offices or city hall and talk to the
politicians and the bureaucrats just as if you were a real reporter
who knew what he was doing. And those public officials, the ones
you read about in the newspaper every day, would actually tolerate
you, and if they were in an expansive mood, actually talk to you, and
give you quotes and facts and figures, just like the real reporters at
the *Tribune* and *Daily News* and *Sun Times* were getting.

I never did get a chance to talk to the mayor, Richard J. Daley. He
was an awfully busy man. Those years, the late 1950s, were Chicago's
salad days. It was "The City that Works," and it was Mayor Daley who
made it work. He ran the city and the Cook County Democratic

Party, and it was usually his choices who sat in the governor's office in Springfield and occupied at least one of the seats in the U.S. Senate. Most all of Chicago and its environs were all-Democrat all the time, and no Democrat of any consequence got elected without Mayor Daley's say-so.

The mayor had made Chicago big and rich by striking up alliances with all sorts of big corporations, which built big offices and factories. He'd reward them if they'd come to Chicago and do their business and find ways to punish them if they didn't. Nobody did business of any consequence in Chicago without Mayor Daley's say-so.

There were those who said the partnership worked both ways; big business helped make the Daley Democratic party machine bigger and more prosperous, too. And the papers were seldom complete without a splashy front-page account of some new graft or payoff scandal and photos of one bureaucrat or another with his coat over his head being hustled off for trial on some bribery charge.

People wondered whether Mayor Daley, who always seemed to know everything that was going on, knew about the darker doings in his political machine. But I don't remember anybody every seriously suggesting Daley himself, who led an Archie Bunker sort of home life, ever profited personally from those shenanigans. Fame and fortune weren't his thing. Richard J. Daley simply wanted power, so he could get things done.

I sat in on one of his city council meetings once. It was almost Soviet. The meetings never took very long. The mayor, or one of his assemblyman factotums, would propose something and everyone would raise his hand high to vote for it. Well, almost everyone. The exception was the lone assemblyman from that northern city ward who always voted Republican. That was simply how the city that works, worked.

The story goes that one dark night shortly before a Democratic primary, in the middle of a cemetery at Bridgeport, a neighborhood where the mayor lived not far from the Chicago stockyards, two Democratic precinct captains were busily at work, scribbling down names from the tombstones to add to the Democratic Party voter lists. One of them was taking a particularly long time trying to make out the name on one badly weathered tombstone. His partner whispered in exasperation, "Paddy, will you hurry up, we got this whole cemetery to canvass before dawn!" And Paddy, in high dudgeon, shot back, "Listen, this fella here has as much right to vote in this election as anybody in this cemetery!"

These days, in Moscow, I often wonder what the late Richard J.

Daley would have made of Yuri Luzhkov. Even if that cemetery story is not apocryphal, Daley certainly wouldn't have needed to fiddle with the votes to get reelected by substantial majorities. Chicago couldn't imagine itself without him.

Yuri Luzhkov is the mayor of Moscow, and without apparently fiddling with the numbers he was reelected last year with 88 percent of the vote. And it's hard to imagine Moscow right now without him. He's built like a fireplug and not much taller. His bald head bursts with ideas and restless energy.

Here is a typical Saturday afternoon with Mayor Yuri: While traffic cops clear the boulevards for miles ahead, and police cars, sirens blaring, send pedestrians scurrying, the mayor's Volga limousine tears around town, followed by a parade of a couple of dozen additional Volgas and buses full of bureaucrats and journalists. The mayor is surveying his handiwork. He might stop at Luzhniki Sports Stadium, which he's rebuilding. He wants to host the World Cup soccer finals there someday. He dons a construction cap and tells the foreman to hurry up. Or he might tour the new underground shopping mall they're constructing near the Kremlin, or the rebuilt Christ the Savior Cathedral nearby, where the mayor decides what color to paint the exterior and the style of fencing around the complex. He tells the foreman to hurry up. Afterward, he might visit a neighborhood soccer field and play a few minutes with some of the local chaps (he's proud of his soccer skills) and then drag the whole entourage to a big lunch at some local restaurant where the tables, the food, and the refreshments are all waiting, courtesy of the restaurateur.

Luzhkov has turned Moscow into the city that works in a remarkably short time. Or so it seems to a casual observer. There is still a lot of poverty, crime, and suffering in the shabby streets behind the glittering facade of new banks and office buildings and casinos and movie theaters and all-night supermarkets. But on a snowy December night from my apartment window, you can look upon the Moscow River, etched in red and green light for as far as you can see, and you can imagine, for a moment at least, you're in Paris.

Mayor Yuri has done all this much the way Mayor Daley did it in Chicago: with a mixture of bribery, flattery, arm-twisting, and threats. Except Daley liked to sit in his office and pull the strings. Luzhkov loves to be out front, a mayor who is every bit as brash and glitzy as the new Moscow he has built.

And as with Daley's Chicago, nobody does business here without Mayor Luzhkov's say-so. Eighty-five percent of all new investment in Russia this decade has been appropriated by Moscow. Anybody who

Moscow mayor Yuri Luzhkov walks on the podium accompanied by two models during the closing ceremony of Haute Couture Fashion Week in Moscow on November 29, 1998. (AP Photo/Mikhail Metzel)

wants to put up a new building or start a new factory better be prepared to pony up a big cash donation to say, helping to resurface the Garden Ring expressway or whatever else the mayor thinks needs doing.

Critics, and publicly at least there aren't many of them, say Luzhkov is too close to the bosses of some of the Russian mafia outfits. In fact, though, hardly anybody does business in Russia these days without having some mafia connections, at least not for long.

And like the elder Mayor Daley, Luzhkov doesn't seem interested in accumulating a vast personal fortune, although he does have a collection of offices, including a very nice office high up in the city hall building, which would put some of those new Manhattan skyscrapers to shame. And there are the requisite rumors about his secret bank accounts and fancy villas somewhere, the sort of stories that follow all of Russia's most powerful. Still, like Daley, Luzhkov seems to prefer power over everything else. The power to Get Things Done.

Lately, Luzhkov seems bound and determined to do for Russia what he has done for Moscow. He claims he only wants to be mayor of Moscow forever, but he's certainly acting as if he wants to succeed President Boris Yeltsin when Yeltsin's term expires.

It would be foolish for Luzhkov to announce this early, since he needs Yeltsin's help to finish what he's started in Moscow. And Yeltsin, who is technically barred from running for another term (although there's a legal dispute about that), most likely wants one of his own young reformers to succeed him.

But if Yuri Luzhkov doesn't want to be president, he's certainly going to a lot of unnecessary trouble. He has, in recent months, announced he is in favor of a Russian treaty with Belarus; demanded that Russia take back control of the big Black Sea port of Sevastopol, which belongs to the Ukraine; and warned that the Kremlin is selling out to unnamed Western interests. How many other big cities do you know that have their own foreign policy?

And when Yeltsin's government announced it was going to end housing subsidies for all Russians within six years, Luzhkov made so much noise that he got a special exception for Moscow. This is popular with Muscovites but ruinous for the Russian budget. Moscow apartment dwellers live rent-free. They pay only about six dollars a month in light, heat, and building expenses. The government pays the rest, about twenty-nine dollars per person, and as Luzhkov must know, Russia can't afford to keep up that subsidy. Luzhkov's stance is bad economics. But it's great politics if you're planning on running for president someday.

You can now keep up on what the mayor's doing by tuning in to the mayor's very own TV station, Center TV, which is owned and operated by the city of Moscow. It is fast becoming Luzhkov's own TV trumpet, and before long he's hoping the signal will reach beyond Moscow to the whole country.

But Yuri Luzhkov has to go some before he can capture the hearts and minds of the rest of Russia. The most recent national polls list him as an also-ran for president in the minds of most Russian voters; barely 9 percent would vote for him today. Most Russians in the hustings view Moscow with the same indifference, if not distaste, with which Americans in the hinterland regard Washington, D.C. Luzhkov will have to find a way to cast himself as an outsider if he expects to succeed Yeltsin. And it doesn't help that the Yeltsin entourage in the Kremlin refers to Luzhkov privately as "The Bandit."

But the mayor is finding new and imaginative ways to keep himself and Moscow prominent. This fall, the city threw itself an 850th birthday party, complete with parades, concerts (including one entitled "The Inextinguishable Light in the Windows of Moscow"), and exhibitions; a sort of MoscowFest. It cost about $350 million, although the mayor assured Muscovites that private business paid for a third of that.

You are wondering why an 850th birthday celebration? Stalin threw the last birthday bash for Moscow back in 1947, when it was 800. Why not wait till 2047, and celebrate the 900th? Well, by that time Yuri Luzhkov, who is sixty, would be 110. He'd never live that long. Although there are those here who swear that Yuri the Great is even working on that problem, too.

[Editor's Note: Yuri Luzhkov is still the mayor of Moscow.]

chapter 23

President "Da"

(November 1997)

I t looms over Smolenskaya Ploschad, one of
Moscow's busiest intersections, one of the few remaining symbols of permanence in Russia's swiftly changing times.

The Russians know it as the MID, the Ministry of Foreign Affairs.
It's a block-square pile of granite and marble, more than 500 feet
high, adorned with bas-reliefs of flags and hammers and sickles.
Stalin built it in the 1940s, along with the other "Seven Sisters," the
ornate wedding-cake buildings he was fond of, as monuments to a
Communist future.

In the years when the Soviet Union was America's bogeyman,
this was where the "Mr. Nyets" of Soviet diplomacy did their work;
Molotov and then Gromyko, fashioning a foreign policy as cold and
gray and stony as the MID itself.

They're all dead now, and so is the Soviet Union, but the diplomats and the functionaries of the new Russia still toil here, trying to
fashion a place for their country in a vastly different but still-dan-
gerous new world.

The MID faces west, which is the way Russia itself has been
facing, more often than not, since the days of Peter the Great. You
can walk out the door of the MID, across the bridge over the Moscow
River, and if you keep walking west, and a little bit south, you'll eventually run into Kiev, Warsaw, Berlin, and Paris.

It wasn't until the early nineteenth century, however, that the
West began looking toward Moscow, and taking Russia seriously as a

major player in Europe's affairs. Under two tsars, the Russians put down Napoleon, restored the monarchies in France and elsewhere around Europe, and spent the better part of thirty years as Europe's policeman, putting down revolutionaries and making it safe for kings and queens again.

Then, for twenty years after 1917, a Communist Russia scared the wits out of the West by reemerging as the self-styled vanguard of world Socialist revolution. Next, it sacrificed twenty million of its citizens and much of its substance in helping to make the West safe from the Nazis. Finally, for forty-some years of Cold War, it once again scared the wits out of the West and the rest of the world as the sinister other half of the nuclear balance of terror. The Evil Empire, as Ronald Reagan liked to call it.

And now? Well, there are times when you half-expect the solemn facade of the old MID to be sporting one of those smiley-faced "Have a Nice Day" signs.

A hale and hearty Boris Yeltsin has become the "Mr. Da" of Russian diplomacy. He's become chummy with President Clinton, a friend of Britain's Prime Minister Tony Blair, and hosted French Prime Minister Jospin in Moscow just the other day. Yeltsin and German Chancellor Kohl are best buddies.

Without much fuss last spring, Yeltsin said yes to an expansion of NATO. Next spring, Russia will likely become a proud new member of the most exclusive club in the world, the G7 (which will become the G8). They are the richest countries on Earth. Russia isn't even among the top ten wealthiest nations, but the other seven members of the club figure that's a cheap price for keeping Yeltsin happy and Russia quiet.

Meantime, Yeltsin's two alter egos, Anatoly Chubais and Boris Nemtsov, who are helping to run Russia's foreign policy, spend much of their time hopping from Washington to London to Brussels chatting with the International Monetary Fund, the World Bank, and various other planetary charities.

Russia's introduction to G8 was made possible because one of the members in good standing, Japan, finally decided to forego its blackball. On paper at least, Japan and Russia are still enemies. The two countries fought four times in the last century, and never signed a peace treaty after World War II ended in 1945. Russia seized the four lonely Kurile Islands from Japan in 1945 (the Japanese insist on referring to them as the Northern Territories) and has refused all these years to give them back. But Russia badly needs and wants Japanese investment, and if Boris Yeltsin is not yet ready to say "Da" regarding the Kuriles, he seems to be saying "Maybe."

That was enough to produce an informal summit meeting last weekend in the middle of Siberia, where Yeltsin and Japanese Prime Minister Hashimoto went fishing. They didn't come to any conclusions on the Kuriles, but Hashimoto enthused, "We agreed to put maximum efforts into concluding a peace treaty."

What's suddenly made Russia so agreeable? For one thing, President Yeltsin seems to genuinely like summiteering. He enjoys chatting up the world's other movers and shakers, the crowds and fanfare and good fellowship. And it seems to be good politics. Russians who don't pay him much respect at home are proud to see him with the other world nabobs, being feted in Washington. A recent poll here found that 73 percent of those Russians sampled would like to visit the United States. Since most of them won't, perhaps Russians take some vicarious pleasure in seeing their president taking the air on the South Lawn of the White House.

And as the months progress, Yeltsin seems more and more aware of the short time remaining before his final term runs out in the year 2000. You have the feeling he's trying to use that time to balance Russia's books with the rest of the world, so that he can at least leave a legacy of peace, if not prosperity, to his countrymen.

It may be, though, that Yeltsin's successors will be most grateful to him for what he's done to patch things up not with the West, but with the East, namely, China.

This week, in the Great Hall of the People in Beijing, Yeltsin and China's head of state, Jiang Zemin, held a sort of public love-in. It was their fifth summit meeting in as many years, and the Russian and Chinese newspapers had a field day, splashing photos of Yeltsin bear-hugging Jiang, and Jiang panda-hugging Boris, all over the front pages.

And it wasn't all for show. Yeltsin and Jiang seem to have a kind of personal chemistry, apart from the fact that they're both grandfathers and enjoy chatting about the grandkids. The two of them seem genuinely fond of each other, rather like Yeltsin's relationship with Chancellor Kohl. There was an evident warmth in Beijing that was absent, for example, when Jiang met President Clinton in the United States a few days ago.

Most important, Yeltsin and Jiang signed a declaration finally settling the fractious question of Sino-Russian relations along the 2,800 miles of border they share. Each country will keep about 130,000 troops inside a sixty-mile-wide border zone.

That was no small accomplishment. China and Russia have been waging hot and cold war ever since the time of the Mongols in the Middle Ages. They were Communist allies for a brief moment in the

1950s, an accommodation that swiftly dissolved into a bitter struggle for power in the Socialist world. As late as 1969, Soviet and Red Chinese border guards were shooting it out on the ice floes along the rivers that separate the two nations.

Since both countries are members of the nuclear weapons club, the prospects of Moscow and Beijing triggering some sort of nuclear Armageddon caused more than a little concern in the West.

These days, the West is worried that perhaps Moscow and Beijing are getting a little too chummy. The two of them certainly have good reason to let bygones be bygones. The Central Asian republics that border them, the leftovers of the old Soviet Union, are mostly run by volatile and inexperienced governments, many of them dictatorships. And they are Muslim nations, potentially susceptible to the sort of religious fundamentalism that has wracked Algeria and Egypt and turned Iran into an international pariah.

Then there's the matter of money. China has become Russia's third-largest trading partner, more than $6 billion every year. The two countries want to triple that in the next few years. In Beijing this week they made a start, signing an agreement for a thirty-year, $12-billion project to pump natural gas from Siberia to China.

Most of the trade right now involves weapons sales. Moscow is already China's biggest arms supplier, especially of new Russian warplanes. And China is swiftly importing Russian technology so that it can one day make bigger and better warplanes and other weapons of its own. In return, Russia is getting the sorts of things it desperately needs: consumer products, and Chinese investment money.

Since the Soviet Union dissolved, Russia has had to come to terms with the fact that, despite its nuclear arsenal, it is no longer a superpower. And despite its economic achievements in the last decade, China still can only dream of becoming a superpower someday. There's only one superpower left in the world; the United States, and neither the Russians nor the Chinese like the prospect of Washington throwing its weight around. If a Russian-Chinese partnership can sober up the Americans before they become drunk with power, the reasoning goes, so much the better.

Yet there remain some big potholes along the road to the future that could take some of the gloss off this new era of good feeling between Moscow and Beijing. If Russians remember Ghengis Khan, the Chinese still rankle over the exploits of one Erofei Khabarov, a Russian fur trader who in 1640 found that much of Siberia was Russia's for the taking, and took it. Now, as then, the Russians regard themselves as the more civilized and developed country sharing a long border with some rude and less-fortunate neighbors.

And then there's the problem of numbers. On the Chinese side of their border, the country is poor but teeming with people. On the Russian side, there's a wealth of natural resources but hardly any people. The entire eastern third of Russia numbers less than twenty million souls. In just three adjoining Chinese provinces, there are five times that many.

With 1.2 billion mouths to feed and fifteen million more of them every year, it may not be long before China begins to covet that Russia east of the Urals which the Chinese have always regarded as a part of the world that would have been Chinese anyway, if it hadn't been hijacked.

It wouldn't take a military invasion for the Chinese to "reclaim" Siberia either. Moscow's relations with the Russian Far East have never been worse. Increasingly, regional bosses in Siberia are going their own way, and Moscow has neither the financial or political wherewithal to do very much about it. In a few decades, with carefully targeted investment, China may well be able to buy Siberia rather than seizing it by force.

History make look back on all this and decide that it might have been more symbolic, in retrospect, for the Russians to build that MID building so it faces east, rather than west. At present, the West can take some comfort in the fact that Russia and China are acting like good neighbors.

And speaking of symbols, if you're looking for something that perfectly sums up the difference between the foreign relations of the old Soviet Union and the New Russia, take a look at President Yeltsin the next time you see him on TV, at one of those fancy G8 dinners. Remember those dumpy old off-the-rack suits the Communist diplomats used to wear? Boris Yeltsin now wears a tuxedo.

chapter 24

Lenin Who?

(November 1997)

I t's a lousy day in Moscow for a celebration—cold
and cloudy with a smattering of sleet. Which is just as well.
There won't be much of a celebration here anyway for this anniversary.

Exactly eighty years ago last night, up in St. Petersburg (Petrograd as it was then known), Lenin and the Bolsheviks staged a coup,
overthrew the government, and established what was to become the
Soviet Union. They call it the October Revolution because under the
old Russian calendar it was October 25.

A few years ago, when this was still the Soviet Union, today
would have been a big deal, no matter the weather. *Pravda*, the Communist newspaper, would have already published an official list of
slogans that people would be permitted to put on their banners and
flags, which varied according to whatever line the Kremlin happened to be pushing at the time: "Down with Capitalism!" "Up with
our Cuban Socialist Comrades!" "No to NATO!" State factories would
be busy distributing holiday packages of food and candy and cakes
to workers' families. All around the Kremlin there would be huge red
flags and Mt. Rushmore-sized portraits of whoever happened to
matter in the Politburo at the time.

And on anniversary day, the whole city would turn out for that
big military parade through Red Square, surveyed from the top of
Lenin's mausoleum by the Soviet leadership in their identical winter
coats and hats. Kremlinologists would speculate for months on the

136

meaning of who was standing next to whom. But you probably remember that part from the little snippets of it they used to show on the TV news back home.

This day is still a holiday in Russia, but this anniversary was remembered, in public, by only a remnant of the faithful. A little corner of Red Square was occupied for an hour by about three thousand pensioners, leftists, and Communist diehards who, like the old monarchists here, still imagine that the past may yet somehow become prologue. Somebody figured out the other day that there are now only six hundred thousand card-carrying Communists in the whole of Russia. Six years ago there were almost seven million.

As for everybody else in Moscow, it's just a Friday off. The streets are blessedly free of traffic. People are sleeping late,

Elderly Russian Communist Party member at Communist rally in Moscow. (© Richard Threlkeld)

doing chores, watching TV, playing with the kids, and figuring out what to do on the weekend. In a national poll last week, 95 percent of the respondents said they planned to observe this day as a nonpolitical day off.

The question I seem to get asked most by friends in America is, "Are the Communists going to take over Russia again?" Here's a bulletin: No Way.

Sure, there's certainly enough fodder to make a revolution here. Neocapitalism has had a vicious effect on most average Russians, especially the elderly. Wages and pensions have gone unpaid, and the ruble gap between the brash, newly rich New Russians and the rest of their countrymen is vast and growing. But the Russians who are most angry, who remember when there was always food of some sort on the table, a roof of one kind or another over everybody's head, a guaranteed job, even if it was usually a dead-end sort of job, and a couple of weeks off in the summer, those Russians are too old and too tired to make a revolution.

You'll see them out in the streets today, with the same old banners and shouting the same old slogans. But when it's all over, according to agreement with the cops, at precisely one o'clock this afternoon, they'll all go home. Then they'll probably crack open a bottle of vodka and reminisce about the Good Old Days.

Maybe there will be another revolution in Russia someday. Who knows? It's instructive to recall that through all of its history except for the past six years or so, Russia's been a dictatorship in one form or another. A millennium of autocracy is a hard habit to break, and it's not altogether impossible that some future man on a white horse may come riding out of the Urals or somewhere to take up where the tsars and Lenin and Stalin left off.

But he won't be a Communist. The Communists had their last best chance to return to power last year in the presidential elections. And Boris Yeltsin, with the help of a pliant media and the big-business barons, dashed that dream.

Since then, the Communists, who still control the Duma, have become reluctant partners in Russia's seemingly relentless march toward a free-market future. They've reluctantly acquiesced in some of the budget cutting demanded by Western lending institutions, endorsed Yeltsin's Western-oriented foreign policy, and when Yeltsin and the Communists went eyeball-to-eyeball the other day over the stringent new budget, it was the Communists who blinked.

The leader of the Communists and Yeltsin's opponent in last year's elections, Gennady Zyuganov, made a ritual trip to St. Petersburg this week to commemorate this anniversary. This is the man who still represents the vanguard of world Socialism, such as it is. Here is what he said about the October Revolution: "Today is a new era and we must avoid such revolutionary uprisings." Say What?

Zyuganov has turned into such a political pushover that he's now in a leadership battle with some of the young firebrands in his party like Viktor Anpilov, who accuse him, with considerable justification, of selling out to the capitalist enemy for a seat at Yeltsin's table.

The ones who make revolutions are the young folks. And they, the Russians under twenty-five, say, are not in what you'd call a revolutionary mood. The best and brightest are out to make money, just like they've been doing most days on Wall Street. Pay a visit to the Moscow Stock Exchange. It has been doing a lot better than Wall Street this year; stocks here are up 100 percent over last year. And the trading rules are, to say the least, exotic. The other day, when all the Asian stocks were tanking, the Moscow Exchange leadership was worried that Russian stocks might fall, too. So they simply closed up for a while, until things began to look better. Maybe the Russians are on to something here. You just keep the market open only when stocks are going up. Should we tell Dow Jones?

Anyway, when you stop by the exchange, you'll be hard put to find anybody among the traders who doesn't look like he just stepped out of the photo in his high-school yearbook. They're kids; smart, ambitious kids who are figuring out how to use the system. The last thing they want to do is to change it, violently or otherwise.

The less talented among the Russian young have found other ways to revolt. You'll see them in clumps on the Moscow street corners at night, wearing cheap leather jackets with a lot of hardware hanging from the pockets, 1950s Marlon Brando look-alikes. There are skinheads and dope freaks and even, God forbid, Neo-Nazis among the Russian youth. But you find the same sort of aimless children on the street corners in Berlin, Paris, London, Rome, and Philadelphia, too.

They don't care about revolution, the Russian youngsters, and they certainly don't care about recent history. Betsy was talking to some Russian nine-year-olds in school the other day and asked one of them who Lenin was. The girl thought for a minute and said, "Isn't he the head of some company?" A better answer, perhaps, than a colleague of mine, David Hoffman of the *Washington Post*, recorded a while back when *he* visited a Russian classroom. The teacher asked the same question of the kids: Who was Lenin? One of her students considered that for a time, shot up her hand, and replied, "Um, he's dead, and, um, he was one of the Beatles!"

It's funny, but it's a little sad, too. Masha Lipman is one of the most thoughtful and inventive of the new generation of Russian news analysts; Moscow's Ellen Goodman, if you will. Masha is the mother of a sixteen-year-old girl, and over dinner the other night, Masha was talking about her own girlhood.

"I grew up in the Brezhnev, Andropov, and Chernyenko years," she said, "when we all thought the Soviet Union would last forever. I was a good student, and a member of the Komsomol, the Young Communist League, which was the only ticket to advancement in the system. But we loved Western music, especially jazz and rock. The Soviet authorities frowned on that, of course, as decadent capitalist music. But every once in a while, at Spasso House, the American ambassador's residence, they'd have a jazz concert, and it was open to any of us Russian kids who wanted to come. The problem was, the KGB would take your name down if they saw you there, and then they'd drum you out of Komsomol, and there would go your future. It was a tough decision."

Masha and some of her girlfriends went to the concerts anyway, and suffered the consequences. I asked her if she'd talked to her daughter about that.

"I've mentioned it to her," Masha replied, "but she's not interested. She's interested in boys and clothes and rock music. Now you don't have to go to Spasso House to hear rock music. It's all over. I guess it's a good thing she's free now to make whatever choices she wants, without somebody taking names. Still, whatever was wrong with our system then, and there were a lot of things wrong with it, we youngsters always felt we were working together, doing good for our country and the world. Now everybody's just in it for themselves."

President Yeltsin, an old Communist himself, had some revealing things to say about Russia then and now, in a remarkable interview he gave the other day to the Moscow newspaper *Sevodnya*.

"We have gone a very long way from the times we remember," he said. "And I believe they have gone forever."

This is an anniversary of sorts for Yeltsin, too. It was ten years ago that, rather like Masha Lipman, he put his own career on the line at a secret party meeting by denouncing a personality cult growing up around Soviet President Mikhail Gorbachev. Yeltsin was booted out of the leadership and wound up leading Russia's new democratic movement, which put him on the path to power, an ex-Communist running an ex-Communist nation.

"Ten years ago," he mused, "I still hoped the party would get well again. It was after that October meeting when I denounced Gorbachev's personality cult that made my hope waiver."

Today, in an address to the nation, Yeltsin said he has ordered the construction of a new monument to those who died in the civil war that followed the October Revolution. It will be a symbol, he said, "of our common will for accord and reconciliation, for civic peace."

So hereafter, today will remain a holiday in Russia. It just won't be called Revolution Day anymore. Henceforth, it will be the Day of Reconciliation and Accord.

chapter 25

Divided
We Fall

(December 1997)

O nce upon a time, when I was reporting from
southern California, I did an interview with a once-famous
movie actress. I'd had a crush on her while I was growing up,
although she never appeared in the sorts of roles that won Academy
Awards. She played supporting parts in the "B" movies of the time,
but I thought she was about the prettiest woman I'd ever seen, and
she certainly would have gotten my vote for an Oscar.

She was about to make a comeback in an obscure new movie,
after she'd been away from pictures for quite a while. As I discovered,
the reason she'd been out of the movies is that she'd spent years
abusing herself with alcohol, drugs, and who knows what else.

The interview, which I'd so much anticipated, was a bust. So was
her comeback. They never made the movie, and we scrapped the
story. She died an early death some months later. If I'd been a better
reporter, I might have realized that that was a better story than the
one I was trying to do.

What I remember most is how appalled I was when I saw my
favorite star. Her raven hair was bleached a terrible yellow, her face
was puffy from the years of dissolution, and the sparkle had gone
from her eyes. I could barely recognize her, and I was depressed for
days afterward.

I sometimes thought about my movie queen while wandering
around Bosnia this month. I'd never been anywhere in what used to
be Yugoslavia, and I was unprepared for how spectacular this little

corner of it truly is. When it comes to Bosnia, God would certainly get my vote for an Oscar for scenic design. As you might have seen, though, the man-made parts of it are pretty messed up. Like that movie actress, the damage is all self-inflicted.

It's a little odd, touring Sarajevo as a first-time visitor, with fellow journalists who spent a lot of time covering three years of war here. You leave the airport, and they all start looking over their shoulders. "This used to be the front line," they'll say, pointing to several blocks of burned-out shells of apartments on the airport road. "The only way to drive this stretch was fast. And seldom."

There are some shell holes in the museum downtown, but it's functioning now. "Over here, if you stood in front of the museum, you had some protection. Every morning you could put up a camera and take pictures of snipers shooting people on their way to work, regular as clockwork."

Sarajevo is the major city of something known as the Republic of Bosnia and Herzegovina. And it's the capital of a lesser entity known as the Croat-Muslim Federation. A few miles away, over the mountains, there is Pale. That's the capital of another piece known as Republika Srpska, or the Serb Republic. In a perfect world, Sarajevo would be the capital city of all of this, with a multiethnic central government, and the various parts of it exercising a certain local autonomy and living in happy prosperity with one another, sharing the gorgeous scenery.

It took me a long time just to sort that much out about Bosnia, and I'm supposed to be in the news business. You can see why people who aren't Bosnian get a little confused, so a little history is in order.

Bosnia is the peculiar consequence of several hundred years of history. It's part Muslim, because it was occupied for some centuries by the Ottoman Turks. It's part Roman Catholic, because it borders on Croatia, which adjoins the Roman Catholic part of Europe. And it's part Serbian Orthodox, because part of it adjoins Serbia, where Russian and Greek Orthodox influences predominated. In fact, for most of the past few centuries, these three people dwelt relatively peacefully.

The troubles between them really started this century, and they came from outside. Bosnia's bigger neighbors started fighting over it. That led to the so-called Balkan Wars which led to a famous assassination here in Sarajevo, in 1914, that started World War I.

The Nazis encouraged more interethnic atrocities in World War II. And afterward, for nearly half a century, a Serb Communist named Marshal Tito imposed peace among all sides with brute force, in a Yugoslavia that was one of the most repressive totalitarian states in Europe.

When Tito died, what was Yugoslavia broke up. The Communists in power, especially in the Serb and Croatian parts of Bosnia, decided the best way to save their jobs was to become militant nationalists, and playing on the religious differences, promptly proceeded to set neighbor against neighbor. The Serbs tried to take most of Bosnia, but the Muslims and Croats united to foil them. Then the Muslims and Croats themselves fell out. Eventually, they were all fighting each other and it went on for three years. A new phrase called "ethnic cleansing" crept into the language, and by the time a U.S.-sponsored agreement signed in Dayton, Ohio, and guaranteed with a UN "stabilization" force of thirty-five thousand troops, went into effect in 1995, Bosnia was effectively partitioned three ways.

Sarajevo is mostly Muslim, although it's the one big city left in Bosnia where some Croats and Serbs still live together with them. When you look up, you can see the snowcapped mountains just outside town, and imagine yourself regarding the Wasatch Range from downtown Salt Lake City.

When you're up in the mountains, among the little villages, you can imagine yourself in the Alto Adige of Italy or Austria's Tyrol. Except instead of a church in the center of town, there's a mosque. And when you look down from the trenches and artillery positions where the Serbs besieged the city, you realize what a sitting duck Sarajevo was for those three terrible years.

Sarajevo is struggling to get back on its feet now that nobody's shooting at anybody anymore. There are blocks and blocks of ruined buildings. Here, a neighborhood that looks like Berlin after World War II. Over there, a huge structure that housed a newspaper with the top blown entirely off, as if somebody had taken a big bite out of the Citicorp Building in Manhattan.

And yet, there's a modicum of traffic on the streets again, the stoplights work, the trams are running, and people can go to work without worrying about snipers. Except that there isn't much work. Two-thirds of Bosnians are unemployed.

But somebody in Bosnia has money. In the center of town, behind the Roman Catholic cathedral, there's a warren of ancient streets that reminds you a little of East Jerusalem, except that there are enough fancy clothing and jewelry shops to fill up the Via Condotti in Rome. And on a Friday night, the pedestrian malls in the area are filled with well-dressed kids on their way to one disco or another. You might be in Amsterdam or Prague. The signs are all in the Bosnian language, with a lot of little squiqqles atop the consonants. It's Slavic and it sounds vaguely like Russian. But with place names like Brcko and Srebrenica, you have the feeling that along with all the foreign aid, Bosnia could use an infusion of vowels.

Indeed, if money and the goodwill of strangers were all that it took, Sarajevo and Bosnia would be Utopia by now. There are more than four hundred relief and other nongovernmental agencies helping out here, spending untold billions of dollars rebuilding homes and the country's infrastructure. But you can't buy reconciliation.

Go over to the Nedzarici neighborhood and you'll see Bosnia's problem. It's full of Muslim refugees who used to live in what is now the Serb side of the country. People like Rahima Mujkic. Her husband and son were killed in the war. She and her daughter-in-law, Maida, are living in a wreck of a house that belongs to a Sarajevo Serb who fled to the Serb side. Technically, Rahima and Maida could go back to their old homes and claim them anytime they wanted. And the Serb owner of where they live could do the same. Will they? Not likely. "I can't go home," says Rahima. "I'm afraid." Maida nods. "Maybe I'll go back someday, but not with my two sons. I don't want them to ever see what I saw. I want them to leave this whole country and get a good education and live a happy life somewhere else."

You can hear much the same thing from people on the Croatian side or the Serb side, which is why there are a million of Bosnia's best and brightest, or simply most fortunate, now dwelling in a new diaspora around the globe.

One consequence is that everything in Bosnia seems temporary, including where you live. Since property rights are so muddled, few residents of Sarajevo, for example, can dare leave their homes or apartments untended, even for a day or two. If you have to go to Vienna, say, for a couple of days, you make sure your brother's staying over at your place while you're gone. Otherwise, somebody just moves in. "We play musical chairs with our addresses," remarked a Sarajevo friend of mine. Bosnia's become a nation of squatters.

It's just fifteen minutes up a newly rebuilt road through the mountains to the Serb Republic capital, Pale. The only way you'd know you crossed the border is the ever-present armored personnel carrier with a soldier in the gun turret and a big, white SFOR sign on the side. SFOR is the UN stabilization force here. The other thing you notice is the change in the alphabet. All the signs are in Cyrillic, the Orthodox characters. But the words are the same ones they use over in Sarajevo, and the people look just the same.

The Serb side obviously got the best of things during the war. There's precious little damage in evidence. But peace has by no means brought prosperity. Just the opposite. Bosnian Serb atrocities during the war and its recalcitrance since have cost dearly in vitally needed foreign aid and investment. Pale is poor. The average income here is only about $45 a month, less than a quarter of what it is down the valley in Sarajevo.

Up in the mountains above Pale was where they staged most of the ski and other Nordic events in the 1984 Olympics. There's still a ski hotel and couple of lifts in evidence, but no skiers. Bosnia's presently no tourist attraction. In the hotel gift shop you can buy an official Serb Republic flag and a necklace and amulet with an official crest on it. Business didn't seem very brisk.

The Serb Republic is a fact. So is the Croat-Muslim Federation. But technically speaking, they are supposed to be parts of a whole called Bosnia-Herzegovina. But it's a nation on paper, without a functioning central government, a currency (the German mark is the money of choice), a flag, or even a national anthem.

It does have a UN ambassador, though, Muhammed Sacirbey, a Muslim. He's a stocky, muscular fellow, born in Sarajevo. He speaks with a kind of New York City accent, tempered with a Cajun drawl, which is positively disarming. He was raised in New York and went to college at Tulane University.

Sacirbey was making money on Wall Street when the war for Bosnia broke out. He was part of the government in Sarajevo and eventually got his UN post. Now he divides his time between Bosnia, the UN headquarters in Manhattan, and his home on Staten Island. You have the feeling that if Bosnia ever sorts itself out, Muhammed Sacirbey would like very much to be one of the people who are running things here, hybrid American accent and all.

Sacirbey is one of Bosnia's few evident optimists. "We are actually putting Humpty Dumpty back together in some places, but it's a long task, and when you take that piece by piece and you try to glue it all together, it's not quite gonna look right and it's not gonna be very easy."

He'd like to see Bosnia become a sort of Little America, and doesn't think that's simplistic. "What's wrong with a democratic, multiethnic society and free market?" he says. "It's worked pretty well in the U.S."

His argument is mostly with Paris and Bonn and London, not Washington. "They've got to stop treating Bosnians and those in the rest of Central Europe as second-class citizens. The test for NATO isn't whether they can add the Czechs or the Hungarians. It's whether NATO can make a brand-new nation here. Otherwise, NATO will become just a gentlemen's club without a purpose. We've got 750,000 refugees in Bosnia who are afraid to go home. And they won't go home until the West gets enough courage to arrest the war criminals that have already been charged. Bosnians aren't stupid.

They know that as long as the bad guys are running around free, the message is, 'You can't go home again!'"

In fact, some of the lesser figures among those accused of war crimes *have* been arrested. But neither Washington nor its allies seems prepared to deal with the violent reaction that picking up those who are accused of giving the orders would doubtless inspire. Most of them, although not all, are Bosnian Serbs with nasty-sounding names like Ratko, and while they've lost some of their political clout, they're living a comfortable and seemingly secure existence at home on the Serbian side.

"There's a sense in the West, and particularly among you reporters, that the victims and perpetrators of this war are all equally guilty," said Sacirbey. "In fact, we Muslims in the middle, between the Croats and Serbs, got the worst of it. Just look at Sarajevo. So when it comes to fingering the guilty, you all think that every time you pick up a Serb or Croat, you need to find a Muslim war criminal, too. Well, we haven't got that many. All the Muslims want is justice."

It occurred to me that in my experience, I've never met many people, not to mention whole peoples, who ever got the justice they thought they deserved, and perhaps he and the Muslims might simply settle for peace and prosperity? But I was too polite, I suppose, to pose the question to him.

Like so many Bosnian Muslims, Sacirbey has a touching faith that somehow, someway, America will make things right here. You can hear it from the ordinary people. We found Mustafa Cosic and Ragib Kokalic strolling down an alley in Sarajevo, a couple of elderly friends who'd been ethnically cleansed from the Serb side and after surviving a Serb concentration camp, are making do among their fellow Muslims. They agreed, simply, "If America wishes us to go home, it will be so." Even Muhammed Sacirbey, the political realist, says proudly, "When the U.S. troops walk by us, there is that little American flag on their shoulder patch. And that means there is an American commitment here."

It's a flesh-and-blood commitment. There are about eight thousand American GIs here, part of SFOR, and, just a few days ago, indefinitely committed to Bosnia by President Clinton. You can find them encamped in Bosnia's north, near Tuzla, a two-hour drive over a couple of mountains. It's been the quietest part of the Bosnian landscape to date, and, happily, U.S. casualties have amounted to only a handful of wounded.

Their forward position is high up on a pinnacle called Mt. Viz, which resembles one of those firebases I used to see in South Vietnam; same noise, same sandbags, same concertina wire, same

Threlkeld (front row, second from left) and crew with American troops atop Mt. Viz. (© Richard Threlkeld)

mud. Except there's no artillery, and they just packed away the last of the mortars that were up there. There are forty or so men and women in uniform, whose job it is to keep the Serbs and Muslims apart. During the war a lot of Muslim boys died trying to take Mt. Viz away from the Serb boys, but never did. Then the U.S. Army came along one day and took it away from both of them. So far, the U.S. presence here has been all that's required to keep the peace.

Says Sgt. Jerry Willis, of Jasper, Alabama, in quiet understatement, "Symbolically, whoever is on top of this hill is considered to have great influence in the area."

Sergeant Willis and most of his fellows are from the U.S. Second Armored Regiment, which moved in last August and will probably be here till summer at the least. The local kids didn't take long to discover them. The GIs have adopted the schoolchildren in the nearby village of Miljanovci, and the day before Christmas, Capt. Ross Coffman, of Williamsburg, Virginia, brought some of his "F" Troop over to hand out pencils and crayons and other school supplies to the third- and fourth-graders. The supplies had been donated from the folks at home. The GI flak jackets and helmets the soldiers wore seemed superfluous.

The children might have been a little confused, since they are

Muslim and they are getting ready for the Holy Month of Ramadan, not Christmas. But they were excited and grateful. Around here, a pencil or a crayon is something precious. Would the soldiers of "F" Troop have cared if they'd known that after they left, the school-teacher, a modestly scarfed intense young woman, resumed her lecture to the children about the strict Muslim law code, the Sharia, and the properly subservient role of women in a Muslim society? Perhaps. Perhaps not.

This was Christmas, after all, and playing Santa to the kids helped save the Americans from getting homesick. "The troops love it," said Captain Coffman. "I mean, there's a classroom full of friendly faces who have no idea where the United States is, let alone where Virginia or Michigan is!"

Lt. Ben Johnson of Detroit said it took some of the sting out of not being at the family dinner table Christmas Day. "I'm in charge of giving the prayer for the meal, so they're gonna have to do without me this year. There's gonna be a lot of tears shed at the table."

There were no evident tears at the Mess Hall on Mt. Viz Christmas Day. In this man's and woman's army, they now call it the Dining Facility. And the Mess Sergeant, or Dining Hall Manager, was Sgt. William Williams, who's an assistant school principal in the Bronx when he is not doing this reserve duty. He cooked a Christmas dinner of turkey, ham, stuffing, mashed potatoes, collard greens, and pumpkin pie, among other things. God knows where he got the ingredients. For Sergeant Williams, his diners this day were all kids in uniform, not much older than the ones he teaches at home. "Most of them are young people away from home for the first time, and my mission is to try to make it as personal and homey as possible." Mission accomplished.

I hadn't seen American GIs on duty anywhere since Operation Desert Storm in Iraq, and I'd forgotten how impressive they are nowadays. Despite all the publicity about "don't ask, don't tell" and the way women are harassed in the U.S. military, the U.S. Army has been quietly building a well-educated, well-spoken, efficient armed force composed of volunteers, most of whom plan to make the military a career. It's a shame they are so woefully underpaid. Still, how blessedly different they are from the unfortunate, unhappy, and unmotivated draftees I remember from the latter stages of the Vietnam War; poor whites and inner-city blacks who hadn't the clout or connections to stay out of combat in a war that they on the ground soon realized wouldn't be won.

The GIs atop Mt. Viz were young enough to be the sons and daughters of those soldiers. And they'd been well briefed, obviously, on what to say to inquiring reporters. Even so, you sensed that they really believed in what they were doing here, and unlike the poor Vietnam draftee in the midst of that long-ago battle for Hue, who asked me, "Sir, where is this place?" they actually know where they are and why.

Most important, they've learned how to be peacekeepers as well as warriors, a discipline other contingents in this UN force—the Norwegians, the Danes, the Italians, the French—learned the hard way over the past generation. In this new age of "stabilization," it's not Rambo that's required but the Cop on the Beat. The diplomats call it "conflict resolution," but any policeman will tell you that the minute you have to draw your gun to settle an argument, you've failed. The soldiers on Mt. Viz understand that. They also seem to understand that most likely, somebody's going to be serving turkey dinner to GIs up on Mt. Viz for a lot of Christmases to come.

If things in Bosnia remain as peaceful as they've been, there'll be somewhat fewer GIs here next year. But the American civilian presence has been growing by leaps and bounds the past few months. Bosnia is crowded with Americans now, everything from consultants to construction workers. If Vietnam finally became an American war in the 1960s, Bosnia has become, for better or worse, an American peace in the 1990s.

It didn't start out that way. Early on, when the fighting started, Washington was on the sidelines and Western Europe attempted to settle things. Eventually, when that didn't work, America, as the lone superpower left in the world, stepped in. Depending on whom you talk to, that was either because the Clinton administration was loath to try to untie a Gordian knot in a little place too far away (the European view) or because the Europeans wanted Washington to stay out while they handled things, or tried to (the American view). Now the Europeans seem to be worried that perhaps America's getting a little too involved here. A diplomat friend of mine in Washington thinks it all goes with the territory. "If America avoids a commitment somewhere, everybody says we're isolationists. If America takes on a commitment somewhere, then we're hegemonists."

That Bosnian commitment is personified by a big, beefy fellow in a blue-serge suit who's perpetually puffing a cigar. He's Jacques Klein, and his official title runs close to a paragraph, but he's the highest-ranking American diplomat here. He operates out of a little office on the second floor of an otherwise wrecked building on Marshal Tito Boulevard in Sarajevo. Those GIs who thus far have seldom had to fire their weapons have Jacques Klein to thank for it. For the past couple of years he has managed conflict resolution so well that few of the tripartite disputes here have ever reached the shooting stage.

Klein did a stretch in the army in Vietnam, then went on to the State Department, and wound up in Berlin during the last years of the Cold War, so he knew all about dividing lines by the time he got here. And he strikes you as a most undiplomatic diplomat; he speaks his mind, and does so in a blue streak. Few of his thoughts go unexpressed.

I mentioned to Klein what I thought was the single most depressing sight I'd seen in Bosnia. It's a map on the wall of the SFOR office, and it's a computer image of all the fields of land mines left in Bosnia from the war. Each one is represented by a red dot. The dots connect and merge into ghastly red arteries that precisely mark the borders of partition between Bosnia's Muslims and Croats and Serbs. The message from each to the other is: "Stay out," and it seems to be written in blood. In fact it amounts to seven hundred and fifty thousand unexploded mines just waiting for somebody to stumble over them. So, I asked, why not just accept this fact on the ground and let Bosnia stay partitioned, since that's the way most people here seem to want it?

"Wrong!" he said. "In fact, I know there's a majority of this population that wants to get the war behind them, that's tired, and that indeed wonders how they were led into all this, and by whom. Togetherness is a possible dream. I know all the arguments about accepting partition, and they're false. What's worse is that they sanctify and bless the concept of ethnic cleansing. They basically say that multiethnic societies can't live together. Now that's a very, very dangerous construct to advocate in this part of Europe in the twentieth century."

As you'd expect, Klein likes to point out that all the news from Bosnia isn't bad. And he's right. Three hundred and fifty thousand refugees have already gone back to where they once lived, even if they remain part of a still-despised ethnic minority. Some of the war criminals have been captured and brought to justice, and other leaders implicated in war crimes or corruption have been either removed from power or deprived of political office. There have been three free local elections since the war ended, and some political moderates have been elected by absentee ballot, even if they dare not try to go their city halls and to take office.

Klein regards all this as the beginning of his possible dream for Bosnia, which sounds a lot like Muhammed Sacirbey's. "The goal," says Klein, "is to have a Bosnia that becomes very quickly part of Europe, and that is a democratic, secular, multiethnic state with a market economy. And that requires America's involvement. Whether by design or accident of history, the United States is a global superpower. That means you're an adult, and that means that at times we have to exercise some adult supervision."

Listening to him, I wondered whether the best that Bosnia might hope for is not the Little America of Muhammed Sacirbey, but perhaps a Little Switzerland, with its distinct French- and German-speaking cantons a part of the whole.

Klein, by the way, is no Pollyanna. He knows the mind-set here is going to have to change before his dream can become reality for Bosnia's Muslims, Croats, and Serbs. "There is still a sense among them that each of these sides is a victim. None of them has ever said to me, 'My people were badly brutalized, however, we also did some egregious and evil things.' No one has said that yet, and a good psychiatrist would probably say, 'Until you understand you have a problem, you don't have a cure.' "

In the end, Bosnians themselves are going to have to devise a cure for what ails them, and it will probably have to start in a place like Mostar. You get to Mostar by driving south and west from Sarajevo for a couple of hours. Every place in Bosnia seems to be about a two-hour drive from someplace else. The highway twists and turns through limestone cliffs along the lime-green waters of the Naretva River, as it tumbles its way to the Adriatic. The Muslim villages along the way look like refugees from some capricious tornado; one village is almost untouched, its neighbor almost obliterated in the fighting.

You should come and see Mostar if the Bosnians ever patch things up among themselves. It's nestled in the mountains, and the old city, in the center along the river, is a labyrinth of narrow cobblestone streets with a park or a tiny plaza to discover around every corner, and even in December, the men are taking their bitter black coffee on the sidewalks outside the little cafés. Tall spires of mosques and church steeples frame the skyline. Mostar used to be a city of two hundred thousand, where Muslims and Catholic Croats had lived side by side in peace. When the fighting began between them, the front line was the river, which is no more than a block wide at this point. There were times when the Naretva River actually ran blood-red.

Now Mostar's down to a population of eighty thousand. Forty thousand Croats in West Mostar. Forty thousand Muslims across the river in East Mostar. Everybody else is either dead or gone. The Starri Most, the four-hundred-year-old bridge that symbolized Mostar's togetherness, was deliberately destroyed in the fighting. The Spanish contingent of SFOR has put up a temporary crossing while they rebuild the Starri Most to look the way it used to. But if and when it's done, there won't be much traffic across it. In Mostar today, East is East and West is West and the twain don't meet.

To an outsider, it's impossible to tell the Mostar Croats from the Mostar Muslims. They look alike, dress mostly alike, speak the same language, and use the same alphabet. In fact, people in Mostar say they can't tell the difference either, unless somebody brings it up. You can tell you're in West Mostar because there are Christmas decorations on the streets and it is considerably less banged up than East Mostar.

On paper, Mostar is supposed to be one city. But it's not. The Mostar Croats have their own local government, their own hospital, their own police force, their own public transportation. It's the same with the Mostar Muslims. If you want to get from one side of the river to someplace on the other side that's more than a walk, you have to take a taxi to the bridge, walk across, then take a different taxi to where you're going. If you're in a hospital on one side of town and you need a heart specialist, say, who's working in the hospital on the other side of town, better find your specialist someplace else. He won't treat you. A Croat in West Mostar might go to Muslim Sarajevo if he needed something, but he'd never cross the river bridge to Muslim East Mostar—and vice versa. On each side there are those who know who killed fathers and brothers and sisters and they know where the perpetrators live. It's all too personal.

The trouble with Mostar is what the trouble in Bosnia is all about. If Bosnians themselves, with the help of America and the rest of Europe, can put Mostar back together, they can probably put Bosnia back together. But that's a very big "if."

There is something for Bosnia to aspire to, a vision of what it once was and could be again. It's called Slovenia. It's a vest-pocket-sized country about half the size of Switzerland, with about two million people, Roman Catholics most of them, who speak the same Serbo-Croatian as their neighbors.

Until this decade, Slovenia had almost always been part of something else—first the Austro-Hungarian Empire, later the northern tip of Yugoslavia. When Tito was running things, the industrious Slovenes produced about a third of the income and a third of exports for the whole country.

When Yugoslavia broke up, Slovenia promptly jumped into the arms of its immediate neighbors, the Swiss, the Italians, the Austrians, and the Hungarians. Belgrade made a half-hearted attempt to hold on to Slovenia, but after a ten-day war in which sixty-six people died, the Yugoslav army gave up and returned to more pressing matters in Croatia and Bosnia.

Now Slovenia is independent and democratic and a de facto member of the European Union. It's hoping to become a full member of that Western European economic and political club in a couple of years. Slovenia already exports about two-thirds of its industrial output, much of it software products, to western Europe.

Ljubljana, the capital, shows no scars of the struggles that have raged across this part of the world in the past few centuries. The Turks never made it this far north. They got only as far as Bosnia. The Austrians, the Italians, and the Russians fought bitterly here during the later stages of World War I, but that damage has been repaired, and Ljubljana's Old Town, complete with a medieval castle and Renaissance cathedrals lining a lovely canal that looks like it belongs in Amsterdam, resembles a corner of EuroDisney outside of Paris, except that it's real.

The Old Town market is full of delectable fruits and vegetables, brimming over with breads and pastries and sausages and spices, and trimmed with dozens of fresh-flower stalls. Ljubljana's eight hundred thousand people are well fed and well dressed, with a standard of living approaching that of their western European neighbors.

Only an hour away to the northwest lies some of Europe's most beautiful scenery. It's the Julian Alps, the "sunny side of the Alps" as the locals refer to it, a haven for hikers in the summer and skiers in the winter. Prices for hotel rooms, food in the excellent restaurants, and carafes of the tasty Slovenian wine are ridiculously low.

Tourists haven't discovered Slovenia yet. Most vacationers still think Slovenia is that part of the former Czechoslovakia that isn't Bohemia. Or that it's still part of that restive, dangerous, and divided place that used to be Tito's Yugoslavia. Up the road, in fact, at the lakeside town of Bled, you can stay in Tito's vacation guest house that's been converted into a thirty-seven-room hotel. You can look out one of Tito's windows in the evening and see the church on the island across the water and hear nothing but the slow peal of the bells and the songs of the crickets. Peace and quiet.

So in relation to Bosnia and Belgrade, Slovenia might as well be on Mars. In Ljubljana's narrow streets beneath the blossomed balconies, or at table along the sidewalk cafés, people smile and laugh and embrace each other, as if celebrating not just their lives and liberty and happiness, but also their good fortune.

You can't come to Slovenia without thinking of Bosnia, and what might have been. Bosnians, after all, have just as much scenery and history and energy and ambition as the Slovenians. What they don't have is peace. And what they don't have is togetherness.

That old movie actress I remember squandered her happy ending. There are not, after all, that many second acts in the lives of us mortals. Not so with nations. Bosnia has a second chance. We're all too familiar with its past and present. Maybe there's a Slovenia in its future.

(Postscript: There were more agonies to come in the former Yugoslavia, as history repeated Bosnia's tragedy in the Serbian province of Kosovo: the same bloodshed, the same ethnic cleansing, the same wretched scenes of refugees fleeing for their lives, this time into neighboring Albania. As in Bosnia, it took an infusion of Western peacekeepers to finally secure a cease-fire in Kosovo and bring a tentative peace to the region. Happily, the Serbian people have finally, and peacefully, removed the man most responsible for the former Yugoslavia's suffering, Serbia's president, Slobodan Milosevic. He was forced into retirement after failing to nullify the results of a presidential election he lost. His successor, the nationalist reformer Vojislav Kostunica, will have his hands full rebuilding Serbia's economy and trying to install a demo-cratic political system. But now that there's a new face in Belgrade, rela-tions with Bosnia may improve. Bosnia itself, though, is no closer to togetherness. The Naretva River and a wall of hate still separate the citi-zens of Mostar. American soldiers, and their counterparts from western Europe, are still required to keep the peace. The best you can say about Bosnia is that so far, they've largely succeeded. And keeping in mind the agony that Kosovo has undergone, that's no small victory.)

chapter 26

Kids

(January 1998)

I suppose it was an editor for one of the penny
paper tabloids at the turn of the century who discovered that
kids make good copy, and that a photo of, or story about, children
will sell lots of newspapers.

By the time the TV news came along, and I joined up, we'd all
learned the same thing. So I've spent a lot of time over the years
doing pieces about children, all over the world. I thought I knew all
about kids, until I got to Russia.

Kids are everybody's passion of course, but Russians seem to dote
on them with a particular intensity. Their own kids or anybody
else's. They are pampered, listened to, and entertained to a degree
that would confound even Hans Christian Andersen. The sighting of
a baby almost anywhere is cause for a spirited conversation among
bystanders. "How old is he/she? My, how big for his/her age! Look at
those beautiful blue/brown/black eyes! Is he/she teething yet? I've
got a remedy if it hurts her/him!"

If you're taking Baby for a walk in the stroller on a cold morning,
better be sure Baby's completely covered up. An errant flap of gar-
ment that exposes Baby's precious cheeks to the weather will draw a
sharp reprimand from complete strangers.

Russian adults who will cheerfully elbow each other out of the
way in the subway or on a street corner without so much as an
"excuse me," or splash a puddle of water all over a little old lady
pedestrian while speeding around the corner in the family car and

Russian children.
(© Richard Threlkeld)

not give it a second thought, seem to regard themselves as loving, caring, surrogate parents of every little Russian boy and girl they encounter. The only other creatures upon which Russians seem to lavish such fond attention are dogs. Like the children, Russian dogs are generally well groomed, well behaved, and come in an astounding variety of shapes and sizes.

So it's hard to fathom why there are an estimated four hundred thousand orphans in Russia. That's not counting the thousands of homeless street kids who inhabit the dark underbellies of Russia's cities. Certainly a lot of them are casualties of the economy. Some are children of parents whose lives have been wasted by strong drink or drugs. Some of them are children of parents who died young of disease or despair. And some are children abandoned because some family simply couldn't afford another mouth to feed.

Plain poverty is also the reason that most Russian families don't adopt these orphaned kids. They can hardly afford to feed their own. One index of the hard times here is that the Russian fertility rate has dropped almost out of sight. In 1920, when Communism was just getting started, Russian women were expected to bear an average of seven children each. They are now averaging one apiece. That's far too few to expand the population.

The luckier orphans are well cared for in places like Children's House Number 29 just outside Moscow. They are clean and healthy and active, these kids, and attended to by people who seem to want the best for them, like the director here, Irina Ivanova, who looks like the sort of person you'd want for your own grandmother.

"We do our best with what money we have," says Mrs. Ivanova, "but the one thing we can't do for most of my children is find them a real home. In practice, when a child is holding my skirt and crying, 'Irina, find me a mama, I want to go home,' well, you need to see this and hear this. It's impossible to get used to it."

Without a real family, the best that most of these orphans can hope for is enough to eat, a roof over their heads, and a rudimentary education until they're sixteen. Then they're out the door and on their own, with no future and no prospects.

For a few, though, there is now an American option. For American couples, Russia has now become the leading source of adopted children from overseas, about thirty-eight hundred of them every year.

One afternoon, we encountered one such new family in their room at the President Hotel near the Kremlin. Jim Georgalas is a lawyer from Pittsburgh. His wife, Jane, is a nurse. They'd just returned from a St. Petersburg orphanage with their new daughters, Natasha, who's three, and Valentina, who's a year old.

The girls were quiet and seemingly content with their new surroundings.

"They make up their beds every morning and pick up after themselves without being told," said Jim. "That's a sign that they've been in an institution. Even so, you can tell they've been loved and cherished by someone before us, and we're the beneficiaries."

The Georgalases have been through this before. A couple of years ago they came here to adopt their first Russian child, Michelle, who's now five, and waiting back home in Pittsburgh.

"I grew up in a large family," said Jane. "I had a wonderful childhood and I think it's important for children to have lots of siblings around."

The Georgalases worked with a reputable Russian adoption agency. Even so, the red tape took several months and cost them a total of about $40,000. It's not clear where all that money goes and who winds up with it, but the Georgalases thought it best not to ask those kinds of questions. At the moment they were most concerned with getting everybody home to Pittsburgh, although they like to think that someday they'll bring their daughters back to Russia, to see where they came from; to know they are Russian, and be proud of it.

"When they walk out of that orphanage, they have only one thing that's truly theirs—their heritage," said Jim. "And that's one thing I promise these kids are going to keep."

But not everybody in Russia is happy with what folks like the Georgalases are doing, some of the politicians especially. There's a bill now being drafted in the Russian parliament that would severely restrict adoption of Russian orphans by Westerners, Americans especially. It's prompted in part by a notion, born out of wounded national pride, that foreigners are "stealing" Russian children, and in part by a couple of well-publicized instances of mistreatment of Russian orphans by their new American parents.

The bill isn't likely to become law in its present form, but it's got people like Mrs. Ivanova at Children's House Number 29 worried and angry.

"I get tears in my eyes every time I look through my scrapbook," she says. Her scrapbook is filled with photos and letters from all her orphans who've been adopted by American families. Faces of happy, healthy kids smile out of the pages, looking just like, well, American kids. There's little Olga who's now growing up in San Francisco, with her hair done up in ribbons and a new red dress. Next to it is a card that reads, in English, "Dear Mrs. Ivanova, I just want you to know I am the happiest little girl in the world."

"If the deputies support this new bill," says Mrs. Ivanova, "there won't be any more stories like Olga's. Our children will be sentenced to stay in the orphanage. It's very bad that our lawmakers never visit us, they do not see the eyes of our children, and never ask us how to help."

Jim Georgalas is just plain perplexed. "It just doesn't make sense to me, what the politicians here are contemplating. I think if anybody wants to limit American adoptions, he ought to go to an orphanage, look at the children, have them call you 'Papa,' and then close the door and lock it against them. I just can't see that."

The last we saw of the Georgalas family they were packing up and heading for the Moscow airport, and Pittsburgh, and home. With any luck, and an outbreak of common sense among Russian nationalists, there'll be a lot more of these happy beginnings to come.

chapter 27

The
Odd Couple
(February 1998)

I spent a little time in Cuba back in the 1980s, when it was a western outpost of the Evil Empire. I'd drop in now and then, the Cuban foreign ministry permitting, just to see how Fidel Castro and the Cubans were getting along. I like Cuba, and I've always been fond of the Cubans for their wit and energy. If you've any doubts about that, go visit the Cuban-American community in South Florida sometime.

In those days, Havana resembled the Soviet Union Lite. The city was full of revolutionary slogans and anti-imperialist graffiti. There wasn't any new construction to speak of, and the old buildings along the Malecon, the seafront boulevard, were unwhitewashed and crumbling. The only evidence that America was just beyond that magic Malecon sunset were some old pre-Castro Chevys and Pontiacs sharing the streets with the Russian Zhigilis and Ladas. And there weren't many of those.

In fact, except for the Havana Libre Hotel and a couple of other big hostelries, which had barely been finished by the Hilton and Sheraton folks when Castro took over, Havana looked more Spanish Colonial than Miami Modern. Surveying the cathedral and the graceful old buildings along the wide tree-lined boulevards, flushed with the mango trees in full bloom, you'd have thought the Spanish had just left yesterday, instead of 1898.

The only tourists in evidence were the burly Russian men, sweating in the Caribbean heat and swigging rum "Mojitos" and vodka in some of the same outdoor cafés Ernest Hemingway used to frequent. Except the Russians were more partial to vodka. Cuba was R and R for the Soviet apparatchiki who'd been on especially good behavior. A week or two in Cuba was a lot more fun than a week or two on the Black Sea coast. The Cubans didn't much like the Russians, but after all, the Soviet Union was buying Cuban sugarcane, the national crop, in return for Soviet oil. Cuba was running on Russian petroleum and staying afloat with Russian rubles, $6 billion worth of them every year. In all, over a generation of Cuban Communism, Moscow poured something like $100 billion into this place.

I didn't really know what to expect now, a decade later, when I landed at Havana with Pope John Paul II, a flock of cardinals and other Vatican dignitaries, and the several dozen members of the Vatican press corps (my particular distinction was that I was the only journalist on the plane who was not fluent in Italian).

That the pope was finally coming here, one of the few places on Earth he had not visited, it seemed, was a sign of some change. When Castro came to power forty years ago, some of the first things he did were to expel much of the Roman Catholic clergy, close down Catholic schools and seminaries, and ban practicing Catholics from Communist Party membership. Only one child in a thousand was baptized. Castro even cancelled Christmas. Henceforth, the official religion was to be no religion at all. Only in recent years had the authorities loosened some of the state controls over the church. And this year, in honor of the pope's arrival, Castro had reinstated Christmas, although most younger Cubans had no idea how to celebrate it.

I figured the Cubans must be having at least as hard a time of it as the last time I visited. After all, the U.S. economic embargo against Cuba (the Cubans call it an "economic blockade") had, like Castro, outlasted eight American presidents and was, if anything, tougher than ever. Cuba's Soviet patron was gone, and along with it all those Soviet ruble subsidies, the oil imports, and the lucrative sugar trade. Moscow had gone capitalist, as almost everywhere else in the world, and now regarded Castro not like a Socialist brother, but rather like some crazy uncle. Communism was now mostly a memory, except in a few places like Cuba, where it remained a fact.

What stunned me was how much Havana has *not* changed. I was used to Moscow, where the scenery is studded with billboard advertising and the skyline is full of old buildings coming down and new ones going up.

Havana, at first glance, looks as if it has been preserved in amber. The old buildings along the Malecon and in the central plaza have just gotten older. I couldn't find a single sign advertising much of anything. But the writing on the walls here is still as full of revolution as before. "We will overcome." "Victory or Death." "The Martyrs of the Twenty-Sixth of July Tire Store." Portraits of Castro's alter ego, the martyred Che Guevara, he of the beard and beret, are everywhere, including one overlooking Revolutionary Plaza that must be six stories tall.

There's more traffic on the streets, which includes, along with the Toyotas and Suzukis, a lot of the same old Chevys and Pontiacs and Ladas from before, kept running by an incredibly elaborate spare-parts market.

Some closet capitalism is in evidence. Street peddlers now hawk fruit ices and other snacks, and minicafés have sprung up here and there.

They're finally fixing up the Cathedral Plaza in Old Havana. I remembered it as one of the loveliest relics of Spanish colonialism anywhere in this hemisphere, delicate and almost dwarfed by the buildings around it, and perfectly proportioned.

It was falling apart then. But UNESCO decided to preserve it as a world heritage site, and restoration is now in progress. I'm worried it's going to wind up looking like an exhibit at Disney World.

In the evenings, on the downtown streets, you're likely to encounter one or more miniparades: a couple of dozen people marching around with red flags and signs demanding "up" or "down" with something or other, singing revolutionary anthems, and purposefully going no place in particular. I remembered that Havana always used to remind me of how America might have looked if the student radicals in Berkeley in the 1960s had somehow managed to take over Washington.

About the best you can say for Havana and Cuba and Castro is that they have survived, if not prospered. The Russian tourists have gone, but they've been replaced by Canadians and Europeans and Latin Americans, who, like the Russians, come here for a cheap good time. And it's not so cheap anymore. There are new fancy resort complexes going up along the famous Veradero and all over the island. Cuba boasts some of the finest beaches in the world.

A million tourists now come here every year and spend more than a billion dollars. U.S. dollars, incidentally, are not only accepted here, they are required from foreigners. And tourism has replaced sugarcane as Cuba's principal means of foreign exchange.

And, if you take the time to look carefully, you can see other changes: new office buildings for some of the three hundred or so joint ventures built with foreign investment. Here a new Mexican telephone system. There a new Canadian nickel-mining firm. Over there a new harbor for cruise ships financed by Europeans. Plus new cafés and discos and fast-food shops.

A couple of years ago, the Cuban government did something uite revolutionary; it wrote a new law giving foreign capitalists permission to fully own their businesses here, acquire real estate, and guaranteed them the right to protect their property and remove profits in hard currency. In that, Communist Cuba today is a lot kinder to foreign investors than is "capitalist" Russia. But Cuba also insisted that any new industry adhere to strict environmental guidelines. Industrial polluters are not welcome here.

All of the above has, predictably enough, made a few Cubans wealthy, as the occasional Mercedes sedan on the street demonstrates. But the government's been singularly careful to ensure that the new foreign investment benefits everybody, not just a few. It has earmarked some of the profits to finance the rebuilding of the country's streets and roads, and to pay for what has always been one of the most impressive and inclusive social-service networks in all of Latin America. What was true in Soviet Russia a decade ago remains a matter of fact in Communist Cuba even today: everybody's entitled to a good education, enough food to eat, adequate and available medical care, and a place to live, no matter what. The social services, including state nurseries for children so that mothers can work, are free. And a bus ride anywhere still costs next to nothing.

The result is that 98 percent of Cuba's eleven million people are literate. One in twenty Cubans has a university degree. Cuba has more doctors and teachers per capita than any of its neighbors (although they earn only a pittance). Cuba's infant-mortality rate is comparable to that in the United States, and life expectancy here, seventy-six years, is considerably longer than that in Cuba's old Soviet patron, Russia.

But there is a dark side to all this, and it's more than periodic power and water shortages, or the state bureaucracy which is so mired in Socialist red tape. It used to be that the manager of a Havana office earned no more than four times what his janitor might be paid. Now that income gap is as much as thirty times as much. A baggage handler at the Havana Libre Hotel (which, after a face-lift, is falling apart again, just like some of the new hotels in Moscow) can, by lugging tourist suitcases, earn ten times what a university professor makes. What does a university professor make in Cuba? About three hundred pesos a month. At the peso-to-dollar rate of twenty-three to one, that's about $13. Petty graft is commonplace and, to hear some of the foreign businessmen talk, is not so petty at the official level. Petty theft has become a problem, too. And the tourist neighborhoods are now alive with hookers, capitalist consequences the Cubans could do without.

As in Communist China, even the army is in for its cut. Through a company called Gaviota, the army runs an airline, several hotels, and some of the car rental agencies. And it's moving in on Cuba's biggest cash crop, sugarcane. Also, there's no sign that Castro is willing to try to break up the big, inefficient state industries that are such a drag on the Cuban economy.

At the same time, Cubans are still putting up with the legacies of Cuban Communism. Committees for the Defense of the Revolution, a sort of Neighborhood Watch from Hell, still make sure every family in the block hews to the party line, at least in public. Cuba's secret-police network, the Vigilantes Revolucionarios, is as extensive as ever, and upward of a thousand political prisoners are believed to be inmates in one or another of Cuba's three hundred prisons. Cuban schoolchildren are still taught to try to grow up and be like Che Guevara and to die to defend the revolution.

Nobody really imagined that Pope John Paul II's visit was going to change much of this. The skeptics said the church should be content merely with the restoration of Christmas. You had to wonder if, at age seventy-seven, suffering from Parkinson's disease and the consequences of various surgeries, not to mention an attempted assassination, the pope could even get through this trip. In fact, he trod the Cuban hustings as if he were running for Castro's job. In five days, he presided at four huge outdoor masses and half a dozen lectures and seminars. He held an impromptu news conference and answered questions in four languages (he speaks seven), and as Cuban worshipers discovered, his Spanish is especially good. As always, the pope seemed to draw energy from the crowds and grew stronger each day, his baritone voice ringing with conviction at every homily.

Castro had rolled out the red carpet for the pope and attendance at his public appearances was encouraged and broadcast live on Cuban TV. Even so, the response was impressive. In Santiago, near San Juan Hill, where Teddy Roosevelt and his Rough Riders charged the Spanish, and not far from that Cold War relic, the U.S. naval base at Guantanamo, three hundred thousand people stood for three hours beneath a searing sun to sing the lilting, rhythmic, Cuban Christian hymns they hadn't been permitted to sing, en masse and in public, for forty years. There were two hundred thousand at Camaguey and half a million in Revolution Square in Havana, under the eyes of that huge portrait of Che, at the papal mass on Sunday.

Pope John Paul II listens as Fidel Castro makes remarks, January 21, 1998, during a welcoming ceremony at Jose Marti Airport in Havana, Cuba. The pope arrived for a historic five-day visit. (AP Photo/Domenico Stinellis)

Why had the pope come here? Simple enough. He's tried to go everywhere he thinks his church needs him. And what he wanted from Castro was a promise for a renaissance for his church here; a rollback of all the restrictions that had hampered it for a generation.

He wanted religious schools, and seminaries for new priests, and an end to discrimination against Christians in public life. And, so his Vatican aides hinted privately, he wanted his church to play a role in making sure that Cuba's transition to whatever it will become after Castro is nonviolent; to ensure a "soft landing" for Cuba.

The pope trod carefully here. He issued his standard denunciations of abortion, and his standard calls for freedom of worship and political freedom. But he was short on specifics, and while he criticized the excesses of state Socialism, he was equally vehement in denouncing "unrestricted capitalism, the international imperialism of money." Take that, Wall Street.

And why did Castro, of all people, invite the pope? That answer is more difficult, and more obscure. Certainly he wanted whatever he could get in the way of a Vatican seal of approval on his stewardship, and doubtless he supposed that letting a few hundred thousand Cubans sing and pray in public was an acceptable risk to Cuban Communism. Certainly Castro wanted the international news coverage the trip would bring. He wanted the world to pay attention to Cuba again, at least for a week or so. (In this he was somewhat disappointed. The pope's arrival in Havana coincided with news that President Clinton had just been accused of infidelity in the Monica Lewinsky affair, and much of the press corps promptly decamped for Washington.) And Castro obviously wanted the pope to denounce the U.S. economic embargo. The pope is opposed to economic warfare in general on the reasonable grounds that the victims are usually ordinary innocent people.

But there seemed to be something else involved in Castro's invitation, something very personal. Castro was educated by Jesuits, and legend has it that he entered Havana in victory in 1959 wearing around his neck a rosary of Cuba's patron saint, the Virgen de Caridad Del Cobre. Yes, it's the same Fidel Castro who officially turned Cuba atheist. But Castro had met the pope at an audience in Rome the year previously, when he first issued his invitation. Witnesses said he left that audience visibly moved, and afterward, Cuban television ran a special hour-long documentary on the meeting, in which Castro remarked dreamily, "When I was young, and reading religious books, I never imagined I would meet the pope."

Throughout the pope's visit, Castro seemed fascinated by John Paul II. He touched him, embraced him, again and again, to the chagrin of the pope's aides, who are sticklers about papal etiquette. Castro was only supposed to meet John Paul formally once, at a state get-together at the Presidential Palace. But Castro brought along his family, and insisted on attending almost all the pope's other visits, including conferences with academics and leaders of Cuba's cultural community. At times, the papal trip seemed like a sort of buddy movie. The two of them just couldn't seem to stay apart, although it wasn't evident whether Castro's fixation with John Paul II was returned.

Fidel Castro is a veteran, accomplished politician and therefore a very good actor, and perhaps his behavior was all for show. But he's also seventy-one years old, and it may be that, like any senior citizen, he's begun to reckon with his own mortality. I don't expect you'll see him in church every Sunday from now on, but it's hard to explain why he's eased up on the Cuban church in recent years, much less his evident star worship of Pope John Paul II. Could it be that Fidel Castro is now wondering whether Heaven is really Communist after all, and is therefore hedging his bets? I don't know, but I'd sure like to ask him.

When he said good-bye to the pope at the airport Sunday night and watched John Paul board the plane, Castro looked like he'd just lost his best friend. Or maybe he was sighing in relief that, at the last, in his departure speech, the pope had finally given him what he'd wanted, a strong public denunciation of the U.S. economic embargo as "unjust and ethically unacceptable."

That's a judgment shared by most of the rest of the world, and increasingly, by a lot of Americans. When the embargo was launched forty years ago, it was regarded as a sort of big American stick which would make life so difficult in Cuba that it would prompt the Cubans themselves to force Castro from power. The Bay of Pigs fiasco put an end to that notion. Since then, the embargo has stayed in force by virtue of its own mean-spiritedness, and as the pope noted, has accomplished what most economic weapons ultimately do; make victims of the poor and powerless, and leave their targets in the leadership unpunished.

Two years ago, the embargo was significantly toughened when President Clinton signed the Helms-Burton Law. That was the brainchild of the venerable Sen. Jesse Helms of North Carolina, the Senate's most hidebound conservative. I firmly believe that deep down somewhere, Jesse Helms is convinced that the collapse of Moscow's Evil Empire a decade ago was just part of a giant Communist conspiracy, and the Soviet Union is really off hiding somewhere, just waiting for America to let down its guard so Moscow can pick up where it left off.

The law includes sanctions against businessmen from countries elsewhere in the world who have dealings with any property expropriated from U.S. citizens. The sanctions include barring executives of foreign countries who violate the law from entering the United

States. As author Robert Scheer observes, the pope himself could be declared persona non grata in America if it could be shown he talked with Castro about returning Cuban church property.

Helms-Burton has enraged the Europeans and other Latin American governments, who regard it, properly, as unwarranted interference in their business affairs and a violation of international law. It's a testament to the tenacity of the world business community and Cuban ingenuity that there has been as much foreign investment in Cuba as there's been to date, but the law has had an intimidating effect. The Cuban economy will probably grow only slightly this year, if at all, mostly because this has been a bad year for Cuban sugarcane. One reason is that Cuba couldn't get the $200 million in foreign funding needed to start the harvest. Helms-Burton again.

But times are changing, and so is public opinion, even in South Florida, that crucible of anti-Castroism. That most recalcitrant of Cuban exile leaders, Jorge Mas Canosa, died late last year, leaving the anti-Castro movement in disarray. And now, four decades after the Cuban revolution, that first generation of Cuban exiles is beginning to die out. Their children, their grandchildren, are American-born-and-bred. To much of that second generation, Castro and Cuba is pre-history. A poll of Cuban-Americans last June by Miami's Florida International University found that more than half of those sampled supported negotiations with the Cuban government. While strong majorities still favor keeping the embargo, about two-thirds of younger Cubans polled, those aged eighteen to twenty-nine, support selling American food and medicines to the island.

In fact, there's a bill now before Congress, supported by an impressive array of American conservatives and business executives, to make it easier to sell Cuba some of the essentials of daily life. A lot of American corporations are tired of ceding the Cuban market to the rest of the world by default.

There's even some talk at the U.S. White House of resuming "mercy" flights to Cuba to deliver humanitarian aid.

But for now at least, the embargo itself is likely to remain hostage to the peculiarities of the American electoral system, as well as to scandal. Florida's electoral votes are vital to the mathematics of any presidential candidate who is putting together a winning combination. So far, no one who is serious about moving into the White House has dared come to Florida and say anything but nasty things about Fidel Castro. As long as the Cuban-American vote is important, that's not likely to change. And it's instructive to note that the three Cuban-American members of Congress all still firmly support the embargo.

Proponents of a thaw in Cuban-American relations had hoped that President Clinton might try to take back the embargo authority he had ceded to Congress as a result of Helms-Burton, and even end the embargo. Forget it. That, along with a lot of other initiatives that might have been on the president's mind, will be stifled for the foreseeable future by the White House's preoccupation with the new accusations regarding Mr. Clinton's sex life. Cuba is only the latest victim of the Lewinsky affair.

Life will go on in Cuba much as before. Fidel Castro is a septuagenarian now. His stooped, lanky frame and splotchy beard are reminiscent of Abraham Lincoln in his last years. But Castro is evidently still in reasonably good health and still capable of stem-winding six-hour speeches. His kid brother, Raul, who is sixty-six, is Fidel's designated successor. Raul is a real Communist hardliner who controls the army and security apparatus. But Raul has none of Fidel's personal charisma and no hold at all on the hearts and minds of the Cuban people. Were Fidel to disappear tomorrow, it's hard to imagine that a Communist Cuba run by the other Castro would last very long.

For now and probably for a while, any questions about Cuba after Fidel are likely to be hypothetical. As Fidel says, "It is the world that is changing. Cuba will not change, even death will not defeat us." Well, we'll see, but not anytime soon, I imagine.

Watching the pope and Fidel Castro say good-bye to each other that night in Havana, probably for the last time, I saw a couple of old men, survivors really, secure in their separate convictions, each determined, by force of will if necessary, to survive with dreams intact into the new millennium. An odd couple, indeed.

chapter 28

Take Two
(March 1998)

" **Y**ou're not going to believe this one!"
Betsy had just come home flushed from another day in the CNN trenches, having broadcast a piece on Russian reaction to President Clinton's latest problem with the opposite sex: Monica Lewinsky et al.

"The Russians think this is great, I mean, they think Clinton is great! And they wish that Boris Yeltsin could be just like him!"

She was right. There on the local TV news was a Russian woman in the street, cheering, "Clinton is a real man. A real man is supposed to behave this way!" "Three thumbs up for Bill," said another.

One of the Moscow newspapers ran a telephone call-in poll from readers, and the calls were nonstop; from husbands and wives, old and young, everybody. And all but a couple of the calls were backing Bill. Said one of the editors, "Absolutely everyone's for Clinton. They say, if the Americans don't need him, we'll take him!"

It must be noted here, as it is too often not noted on the news back in America, that at this writing, President Clinton's recent dalliance is only alleged. With one exception, the admission of a moment of weakness with Gennifer Flowers some years ago, Mr. Clinton has steadfastly denied all accusations regarding his infidelity. And until proven otherwise, we may assume the president has been as faithful to the First Lady as Socks, the First Cat—even though the opinion polls indicate most Americans don't share that assumption. They assume that the president is guilty of fooling around, but they're apparently willing to tolerate that as long as the stock market is up and gasoline prices are down. They wish the news media would get off his case. They certainly don't want Bill Clinton impeached, although they might not object if he were neutered.

Toleration of sexual indiscretion in high office, true or not, is one thing. Downright applause for it, which seems to be the view of ordinary Russians, is quite another. Maybe it's a consequence of Russian society, which is still maddeningly male-oriented. Here a man's mistress is not a symbol of his moral failing, but rather of his wealth, attractiveness, and physical vigor. So a lot of Russians would dearly love to have some teenybopper from Rostov-on-Don show up one day to declare in public that she'd been romping among the bedclothes with President Boris Yeltsin, just to show he's still alive.

In his youth, Mr. Yeltsin was known to have an eye for the ladies. Rumor has it that, as a young commissar in the provinces, he was nearly surprised in flagrante delicto with the wife of a local bureaucrat, and had to jump out her bedroom window and into a freezing river to preserve her reputation.

The president is now sixty-seven, and unhappily for the Kremlin's spin doctors, there's hasn't been a hint of sexual scandal associated with him in a long time. His first love, apart from Mrs. Yeltsin, seems to be strong drink, although he's apparently taking that in moderation these days since his heart surgery in 1996.

For a week this month, Boris Yeltsin was home in bed, sick again, it was said, with a bad cold. He was alleged to be taking antibiotics and feeling lousy. And, like most shut-ins, he was doubtless reading the newspapers and watching TV. And what he read and heard undoubtedly made him feel even worse. The commentators in Moscow and in the West were doing virtual obituaries on him. "A Wan and Only Leader?" headlined the *Economist*. Given the Kremlin's customary lack of candor about the president's health, and his periodic absences from the Kremlin due to illness, much of the media assumed whatever was ailing him was a lot worse than a cold. Wrongly, as it turned out.

In Washington and London and Bonn they were saying off-the-record that Yeltsin's health wasn't as important as it used to be, because for the last year-and-a-half of his part-time presidency, the Russian government had managed to run itself, and even if Yeltsin met an untimely demise, Western governments now had enough personal relationships with other Russian government leaders that continuity could always be preserved, etc., etc. All that off-the-record material made it on the record in the media, of course, and it wasn't lost on Yeltsin himself.

Nor was it lost on the president that his loyal foot soldier of the past five years, Prime Minister Victor Chernomyrdin, was already said to be starting his own campaign for president to succeed Yeltsin in the year 2000.

Chernomyrdin, whose public persona can make his best friend in Washington, Vice President Al Gore, look positively magnetic by comparison, was nevertheless said to be the favorite of the dozen or so Russian business tycoons who will try to make certain their candidate is Russia's next president, much as they did with Yeltsin two years ago.

It appears now, at least to me, that Boris Yeltsin made two big decisions while he was home stewing in his bad press. The first was that he ought not to try to run for a third term, his age and health being what it is. Second, that he ought to spend his energy finding and supporting a successor and securing a decent place in history. Yeltsin is said to have been mulling over whether to run again, which is problematical. The Russian constitution limits a president to two terms, which in Yeltsin's case, would expire in 2000. But the Constitutional Court, which predates the recent constitution, has been asked to rule on whether Yeltsin could seek a third term if he chose. Few doubt that the judges will rule in Yeltsin's favor.

But every time you see Boris Yeltsin on TV lately, he looks and acts like a man in some discomfort. His walk has come to resemble Boris Karloff doing a Frankenstein. So he sits down a lot. I'm guessing that whatever aches and pains he now suffers, he reasons, will be made immeasurably worse by another stint in the Kremlin. He'd be seventy-three, if he survived, by the time he concluded a third term, and he may have decided that by then he really would be a "wan and only president" of Russia. Then, perhaps, but not just now.

I think Boris Yeltsin and the late President Lyndon Johnson would have gotten along famously. They're peas in a pod. Like Johnson, Yeltsin reads his press clippings, and seldom enjoys it. Nothing makes him more furious than the suggestion that he is losing his authority, or that he is not up to running Russia. Like LBJ (who out of spite sometimes cancelled the appointment of some assistant secretary he'd plan to announce or tabled some new legislation he'd planned to offer if advance word of it wound up in the newspapers) Yeltsin loves surprises.

I'm convinced that's the other decision Boris Yeltsin made that week he was bedridden. He decided to spring a surprise.

So it's a Monday morning in the office. I'm in at 9 A.M., earlier than usual because we are eight hours ahead of our masters in New York. It's just me and Tanya, the receptionist. It's quiet; the Duma is in recess for the week and most of the politicians are out visiting their constituencies scattered from Siberia to the Caucasus. The only thing going on is that a couple of young Mormon missionaries, Americans, have been released, relatively unharmed, after they were kidnaped and held for ransom in the provincial city of Saratov. The missionaries aren't talking and neither are the authorities, so I'm wondering how to make a television story out of that.

I happened to check the news wires. And on the Reuters news-service wire there was just one word: "Flash." I hadn't seen a "flash" on the news wires very often in my career. That's usually a label for a very big story: "Flash. Nazi Germany invades Poland." "Flash. An Atomic Bomb is dropped on Hiroshima." Like that. This morning Reuters printed: "Flash." Then it printed, "President Yeltsin Fires Entire Russian Government." (A Reuters colleague later explained to me that the news service is trying to draw more attention to its stories, so now they routinely put "flash" on most any story that's more important than a traffic accident, but no matter.)

There aren't many democracies in the world where the chief of state can simply fire his entire government, but Russia is one of them. Bill Clinton must envy Boris Yeltsin. The Russian president can sack his cabinet, and even rule by decree for a time if he so chooses. This day, Yeltsin had chosen the former, without apparently telling anybody, Washington and the rest of the Western governments included. I'll bet Boris was watching the Moscow TV bulletins that morning and feeling better than he'd felt in months.

Like all the Western newshounds in Moscow, I spent the next few hours trying to tell our audience what had happened, and then tried to sit and figure out what it all meant. I didn't get much help. Most of the Moscow political analysts we talked to didn't even know about what Yeltsin had just done. They wound up asking *us* questions.

Out went his economic tsar, Anatoly Chubais, whose budget cutbacks and privatization reforms had been blamed for so much suffering among ordinary folks. Chubais was now easily the most unpopular man in Russia. Out went Anatoly Kulikov, the Internal Affairs Minister. He was the last of the "war party" around Yeltsin that had started the disastrous war against the rebels in Chechnya. Nobody would much miss him.

And out went Prime Minister Chernomyrdin. That was a real surprise. Yeltsin had fired his cabinet a year previously, but promptly rehired most of the members, including Chernomyrdin, in a new cabinet. Not this time. Yeltsin praised his ex-prime minister for five years of loyal service and said he was reluctantly letting him go, so Chernomyrdin could devote full time to running for president. That was not exactly what you'd call a ringing endorsement. In fact, the assumption was that this would completely derail Chernomyrdin's fledgling campaign, since his only political base was his big office in the Kremlin. In national political polls here, Chernomyrdin barely registers. Apparently in Yeltsin's view, oddly enough, Chernomyrdin was becoming too well known.

The prime minister apparently had no warning of his dismissal either, and observed merely that, "This is not a catastrophe." He was noncommittal about his future political plans. But there was little doubt that Chernomyrdin, having played second fiddle to Yeltsin all those years, would decide to have a fling at being Number One, his poll numbers notwithstanding. With the right support from Russia's media and financial barons, he just might succeed.

Yeltsin went on Russian TV that morning and told the Russian people he'd dismissed his cabinet because Russia wasn't moving fast enough along the route of economic reform, and he wanted some new faces that would bring a more dynamic, energetic approach to solving Russia's problems. "No government is irreplaceable," he said. Evidently.

Yeltsin has a couple of weeks to name a new prime minister, who must be approved by the Duma. Even though it is controlled by Yeltsin's Communist rivals, most likely the Duma will give Yeltsin who he wants. If they turned the candidate down, there would need to be new elections, and the Communists, who've lost a lot of their popularity in recent months, probably don't want to risk losing all the perks of office just now.

The president first named himself as interim prime minister, until his aides gently informed him that that was unconstitutional. So Yeltsin promptly named a thirty-five-year-old rookie as interim prime minister instead. He's Sergei Kiriyenko, an obscure fuel and energy minister, who was a bank executive in Nizhny Novgorod just four years ago. Kiriyenko, who is short, bespectacled, and prematurely bald, is a protégé of another of Yeltsin's economic reformers, Boris Nemtsov.

What's Kiriyenko's future? Well, six years ago, Yeltsin appointed another obscurity to the job—a portly young free-market economist named Yegor Gaidar. Prime Minister Gaidar lasted less than six months.

If history is any guide, Yeltsin will include a lot of the old names in his cabinet in the new one, including his defense minister, Igor Sergeyev, and Foreign Minister Yevgeny Primakov who is, among other things, the Arab world's best friend in Moscow.

What's Boris Yeltsin up to? There are two schools of thought. One is that Yeltsin has demonstrated once again what a master politician he is. All during his presidency, Yeltsin has set the goals for improving the lives of the Russian people, and simply told his underlings to handle it. When they prove to be underachievers (and who wouldn't be, considering the damnably difficult problems Russia faces), he fires them and hires some others. Wages and pensions unpaid? Don't blame Boris. Unemployment rising, agriculture in ruins? Not to worry, Boris will sack the laggards. Sergei Kiriyenko, pay attention.

I recall that Ronald Reagan used to do this with uncanny success. Don't blame Number One for anything that goes wrong. He means well, after all. Except that Reagan seldom fired anybody. He couldn't bear it. He just smiled and shrugged. Boris Yeltsin is President Sack. In the months before this latest housecleaning, he'd fired half a dozen members of his cabinet for nonperformance. You have to wonder why anybody would want to be in the Russian cabinet.

But as with Reagan, few people ever seem to ask, "Isn't the trouble at the top?" On the contrary, with his Monday Morning Massacre, Yeltsin has shown once again that he's still pulling all the strings in the Kremlin.

A contrary explanation for Yeltsin's action is that he hasn't the foggiest notion of how to rescue Russia from the doldrums, and it's all a song and dance, and a tiresome one at that. As one Russian commentator here put it to us, "If you don't know what to do, you do what you know. Yeltsin knows to fire everybody." In short, the other school of thought is that Boris Yeltsin is just this side of nuts.

Yeltsin himself has contributed to that notion. He's been acting strangely the past few months. He momentarily scared the wits out of Washington during the latest confrontation with Iraq by predicting it could lead to a "world war."

He seems easily confused. When he was visiting Sweden not long ago, he seemed to think he was in Finland. And he noted in passing that Germany and Japan were fellow members of the nuclear weapons club. Not everybody knows that Germany and Japan don't have nuclear weapons, but Yeltsin should.

Of course he wouldn't be the first president to forget where he is, or who's who in his cabinet. That's been known to happen to American presidents, too. And so far, happily, his gaffes have been limited to little things.

A Russian colleague of mine, Alexei Pushkov, a political analyst for one of the Moscow newspapers, thinks Yeltsin's government shuffle was a masterstroke. But Yeltsin's public blunders haven't escaped him, although Pushkov thinks they are silly, not serious—yet.

"It's interesting," he says, "that those mental lapses come at the moments when things are more or less quiet, as if he were thinking of something else. When there is a big fight, it is as if Yeltsin is mobilizing himself, and you don't see any lapses. He is completely . . . adequate."

Poor Boris. Damned by faint praise again. But why worry about Boris Yeltsin's mental health anyway? Well, maybe it's okay for the president of Russia to get mixed up about the little things. But he's in command of the second-largest nuclear arsenal in the world. What if he starts getting mixed up about the big things?

Right now, though, all the Moscow wise men are worrying about who and

President Boris Yeltsin smiles as his daughter Tatyana Dyachenko talks to him after a meeting with his election campaign staff in a residence outside Moscow in this June 1996 photo. Yeltsin, June 30, 1997, named Dyachenko, his younger daughter, as his official image adviser, boosting the power she gained while heading her father's successful re-election campaign. (AP Photo)

what next? Who's the new prime minister going to be? Is Boris Nemtsov in or out? Is Kiriyenko a player? Did Tatyana, Yeltsin's daughter and closest political aide, put her dad up to this? Is Boris Berezovsky, the zillionaire manufacturing and media magnate who wants to be kingmaker, involved? Things may be clearer by next week, when Yeltsin will name his new roster of sacrificial lambs. But I wouldn't bet much on it.

Winston Churchill had it right about Russia, sixty years ago, and now. "It is a riddle wrapped in a mystery inside an enigma."

chapter 29

Taxing Times
(April 1998)

Every night lately, on the state TV channel in Moscow, you see the same commercial over and over. A poor fellow sitting on the edge of his bed, flipping the night lamp on and off, and a beautiful woman lying next to him, expectantly. He sighs and shrugs, and she sighs and rolls over and goes to sleep.

No, it's not an ad for some new sex tonic or a marriage therapist. The announcer's voice says, "Lost your desire? Pay your taxes and you'll have peace of mind." It's a public service announcement from the Russian government, urging people to file their income taxes and pay up before the deadline, April 1.

There are variations of this. A man sitting at his desk, looking guilty, and jumping when the phone rings. "Lost your nerve?" says the announcer. "Pay your taxes and you'll have peace of mind." Another fellow can't eat the nice dinner the waiter has set before him at a fancy restaurant. The message, "Lost your appetite? Pay your taxes, etc."

The federal tax people are spending more than a million dollars on this TV ad blitz and the distribution of leaflets for those Russians who don't watch TV, or can't afford one, reminding citizens that today's Russian is "Master of his property, his labor, and his income," and has a duty to pay taxes for "What everyone needs: health care, education, public sanitation, police, and the environment."

Today's Russian, if he's average, must find all this very amusing. He hardly feels master of anything. He's lucky if he's got a little shack out in the woods that passes for a *dacha* when his tiny apartment gets too claustrophobic. He's lucky if he's got a job. And even luckier if he gets paid regularly. Tens of millions of Russians are still waiting to collect months of back pay that the government owes them. And he'll hardly have to worry about the income tax. He doesn't make nearly enough to owe much of anything.

The government's targets are the *Novy Russky*: the "New Russians," the middle and upper classes, many of whom have made out like bandits as the Russian economy has switched from Communism to entrepreneurial capitalism.

No question, Russia's taxpayers need some educating. Before 1992, Russians never had to file an income tax form. Under the old Soviet system, the government simply figured out how much it needed to spend, took that out of everybody's wages, and gave the workers whatever was left over. You didn't have to do your taxes. The government did it for you, and did it to you, so to speak.

So when Russia went capitalist, the government here set up an income tax system. And they're proud to say here that they sought and received a lot of good advice on how to do that from your friend and mine, the Internal Revenue Service in Washington, D.C.

It may be the Russians overdid it, though. The current Russian tax code contains one hundred seventy separate taxes and four thousand laws and regulations. It is bigger than the Bible. It could be bigger than the *Encyclopedia Britannica*. There are taxes on business, a 20 percent value-added tax on things you buy, and a 35 percent top bracket for individuals with incomes of $8,000 a year or more. Not too many individuals here have to worry about that top bracket.

Taxes are high, though, for those who do. And there are no deductions to speak of; not for home mortgage interest, or charitable contributions, or medical costs, or local taxes, or business expenses. At least it sounds like you could do your taxes on one-half of a Form 1040. Nope. Not in Russia. The simplest tax form runs to page after page after page.

On the other hand, most Russians simply avoid paying their income taxes. Tax avoidance is a very old and honorable habit among Russians, going back to the days when peasants bravely refused to pay their Mongol conquerors tribute.

Companies pay their profits into dummy corporations. They will give their employees a wage that's a pittance, but throw in a nice apartment and a car, or a big personal loan, or a multimillion-dollar life insurance policy, "for free." The government doesn't have enough auditors to keep up with all of this, not to mention that under the current tax code, a lot of this chicanery is perfectly legal.

And the politicians haven't been setting the best personal examples. Last year, President Boris Yeltsin claimed he made only $5,500. His ex-prime minister and reputedly one of Russia's wealthiest men, Victor Chernomyrdin, claimed a personal income of just $8,000. This year, they apparently thought they'd best keep up appearances. Chernomyrdin listed an income of $233,000, and Yeltsin said he made $320,000, mostly from royalties from his book. (Yes, Boris Yeltsin wrote a book. Don't they all?)

The consequence of all the red tape, and this culture of noncompliance, is that, by some estimates, $100 billion a year in Russian taxes goes uncollected, and the government is just this side of broke. In most countries in the West, the personal income tax accounts for 80 percent of government revenue. In Russia, it's just 6 percent. The result is that the tax burden falls most heavily on businesses and industries, many of which simply can't make a profit as a result, and therefore, can't pay their taxes. But President Yeltsin is determined to change that. He announced proudly the other day that so far this year, five million Russians had paid their personal income taxes. That's in a nation of one hundred fifty million.

No wonder the Kremlin's trying to get individuals to pay up, first asking nicely, and then scaring the wits out of them with the tax police. There are thirty-eight thousand of them roaming the country looking for tax evaders, and the TV news is full of scenes of the black-leather-jacketed tax police hit squads bashing down apartment doors and hustling the alleged tax miscreants inside to pay up or else. A couple of weeks ago, in response to some bad publicity, the tax police announced that henceforth they'd make an attempt to get search warrants before invading any more Russian homes. And you think the Internal Revenue Service is tough!

In a tacit acknowledgment of the failure of the present tax system, the Russian parliament is now considering a brand-new tax law. Russia's under pressure from the International Monetary Fund and other Western lenders, who've threatened to stop giving Russia any more loans until the government comes up with a tax system that is equitable, enforceable, and comprehensible. Also, please, it would be nice if it didn't penalize Western investors. Good luck.

A new tax code will mean, of course, that the thoroughly confused Russians who now do their taxes will have to face a whole new system next April. But the TV executives here, at least, are betting that the Russian public isn't totally turned off to taxes. Starting later this year, Russian TV is going to be showing a brand-new soap opera about the tax police; a sixteen-part series to dramatize the "work, loves, hopes, and fears" of the tax police on and off the job. Sort of

Russian tax police special forces officers arrest suspects during an operation in the Moscow suburbs, January 28, 1998. Police arrested a group of dealers who were suspected of illegally selling automobiles for hard currency. Low tax collections have been a perennial problem for the government, with the taxman's take falling steadily since 1992. Short of cash, the government has been unable to meet spending targets, running up massive debts. (AP Photo/ Alexander Salukov)

like, *ER*, I suppose, except these guys seem to put people in the emergency rooms instead of caring for them there.

Tax cops and tax codes aside, the truth is there are still tens of millions of Russian tax deadbeats who are going to get away with it, at least for a while. Benjamin Franklin observed that "Nothing is certain but death and taxes." Benjamin Franklin never came to Russia. Here, he'd be only half right.

chapter 30

Very Senior Citizens

(April 1998)

As the twentieth century dwindles into yesterday, it's becoming harder and harder for the children of
those who grew up in the Communist world to imagine what life was
like in those three generations. Most of the kids, truth to tell, don't
much care.

And, of course, it's even more difficult to find people who can
remember what life was like before Lenin. But there are a few. More
than you'd expect, actually.

A case in point is Mirzahan Movlamov. He celebrated his 122nd
birthday this month. Mr. Movlamov was already forty-one years old
when the Bolsheviks took over Russia. When he was born, in 1876,
General Custer hadn't yet made his last stand at the Little Bighorn.
The president of the United States was Ulysses S. Grant.

All right, I know what you're thinking. Just because Mr.
Movlamov and his family *say* he's 122, how do we know? Well, we
don't really. He has no birth certificate. Where he lives, they weren't
much at record keeping in 1876. But, like all of his neighbors of a
certain age, he has an old Soviet passport which has his year of birth
written right in the front.

"Actually, I'm probably a few years older than 122," he says.
"When the Communists came here in 1920, they gave us all identity
documents and just guessed our ages from the way we looked. I was
going on fifty by then, but I looked like I was in my twenties, or at
least the girls thought so," he chuckles.

The Bolsheviks didn't get around to visiting Mr. Movlamov and his neighbors until 1920 because where he lives is a little hard to get to. He's one of the Talish people who've lived for centuries in an isolated string of villages four thousand feet up the Southern Caucasus Mountains in what is now Azerbaijan. Climb the steep, snowcapped peaks to the south and you'll be in Iran. Follow the streambeds northeast and you'll be on the shores of the Caspian Sea.

It's a land of deep valleys slashed by rivers running bank-to-bank brown with the spring snowmelt, and steep green hills dotted with bright red poppies and the yellow blossoms of *Lutiki*, a kind of buttercup. Small herds of sheep and goats meander through the uplands, tended by little boys with their switches and sheepdogs. The sky is as blue as the Caspian, and the air is clean and pure and swollen with the perfumes of the mountain flowers. The mornings start cold and clear and by midday the puffy white clouds are drifting through the hills below, drenching them in mist one minute and bright sunlight the next. The clouds retreat at day's end to make way for another glorious sunset. That's spring and summer. Winter's different here. Remarked one villager, "We Kalish say that five months of the year this is Heaven. The rest of the time it's the other place."

It puts you in mind of the high country in Nepal; what few roads there are amount to not much more than muddy tracks. People get around by walking the goat paths from here to there.

Television news correspondents, like this one, get around by taking an ancient drab-green military van provided by the local provincial governor, and dodging the potholes and wallows in the only road for hours on end. It's slow going. It'd be faster to walk, but walking around here is mostly straight up. Still, the trip is worth it.

Perched on almost every hilltop is a little Kalish village. They follow the same formula: a couple of dozen substantial two-story mud-and-timber homes, clean and well kept, a school, a soccer field, a tiny village square, and a mosque. Somewhere near the center is a memorial wall with the names and photos, etched in marble, of the young men (and they're always young men) who've died in battles against neighboring Armenia. That war is supposed to be over, but the dates on a lot of the photos are 1998, good evidence that it's not. At the edge of each village is a stone marker which features a picture of the Azeri president, Heydar Aliyev, along with a salient quotation from him, like, "I give the rest of my lifetime to serve my people."

President Aliyev is seventy-four. If he were a Kalish, he might be able to go on serving his people for decades to come. For among the sixty-seven thousand Kalish in this region, there are almost one hundred people who have already lived more than a century, a truly remarkable statistic.

But even though there's rumored to be a 127-year-old fellow who lives in the mountains a couple of hundred miles from here and who still goes bear hunting, Mr. Movlamov has the bragging rights. He is evident. He lives in a two-room mud house in the district's capital, Lerik, with his wife and his memories and surrounded by most of his seven sons and sixty or so grandchildren and their children. He forgets just how many.

His wife, his third, is sixty-three, a teenager by standards here. He married her when he was ninety and she bore him five children, including two sets of twins. She's confined to a bed in the corner and looks considerably older than her years. Perhaps it was rearing all those kids.

As for Mr. Movlamov, he doesn't look too well either. He lies on a cloth mattress on the floor (he doesn't like spring beds, he says), a sheepskin cap on his head, covered with blankets and attended by his eighty-four-year-old grandson and a couple of daughters-in-law. He's functionally blind and his eyes water a bit, but his mind and memory are still sharp.

His grandson shouts a Kalish translation of my questions into his right ear, for he's losing his hearing, too. How's he feeling? "I'm 122 years old," replies Mr. Movlamov. "How do you think I feel?"

Like many of the very old, he remembers his early years a lot better than the most recent ones. He married his first wife when she was twelve, in 1905. He rode up to her village one day and simply kidnaped her. That was the custom back then. Mr. Movlamov was a soldier in tsar's cavalry, and had a handsome horse. He remembers fighting in a big cavalry battle when the tsar was on hand, a battle his cavalry won, by the way.

After the First World War he returned to farming in his village, and then the Communists came and turned all the little farms into *Kolkhoza*, or communes. The fields around here are no more than a few yards square, so you can imagine the confusion and inefficiencies involved in communizing Talish agriculture. Only now, since Azerbaijan's independent again, is the government reprivatizing this countryside. Mr. Movlamov was a commune worker for many years and then took part in the Great Patriotic War, as they refer to it around here, that kept the Nazis out of the Caucasus and away from the oil fields of the Caspian.

Mr. Movlamov didn't seem to mind the Communists very much. "They came here one day, combined all our farms, told us all we were Soviet citizens, and after that left us pretty much alone."

He's most proud of fighting off the Germans. Twice in his life, as it turned out. That, and living long enough to see Azerbaijan free again.

How to account for Mr. Movlamov and his fellow Talish centenarians? He says it's because he worked hard and had a happy life. His older sister, he says, lived to 123.

Down the coast in Baku, the capital, Dr. Chengiz Kasumov, a gerontologist with the Baku Institute of Physiology, thinks Mr. Movlamov has got something special in his genes. Dr. Kasumov is convinced that the Talish penchant for longevity has mostly to do with heredity. In fact, most of the really elderly among the Talish tend to be somehow related. Dr. Kasumov has been studying the Talish, and recalls that for some generations a community of Russian settlers lived right next to the Talish. But the Russians, he said, still lived only into their sixties and seventies.

Dr. Kasumov is a trifle embarrassed about his research facilities. His laboratory consists of a small room inside an auto-repair garage in a dirty alley behind the institute. He's underfunded, to say the least, and the only lab experiments he can afford to do are on white rats. Currently, he's been injecting them with petrochemicals and has discovered that too much of that will hasten the aging process. But apparently that can be reversed with massive doses of malt. The conclusion seems to be that if you live someplace where there's a lot of smog, you should be drinking a lot of beer.

And Dr. Kasumov doesn't discount the effects of diet and the herbal medicines the Talish take to cure their aches and pains, for none of the centenarians we talked to had ever seen a medical doctor.

In the Talish village of Monededjar, on the other hand, Simuzar the Widow has been treating real people, three generations of Monededjar villagers. Simuzar is a *babushka*, which, in Talishtalk, means a kind of medicine woman, minus the magic and spells and incantations associated with that term. Each village has its own *babushka*, a woman who functions as doctor, nurse, and midwife, dispensing her own home remedies handed down from family to family.

Simuzar has apparently managed to do a pretty good job of treating herself. She's 110. She's about four inches shy of five feet tall, and when she smiles, which is often, the wrinkles of her dark face become a collection of happy dimples. It belies her personal history. Her husband died fighting in the Great Patriotic War in 1941, soon after the Germans invaded, and left her with two young sons and two young daughters. They're all grown now with grandchildren of their own.

To meet Simuzar the Widow for the first time is enough to make

Simuzar the Widow dancing
with her grandson.
(© Richard Threlkeld)

any man pushing retirement, like this one, feel like a kid again. A big smile, a hug, a kiss on the hand and on both cheeks, and the conviction that if she knew the word, she'd refer to you as "Sonny."

"There's no secret to long life," she says. "It's hard work. I love hard work."

But Simuzar plays hard, too. It didn't take much coaching from the rest of the village for her to start dancing to the beat of the little drummer boy, who's the percussion section for the Mondedjar dance troup. Her dance partner in this mountain jig was her grandson. He's sixty-five.

Later, she took us around the garden she tends. She picked us a collection of stinging nettles, and light-green burdock. "Now you take these, and brew them into a tea, and it's good for backache, headache, and liver troubles." She also introduced us to some mint that, Dr. Kasumov claims, removes cholesterol from the blood.

We wanted to stay and talk more with Simuzar the Widow, but she politely begged off. It was time to get back to work. We left her in the company of her garden spade, earnestly weeding her orchard.

At Chairut, the next village, we had a lunch with Mrs. Kizil Dzahneeyev and her family. That was right after the prayer service at the mosque. The village goes there every day at midday for prayers and a sort of village meeting where problems are threshed out, arguments settled, and gossip traded. The men pray separately from the women and children, but the Shia Muslim service here is a lot more inclusive than over the mountains in Iran.

Lunch at the Dzahneeyev household was fresh cheese and butter and *churek* (warm bread) and a few mouthfuls of parsley, cilantro, and watercress, washed down with flower-blossom tea and thick, dark wild honey with bits of beeswax still inside. This was a period of religious mourning in the Shia faith, or they'd have been drinking some sweet red wine, too. The Talish eat sparely and simply, and the food is as fresh as today. Certainly, diet must have something to do with the Talish longevity. Mrs. Dzahneeyev had the best appetite of anybody at the table. She's 108.

You can judge for yourself if there's anything about the Talish lifestyle you think worth copying, in case you're hoping to live well into the next millennium. But remember a few other factors that we noticed while visiting these generous and hospitable people: Beautiful scenery. A strong faith in God and each other. An abiding respect for the elderly. And the love of friends and family. Things that seem to make a very long life worth living.

I couldn't resist asking Mr. Movlamov what wisdom he may have gained in living all those years, since you don't come across a 122-year-old every day. Was there, we asked, a simple phrase into which he could put his life's experience? They had to translate his reply from Talish to Azeri to English, but I think what he said was, "Buy low, sell high."

chapter 31

Not the News

(May 1998)

Watching commercial television in Russia is, to say the least, an educational experience. One night you can tune to a TV newsmagazine and watch an investigative report on unscrupulous Moscow building contractors who are importing foreign laborers on the cheap, confiscating their passports, and turning them into virtual slave labor. It is every bit as well shot, well reported, well scripted, and well edited as anything you might see on *60 Minutes*. Or you can flip the channel and watch another series devoted entirely to crime: auto accidents, dead bodies, cops wrestling bad guys to the ground, all real-life and all blood and guts all the time.

That's a world of difference from the TV I used to watch when I first started coming to the then-Soviet Union in the early 1980s, before Gorbachev and glasnost, etc.

Lenin and the Bolsheviks understood the power of broadcasting early on, even though radio was still in its infancy when they came to power. Like the Nazis in Germany, they lavished what money there was to hook up the entire country. First it was radio and by the 1950s, television. There were only a couple of channels, run by the government of course, and slavishly promoting the party line. There was no advertising. Well, actually, the whole broadcasting enterprise was just one long advertisement for the Soviet Union and Communism. And it extended overseas. No matter in what forlorn and isolated little corner of the world I happened to find myself in those years, I knew I could

186

Ostankino TV tower. (© 1995 Jonathan Sanders)

always turn on my shortwave radio and find the voice of Radio Moscow booming back at me. It was always the strongest signal.

On television, Soviet viewers had a choice of watching the strictly censored and dull news programs like *Vremya*, highbrow arts and culture broadcasts featuring *Swan Lake,* and several hours of the Moscow Symphony playing Tchaikovsky, or reruns of Sergei Eisenstein's classic motion picture *Alexander Nevsky.*

The closest thing to a dramatic program or sitcom you could find were the old World War II Soviet movies or the socialist realism potboilers from the 1930s and 1940s; collective farm boy meets tractor, boy and tractor meet collective farm girl, and all three of them live happily ever after.

No more. Now anything goes, at least in the realm of what passes for TV entertainment here. You can flip to a TV call-in talk show, where the topic of the day is, "Are the Protocols of Zion an Authentic Jewish Historical Document?" If you want to stay up past midnight, you can tune in *About That,* where Yelena Khanga, an African-American-Russian TV host sprouting a platinum-blond wig, chats frankly and explicitly about sex with a panel of "sex experts" and a studio audience. Topics include the joy of sex with older men, and tips on how to carry on with your mistress without your wife finding out.

They're even trying to bring back those old Soviet tractor movies, which, believe it or not, still have a loyal following among Russians old enough to become nostalgic about them. Mosfilm, founded by Lenin himself and for generations one of the world's biggest movie studios, has been dickering with the Russian networks to sell off its library of two thousand old movies. Mosfilm is finally being privatized, and its executives figure those old movies are worth several hundred million dollars, which will help Mosfilm get back into the movie business in a big way, and earn the sobriquet it once had among Russians, "Hollywood on the Moscow River."

As in much of the rest of the world, Russian TV has been importing reruns of Western sitcoms, most of them American, but also some Spanish and Mexican soap operas, along with the inevitable crime shows, everything dubbed into Russian. But because it costs a fortune to buy the rights to what's available in foreign syndication, now there are a couple of Russian sitcoms that have just debuted, borrowing heavily from the American TV formulas. *Funny Business, Family Business* is a takeoff on *All in the Family*, and *Café Strawberry*, which will remind you a little of *Cheers*.

The scriptwriters are still feeling their way with the audience. In Russia during the past century, not an awful lot has happened that is fodder for what you'd call comedy. On the other hand, the Russians have a special fondness for the sardonic and the absurd. There is a mother lode of humor in this country, but you need to see the subtleties, and mine it with a scalpel rather than a pickax.

And there's no better example of that than *Kukly*, a weekly program of political satire, Russian-style. *Kukly* means "puppets" in Russian, and that's what the characters are; handpuppets every bit as fetching as the ones the late Jim Henson used to produce. In fact, the whole show is a little like "The Muppets Go to the Kremlin." One episode featured the entire government leadership, from President Boris Yeltsin on down, depicted as homeless bums, with Yeltsin begging for money among startled passengers on a subway train. The then-prime minister, Victor Chernomyrdin, who remains associated with Russia's huge gas monopoly, Gazprom, and is reputedly one of Russia's richest men, was shown trying to earn a living selling spare parts for gas stoves. A more recent episode had President Clinton whining to Yeltsin about the Monica Lewinsky affair and that he, Clinton, was being undone by the provisions of America's constitution.

Yeltsin's puppet: "What's the problem? You send in the tanks and then change the constitution."

Clinton's puppet: "That's impossible."

Yeltsin's puppet: "Look, if it doesn't work and you are still in trouble, come over to Russia. I'm looking for a successor, you know!"

A couple of decades ago, that kind of stuff would have prompted the Kremlin to pack the puppets and the producers off to Siberia. Two years ago, criminal charges were actually brought against the producers of *Kukly* for making fun of Yeltsin and his Kremlin cohorts. The charges were eventually dropped. But it's evidence of how emboldened this country's mass media have become. These days, parody is not only permitted, it is popular. And in fact that new constitution Boris Yeltsin drew up a few years ago, after he sent the tanks into Moscow's streets to quell a Communist coup, explicitly provides for freedom of the press and freedom of expression.

Of course the old Soviet constitution had those same guarantees. And now, as then, there's quite a gap between freedom of the press on paper, and the reality.

And Yeltsin himself is not above reminding TV journalists that there is a real world. This month he called in the directors of the three biggest national TV networks to complain about their coverage of the biggest Russian story of this spring, the sit-in of striking coal miners on the tracks of the Trans-Siberian railroad. The coverage was, he felt, excessive and unnecessarily negative.

"We have the right to, I don't want to use the word 'demand,' we have the right to ask you to carry out state policy on television," said the president.

It wasn't clear whether Yeltsin meant that "state policy" required the reporting on TV of only the good news, of which there has been precious little of late. And it wasn't clear who he meant by "we."

But the TV bosses probably had a pretty good idea. The Russian government is now in the process of forming a new state agency that is supposed to "coordinate" the operations of state-owned broadcast outlets around the country, as well as the transmission of private channels. It's proposed name, the All State Television and Radio Company, has a familiar ring to those Russians who remember the old Soviet broadcasting bureaucracy, Gostelradio.

Nobody in the Kremlin is likely to try to resurrect Gostelradio, much as the Kremlin might prefer it. Russian broadcast journalism has come a long way in its seven years of relative freedom. It was the Russian TV news' unfettered combat reporting of the hideous military debacle in Chechnya that more than anything prompted the Russian government to put an end to that tragedy. Russian viewers and listeners are beginning to pay attention to their news again, in a way they never did in the Soviet period, in the expectation that these days, at least some of what they hear and see may actually be true. So no Russian bureaucrat with any sense is going to try to take away Russians' TV news now. But, as President Yeltsin pointed out to the network TV bosses, there is a real world in Russia's broadcast news, with real limits. And those limits are most often apparent outside of Moscow.

Betsy and I occasionally spend time talking to young reporters and anchors from some of the TV stations around Russia. It's fun because they are young and earnest and full of journalistic zeal. But it's also depressing because while you can tell them how to shoot tape and write and edit, you have to be very careful when you start talking to them about what sort of stories they should report, especially the investigative kind. You know it and they know it. Many of their stations are owned by big businessmen with ties to organized crime. You don't get to be a big businessman in Russia without some friends in one mafia or another. So the ambitious young street reporter from Volgograd or Minsk better be careful about trying to become another Mike Wallace, particularly if his story treads on some friends or associates of the station's management. Imagine if, say, WGN-TV in Chicago was owned not by the *Chicago Tribune*, but by Al Capone. So, observing the journalists' maxim of "Comfort the afflicted and afflict the comfortable" can get you into a lot of trouble in Russia. And trouble here isn't the risk of becoming unemployed; it's the risk of being fitted out for a cement overcoat.

And it's not just the TV out in the hinterlands that has boundaries beyond which the prudent TV newsman will fear to tread. The national channels are mostly owned by big businessmen, too, much bigger businessmen. The government still has its hand in TV, of course. It owns all of the government channel, RTR. It owns 51 percent of one of the big commercial channels, ORT. Part of ORT is owned by Boris Berezovsky, a multibillionaire who makes no secret of his political ambitions. Berezovsky also owns part of another "independent" channel, TV 6, another part of which is owned by the big Russian oil company Lukoil. The biggest and best of the commercial networks, NTV, is partly owned by Gazprom (remember Mr. Chernomyrdin?) and run by another media magnate, Rem Vyakhirev, a Chernomyrdin man. Another part owner is Vladimir Gusinski, the head of MOST group, a media conglomerate. Mr. Gusinski, at this writing, hasn't decided whether to cast his lot with Mr. Chernomyrdin or Moscow's mayor, Yuri Luzhkov.

And Luzhkov himself is taking no chances. He's founded a brand new TV channel of his own, Center TV in Moscow. Luzhkov is considered a prime candidate to eventually succeed President Yeltsin. Next year, Mayor Luzhkov hopes to put Center TV on the air in

Russia nationwide. Even if you've by now found yourself hopelessly lost in this maze of multiple ownerships, you get the point; Russian TV is brought to you by The Tycoons. President Yeltsin's proposed All State Television and Radio Company may be less of an effort to reimpose state controls on broadcasting than to take the authority away from the media oligarchs who now effectively have it.

Yes, you say, but how is that any different from America? The difference, in fact, is simply one of degree. In both countries, all the big commercial networks are owned by big corporations. And they are mostly interested in making money. So in both countries, the broadcasters give lots of money to the politicians so the government won't interfere with business.

The difference is, if you're a U.S. broadcaster and you don't have a friend in Washington, maybe you won't get to buy that TV station you wanted. If you're a Russian media mogul and you don't have a friend in the Kremlin, maybe they'll take your network away and put you in prison for tax evasion, guilty or not.

So Russian broadcasters shamelessly show praise on their favorite politicians and throw mud on their opponents with an abandon that would cause even a William Randolph Hearst to blush. During the last presidential election, the media barons, having committed themselves to Boris Yeltsin, turned their newscasts into one big Yeltsin commercial. His opponent, Gennady Zyuganov, when he was mentioned at all, was portrayed as something close to the Antichrist. So much for editorial objectivity.

And that's not just one man's opinion. It's also the observation of someone who really ought to know: Vladimir Posner. You probably remember him. In the 1980s, when Mikhail Gorbachev was running the Soviet Union and Glasnost was breaking out all over, Vladimir Posner was the Kremlin's Designated Explainer To America. You'd see him from time to time talking with Ted Koppel on *Nightline*, giving Moscow's view of things after, say, President Reagan had just called the Soviet Union an "evil empire." Posner spoke in perfect colloquial American English, with a New York City accent. And no wonder. He is a New Yorker, or was.

Posner's father was born in St. Petersburg, or Petrograd as it was then known. He moved to Paris soon after the Russian Revolution and met and married a Parisian woman. Posner was born in Paris. His father fought for the French against the Nazi invasion, and the family escaped to America with the fall of France, and moved to New York City, where Posner grew up and graduated from Stuyvesant High School.

Then came the Cold War and the McCarthy hysteria of the 1950s.

Posner's father, still a Soviet citizen, worked in the U.S. movie industry, which, some U.S. congressmen were convinced, had been dishing out Communist propaganda. Posner's father could have become a U.S. citizen and remained in America. But he regarded himself as a Russian patriot and still had some fond, sentimental memories of the early years of the Bolshevik revolution.

So he accepted an offer from the Kremlin to help administer what became Communist East Germany. Posner himself thinks that the posting, far away from Moscow, probably saved the family's life. Those were the last paranoid years of Stalinism, and Posner's father's time in capitalist America, plus his Jewish origins, might well have doomed them. As it was, they arrived in Moscow a couple of months before Stalin died, when, of course, things changed.

For most of the next four decades, Vladimir Posner was a good Communist. He couldn't get into Moscow University because he was a Jew. But the Soviet Army's espionage school was anxious to have him, an erstwhile American who could handle English like a native speaker. He worked in the Young Communist youth brigades, building hydroelectric complexes and helping plant the "virgin lands," Premier Krushchev's scheme to try to turn much of Soviet Central Asia into one gigantic Kansas wheatfield (it didn't work).

Eventually, the Gorbachevites let him deliver an occasional Moscow reaction on American TV to whatever happened to be going on between the United States and the Soviet Union. "The Kremlin people never interfered with me," he says. "Of course, I knew my limits, but they figured that if it came out all right, they could take the credit, and if I screwed up, they could just blame me."

When the Soviet Union disintegrated, Posner was able to travel freely for the first time in forty years. He moved back to New York in 1991 and for a time did a talk show with Phil Donahue on one of the American networks.

"One day in 1997, the producers told us that from then on, we'd have to clear our topics and scripts with management before every show," says Posner. "They never did that to me even back in Moscow. So Phil and I quit."

And last year, Vladimir Posner returned to Russia for the second time. Now trim and tanned and sixty-four, he has apparently returned for good. He does a couple of TV talk shows now on Russian TV: *The Man in the Mask*, a kind of tabloid interview program, and *We*, an interview show devoted to more serious topics in the worlds of politics and foreign affairs. Says Posner, "I felt that I could probably do more here, and felt that what I could do here was more important than anything I could possibly do in America."

Offhand, I don't know of anybody who has more of a personal acquaintance with both the America that was and is, and the Russia that was and is, than Vladimir Posner.

And he is worried about Russian television. Mostly he is worried about the news. "Of course they manage the news as the networks here," he says. "There are walls, editorial walls, and if you don't want to bang your head against them, you just don't. I've never been specifically told to say this or that, but you just know. I think that's true for journalists no matter where they work, it's just that the walls are a little more confining here."

And more obvious. "It's very clear that today your number-one commentator will say this or that about this political figure, and tomorrow he may say the exact opposite, because he's been told to do that without ever changing his expression."

Posner remembers when one of his anchor acquaintances, a woman, was getting ready to read an item about Boris Berezovsky on her nightly news program on the government channel. It described Berezovsky as a well-known mathematician, which he in fact is, in addition to being rich as Croesus. "And overnight," Posner says, "the government's opinion of Berezovsky changed, positive to negative. They told the anchorwoman to remove that passage. She refused and read it anyway. She did that three times and they fired her. But eventually she got a good anchor job at another network. I suppose the good thing is that at least in the new Russia she can get another job. In the old Soviet Union, she'd have lost her job, her apartment, everything."

The tycoons who own Russian TV and manage the TV news don't need Lenin to tell them how powerful a medium broadcasting can be. They learned that in the 1996 presidential elections here. When it looked as if the Communist leader, Gennady Zhuganov, might defeat Boris Yeltsin, the TV networks simply stopped reporting on Zhuganov and turned themselves into Yeltsin propaganda machines in the weeks leading up to the election. Though Yeltsin, as it developed, was suffering the effects of a massive heart attack and was out of public view, you'd never have known it watching Russian TV news coverage. Yeltsin, of course, won handily. What made his reelection so vital to the tycoons?

Says Posner, "The robber barons, as we call them, are people who have made huge sums of money, thanks to what one calls here, a market economy. The Communists, the ones on the Left, the Nationalists, would go back to something close to the old Soviet system, taking away what the robber barons have. As long as that possibility exists, television is going to be political in this country, and the principal weapon for political infighting."

And that, Posner thinks, is bad for Russian TV and for the people who watch it. "There's less and less respect and less and less credibility as far as many Russians are concerned. They're always saying, 'How can you believe these people when I heard this man the day before yesterday say that Ivanov is wonderful, and today he is saying Ivanov is a jerk! I mean, come on!'"

And it may be even worse a couple of years from now, when there will be another election to choose Yeltsin's successor. This next time, the tycoons may not band together to fight the Communists, whose strength has dwindled. Their rivalry is likely to dissolve into political squabbles, with each of them using this TV news weapon to support his own particular candidate.

"As we move toward the year 2000 and the next presidential election," says Posner, "television is going to be more and more politicized and more and more polarized. That's an absolute certainty."

And even that may not be the worst of it when it comes to managing the news, Moscow-style. There is now a move afoot in the Duma to censor what is presented on Russian television. The politicians claim to be scandalized by all the sex and violence. Posner says he has no objection to a system like Britain's, where an impartial nongovernment committee, voluntarily set up and paid for by the networks, examines TV programs after the fact, and fines or otherwise punishes the networks if they violate the terms of their own broadcast code. But Posner doesn't trust Russian politicians to come up with anything nearly so innocuous.

"Let's not forget that most of these politicians in the Duma grew up in the Soviet Union. They have a knee-jerk reaction whenever there's a public controversy. You know, 'Let's shut up the media,' basically. That's censorship, and you've got to stop the politicians before that sort of thing gets into law."

Well, there are a lot of reasons to worry about the TV news in Russia. And maybe not just in Russia. I was the guest a couple of weeks ago on a current-events program on one of the Moscow TV channels. We talked on camera for an hour about how Western networks report the news in Russia and why we choose the topics we do. I'm not so sure how much the Russian viewers learned from what I had to say, but I certainly learned a lot.

After the program was over, I was chatting with the Russian host, a very sophisticated fellow who'd spent more than a little time in the United States, and much of that watching the news on American networks. "I know we've got our own problems with those who want to manage our news," he said. "But what's the real difference between the political consultants over here, who tell us what to report and not to report to gain some political advantage for our owners, and the news consultants in your country who tell you what sort of news subjects to emphasize, like lifestyles and celebrities and health and beauty tips that will get the biggest audience and make the most money for your owners?"

I was glad that that part of our talk wasn't on live TV, because for one of the few times in my career, I could think of absolutely nothing to say.

chapter 32

G-Willikers!
(May 1998)

One summer when I was a kid growing up in a little town in the Midwest, my friends and I organized a neighborhood baseball club. There were nine of us, and we called ourselves the "PAKLATONS," a word which included the first letter of everybody's last name, and the invention of which required no small amount of effort on our parts.

We scratched out a nice little baseball diamond in Andy's backyard. Andy wasn't a member of our club. He was a fat little mouthy kid whom we considered something of a pain in the neck, when we considered him at all.

The morning before our first big Saturday-afternoon game with the LaPoint kids and their friends over on the next block, we broke our baseball bat while practicing. It was our only bat.

My pal Bruce, the catcher, absented himself from practice for a little while, announcing he would seek a solution.

Just before game time, Bruce showed up with a new baseball bat, and Andy.

"What's Andy doing here?" I asked Bruce.

"We've got to put him on the team," he replied.

"What? We've already got nine guys. He's a dork. And besides, where would you put a 'Z' in 'PAKLATONS'?"

"He wants in," Bruce explained patiently. "Andy's folks own the ball field. And Andy owns the bat."

So we played baseball that summer. We platooned at shortstop.

We changed the name to "PAKLATONSZ." I don't know whatever happened to Andy, but my pal Bruce went on to become a labor-relations specialist. Honest.

The "PAKLATONSZ" came to mind this week while I was reading the dispatches from Birmingham, England, about the spring meeting of the leaders of the G8 "group of leading industrialized nations," as they are invariably called.

It used to be the G7, and no question they are leaders in the industrialized world: the United States, Japan, Britain, France, Germany, Italy, and Canada.

A year ago, you may recall, they started calling it the G8, when Russia was invited along as an observer. By this spring, Russia had become, in effect, a regular member. President Boris Yeltsin was in all the group photographs along with Messrs. Clinton, Blair, Kohl, Chirac, and the others.

Russia, as everyone knows, is manifestly not a leading industrialized nation. But Russia's part of the club, nonetheless. Russia is the G7's Andy. Russia owns the bat, which in this case is about twenty-four-thousand nuclear weapons, second in number only to the United States.

So in hopes of keeping Russia democratic and peaceable, the G7 has been doing a lot to make nice to Russia, and to nurture it through what the economists call its "transitional recession" from Communism to capitalism. That's the term that describes the economic pain former Communist countries are said to be required to undergo before they can begin to enjoy the benefits of a market economy. It's a pattern that seems to be working after a fashion in some of the old Iron Curtain nations, like Poland and Hungary.

In Russia, however, that "transitional recession" has really been a depression. It's been underway for a decade now. The total value of goods and services produced by the Russian economy dropped by almost half after Communism collapsed. Last year (1997), for the first time since then, the Russian economy grew, but by a niggling four-tenths of 1 percent. And the government itself has conceded that one-third of all Russians are now living at or below the poverty level.

There was no better demonstration of Russia's misfit membership in the G8 group of "leading industrialized nations" than what confronted President Yeltsin right after he got home from Birmingham. In a space of twenty-four hours, the Russian economy went into free fall. Shares on the Moscow stock exchange dropped 12 percent. Since January, the market has lost 50 percent of its value. Speculators started a run on the Russian ruble, and the Central Bank had to spend $1.5 billion of its dwindling dollars to keep the price stable.

On top of that, it had to raise rates on refinancing the government's debt to a whopping 150 percent. That means that if you're willing to loan Russia, say, $100, you'll get back $250 dollars. That's if the Russian government will be able to pay you back. That "if" is why the interest rate is 150 percent.

If something like that meltdown had happened on Wall Street, as in 1929, you'd have had brokers jumping out of windows and fellows in nice suits selling apples on the streets.

Not in Russia. Most Russians can't afford to own much of anything, least of all stocks. It's the get-rich-quick New Russians who play the market, the ones who eat at the fancy Moscow restaurants and drive hell-bent-for-leather around town in their new Mercedes and BMWs with the blue lights flashing to show how important they are. And a lot of those New Russians have lost their shirts, not to mention their posh country *dachas*, in the past few months. For them, the ordinary folks are crying crocodile tears.

Step out on the street here and mention the stock market. Katya, a secretary, giggles. "I don't own any stocks. I keep my savings in dollars, like everybody else. And I'm not a bit sorry for those parasites who do own stock. They'll make out. They always do."

"Me, own stocks? You kidding?" says Sergei the electrician. "This stock thing isn't about us, it's about the tycoons, and they're getting what they deserve. As for the rest of us Russians, we'll muddle through. We've been through this all before."

Yevgeny, a computer salesman, says he keeps all his money at home. ("I won't tell you where," he smiles.) "Look, at least we've got freedom now. You can be your own boss. Freedom's more precious than anything for sale on the stock market."

Needless to say, the people in the Kremlin can't afford to be quite so philosophical. Yeltsin and his cabinet have now gone into Reassurance Mode, promising that the ruble will be protected and that "Heads will roll" among those he deems responsible for this latest Russian crisis, presumably not his own head. Yeltsin always fires somebody when there's a problem. Now he's fired the head of the tax service. Which is too bad for the former head of the tax service. It means he won't get to move into his office in the biggest, fanciest building currently under construction in downtown Moscow. It's a hideous pink structure and it will house—the guess what?—the Federal Tax Inspectorate.

Although the Russian government has found enough money to keep the tax inspectors living in the style to which they've become accustomed, it hasn't got enough money for much of anything else. The reason, of course, is that it's not collecting the taxes it's due. The biggest industries bribe their way around the tax laws. A lot of the ordinary folks just don't pay taxes because they feel, justifiably, they're not getting much in the way of services from their government anyway. Yeltsin insists he's going to change that. "People must be forced to pay their taxes," he trumpeted. "And some must be prosecuted. We have names."

Well, presumably he has my name. I'm a resident of Russia, and even though I'm a U.S. citizen, I'm legally required to pay Russian income taxes. Okay, how much? My first income tax payment for this year was due two weeks ago. But I still haven't received a bill from the tax people. I don't know how much I'm supposed to pay. Nobody else I know has received a tax bill, either. How's the government supposed to collect my taxes if they can't get around to sending me a statement? Multiply my story by a few tens of millions and you begin to see the problem. No wonder Yeltsin fired the head tax man.

And it's not just a tax problem. Apart from a pledge to cut the federal budget by a draconian 12 percent, the Kremlin's done precious little to reassure Western investors that Russia's ever going to be a best buy. Partly because of opposition from the recalcitrant Communists who control the parliament, Yeltsin's government has failed to create a rational tax system, or privatize agriculture, or trim the vast state bureaucracy, or reform the banking system, or fashion new bankruptcy legislation to stem the financial hemorrhaging of the huge network of unprofitable state industries.

The result is that Western investors, who are much less forgiving when it comes to Russia than are Western statesmen, have suddenly started to take their investment money and head for the exits. Investing in Russia has become about as popular as putting your money in hula hoops. A few days ago, the government tried to sell off the last of its big state-owned oil companies, Rosneft. The price was about $2 billion for a controlling interest in Rosneft, and the government was hoping to use the money to make up some of its budget shortfalls. There were no bidders for Rosneft. None.

That news triggered the Moscow market crash, along with the revelation that the Russian government is pretty close to broke. How close? Well, foreign investors currently have loaned the Russian government about $20 billion in short-term debt. They could call that in any time, if they lose confidence in the Russian economy, and they may. The Central Bank here only has $10 billion left to back up the Russian ruble. You do the math.

If the ruble collapses, so could what's left of the entire Russian economy. Consider Indonesia for a moment. If you've been watching the riots on TV from Jakarta lately, you'll know what could happen here if one day one hundred fifty million Russians woke up and discovered what few rubles they had left were worthless.

In fact, the Communists in the Russian parliament seem to be hoping for some kind of Indonesian scenario. They've started proceedings to impeach President Yeltsin for economic mismanagement and other perceived misdeeds, hoping he'll just resign, like President Suharto. Fat chance.

But there are some troubling similarities between what's happened with the Russian economy, and what got the Indonesian economy into trouble recently. Call it Crony Capitalism. In Indonesia, most everything worth owning is owned by Suharto's friends and family. When the big-money types started making bizarre investments out of love and loyalty instead of common sense, Indonesia's economy tanked. Most of Russia's big business is run the same way, by a dozen or so vastly rich tycoons with close ties to the Kremlin.

Well, not to worry. If history is any guide, before the Russian economy goes off the cliff, the International Monetary Fund will likely ride to the rescue. It's already in the process of giving the Kremlin another installment on a $10 billion low-interest loan it has promised, and probably will wind up loaning another $10 or $20 billion before this panic is over. Just the news that the IMF fellows had arrived here with their briefcases was enough to settle down the Moscow stock market, at least for the moment.

It has always amazed me how, when governments are about to go broke, the rest of the world lines up to loan them money. If you or I were to take a balance sheet like the one just described to our banker, and ask for a big loan, he'd laugh us out of his office. Then he'd call the sheriff. But countries, especially great big countries with lots of nuclear bombs, are different from you and me. International lenders will doubtless shell out what's needed to tide the Russians over, firmly convinced that, unlike ordinary folks, governments can't really go bankrupt. Well, we'll see. Russia's borrowing may see it through today, but as for tomorrow, I sure wouldn't want to co-sign any of those new loans.

One thing's for certain. None of these shenanigans have fooled the ordinary folks here. The other thing Boris Yeltsin discovered when he returned from hobnobbing with the rest of the G8 was that you couldn't get from Siberia to Moscow anymore. Not by train, anyway. Thousands of striking coal miners had blocked the tracks of the Trans-Siberian railway, and vowed to stay there until they got the back pay that is owed them.

The government has been promising for more than two years to

Miners from Siberia sit at the Russian government headquarters in Moscow, June 11, 1998, to protest the government's failure to pay months' backlog of wages, as state
officials had promised in May in an attempt to quell
miners' strikes. Miners had returned to work after days of
protests that included crippling several stretches of
Russia's railway system by blocking tracks. (AP Photo/Ivan
Sekretarev)

pay up the arrears owed in salaries and pensions to ordinary Russians, but they haven't been paid, and in the past several months, the
total's grown to more than $10 billion. The government says it's the
fault of the mine owners. The mine owners say it's the fault of their
customers, mostly the state-owned industries, who won't pay their
bills. The industries say the mine owners are just stuffing their own
pockets. Anyway, the miners aren't getting paid.

This month the miners finally decided they couldn't take it anymore. They'd tried voting for the Communists in protest, but the
Communists in the Russian parliament have become paper tigers.
They tried protest marches with the teachers, medical workers, and
other state employees, but that got them nothing except a little publicity. They went on strike at the mines, but it's coming on to
summer here, and Russia won't need a lot of coal till next winter.

So the miners decided maybe it would be a good idea just to go
out and lie on the tracks of the Trans-Siberian railroad until somebody took notice. Within a week there were six hundred freight and

passenger cars stuck in Siberia, and factories from Vladivostok to Nizhny Novgorod were shutting down. The Kremlin took notice in a hurry. A flock of government officials, led by Deputy Prime Minister Boris Nemtsov, dashed out to Siberia with suitcases full of cash and promises. After vowing to start paying back wages directly to the miners so they can buy apartments and/or start their own businesses (thereby preventing mine owners and local bureaucrats from siphoning off most of the back pay that's supposed to go to the miners), Nemtsov negotiated an end to the Siberian sit-down strike, and most of the trains are now moving again.

Nobody pretends Nemstov's fix is anything but temporary. And the ruinous interest the Russian government now has to pay to lenders isn't going to make it any easier to find the wherewithal to pay those back wages.

It has become a familiar Russian ritual. The miners and state workers, tens of millions of them, go unpaid for months, sometimes years. Eventually they take some sort of strike action. The Kremlin applies a Band-Aid and everybody quietly goes back to work. Until the next time.

A Russian acquaintance has decided that the Russians, having been captives of Communism for seventy years, are now captives of Crony Capitalism. "A long-oppressed society eventually loses it's natural qualities of love and self-respect," he concludes. "Russia is such a society. And now those natural qualities, those gifts of God, have been replaced by a tendency to despise ourselves, to become toadies. Such a society cannot enjoy the fruits of its freedom, even if this freedom was acquired by accident, as ours was when Communism collapsed. In our minds and our hearts, we are, most of us, prisoners still."

While the Russian economy has been in freefall, the political system's been operating strictly by the book. President Yeltsin dismissed his prime minister, Victor Chernomyrdin, along with the cabinet, and replaced him with a thirty-five-year-old nonentity, Sergei Kiriyenko. After some brinkmanship, the Duma, which is controlled by the Communists, finally rolled over and approved all of this to avoid new elections. It was the first acid test of Russia's new constitution, and it worked.

Whether young Mr. Kiriyenko will be able to manage things any better than his predecessor remains to be seen. The best you can say for him is that he claims to be committed to the same reforms that Western investors are insisting on.

Chernomyrdin, who is now busy running for Boris Yeltsin's job in the year 2000, must be happy to be rid of the Kremlin, in view of what's happened since his departure. Kiriyenko, in his public appearances, has appeared somewhat overwhelmed by his new responsibilities, or perhaps, since he's still such an unknown quantity, that's the way he generally appears. His most notable public utterance to date has been, "We must honestly tell the people that Russia is a rather poor country." As if those Siberian miners didn't know! I suspect that before long, President Yeltsin will wish he hadn't fired good old reliable Victor Chernomyrdin in a fit of pique.

Still, you've got to give Boris Yeltsin credit for chutzpah. To judge from the way the Kremlin's been throwing its weight around in world affairs, you'd never suspect Russia was "a rather poor country." Yeltsin and his foreign minister, Yevgeny Primakov, who survived the latest cabinet shake-up, have been playing Good Cop-Bad Cop with the West. Yeltsin makes the rounds of the summit meetings, glad-handing with presidents and prime ministers, and even organized a little "troika" summit of his own a few weeks back, inviting Germany's chancellor Helmut Kohl and French president Jacques Chirac to Moscow, apparently just to get reacquainted, since nothing meaningful was signed or sealed as a result. Yeltsin looked ecstatic. Kohl and Chirac just looked confused.

Meanwhile, Primakov spent last winter giving Washington fits by undermining American diplomacy in the Balkans and the Persian Gulf, among other trouble spots.

Russia, in short, is behaving less like the international bindle stiff it has become, begging for handouts from the IMF, and more like that other power in what used to be, in the days of the Cold War with the United States, a bipolar world.

Even though now, in practical fact, Moscow is too weak to even manage relations with the newly independent nations of the old Soviet Union, the Commonwealth of Independent States. Most of them have chosen to go their own way in international relations, which is basically Westward. So far Russia hasn't even been able to ratify the new borders with most of the new states that surround it.

Apart from adding on a few countries to NATO, something adorned with all sorts of provisions for Russian face-saving, the West has thus far been reluctant to remind Russia that it isn't what it once was, hoping that Russia will stay peaceful and quiet until it gets out of hock, eventually begins to prosper, and find its new place in the world.

Russia may be down on its uppers, but it has still got those twenty-four-thousand nuclear weapons. And so far it shows no wish to start getting rid of them. The parliament still refuses to ratify the START II arms-reduction treaty, signed with the United States five years ago. Maybe those Communists who dominate the parliament aren't so dumb. With all its troubles, like Andy, Russia still owns the bat.

chapter 33
Awl Bitnet
(June 1998)

A few miles outside Baku, past the forest of rusty old oil derricks and the stinking pools of oily water on the Azerbaijan coast of the Caspian Sea, there's a quiet little hillside, blooming with spring flowers and the remains of what was once a little tourist restaurant. If you look east, you can see a pleasant-looking community of fancy seaside homes, white against the rosy clouds of the evening sunset. It resembles the Hamptons on Long Island, outside of New York City. In fact it's a local version, where the new Azeri rich spend their summer weekends, defending themselves against the fierce heat.

But that's not the real attraction on this particular hillside. It's the fire. The whole hillside is ablaze with an eerie blue flame, whooshing into the air as if somebody's gas stove had just exploded. The fire is fueled by natural gas pouring into the air from a natural reservoir thousands and thousands of feet deep in the Earth. It's called Yanar Dag, the Burning Mountain, and it has been burning like this for at least a thousand years. Once, Hindus from India came west to worship at Yanar Dag. And Zoroastrians from Persia. Marco Polo stopped off here in the thirteenth century while traveling the Great Silk Road from Venice to China. He wrote of a black oily substance that oozed right from the ground and was "good to burn."

If the ancient Azeris weren't the first to discover oil, they were among the first to figure out what best to do with it, although that took almost a millennium and the invention of the internal combustion engine. They sank the first oil well and brought in their first gusher on the shoreline here back in 1873. By the 1890s, Azerbaijan was producing half the oil in the whole world, and making fortunes for families like the Rothschilds, the Rockefellers, and the Nobels. It was the beginning of a pattern. Azerbaijan had the oil, so other people came along and pumped it out, and took the oil and the money and went their way. And the Azeris were left with those rusty old oil derricks and stinking pools of oil on the Caspian shoreline.

Well, that's not quite all. There are some remains of that first oil boom. Baku, the Azeri capital, is adorned with them. The old city center is full of graceful, wide boulevards, lined with palms and cypress and sooyid, a sycamore look-alike. Blue and yellow blossoms rustle in the breeze on a gentle spring day. You could imagine yourself in Rome. The public buildings are ornate and neoclassical, with lots of statues and colonnades and stone curlicues.

The six-story apartment buildings, with shops and cafés on the ground floor, seem to belong somewhere on Paris's Left Bank. An Azeri acquaintance confided to me, "Our little secret is, we really want to be European."

But the Azeris are Muslim, Shia Muslims like the Iranians just over the Caucasus Mountains. The Azeris and Iranians don't much get along. Iran's mullahs are scandalized by the Azeris' casual approach to their religion. No veils, no chadors here. Baku women go about in high heels and short skirts over their pantyhose, and proudly bareheaded. There are a few mosques in evidence, but in a week of looking around, I never heard a single call to prayer. The men, those who can afford it, wear well-tailored suits or expensive sweaters casually thrown about their shoulders, Milan-style. And they've learned that Italian way of carrying themselves, even while talking on their cell phones.

It's a nice pose, but it doesn't quite come off. In the evening, when you stroll with the rest of Baku's upper middle class through the city's version of the Piazza Navonna, you can't escape Central Asia. On the balconies, you'll see the same delicate Islamic stone latticework you might find in Cairo or Istanbul. Around the corner is a cozy cobblestoned alley with cool green vines climbing the old stone walls, as if they belonged in West Beirut.

The older men have assembled in the outdoor cafés, playing backgammon and fingering their worry beads, sipping their tea *mas boot*, and listening to the wail of the latest Azeri love song on cassette and CD. It is the sort of music that, to my tin American ear, always seems to have no beginning and certainly no end, except when the performers seem to tire of repeating the same eight bars over and over. I can't imagine Azeri boys and girls ever falling in love to that kind of music, but I guess they must. There are seven-and-a-half million Azeris.

Baku's whole history is written in brick and stone, the most recent history, too. Along the seawalk is the former headquarters of the Supreme Soviet, a vast Stalinist pile of concrete and marble with a huge open plaza where the troops and tanks would parade every May Day for most of seventy years.

Azerbaijan became Russian property as early as the seventeenth century when Peter the Great's army conquered it. The Azeris won their country back for a while, but the tsars reconquered it again in the ninteenth century. After World War I and the Bolshevik revolution, Azerbaijan enjoyed a brief moment of independence until 1920, when Lenin decided he wanted Azeri oil to fuel the Communists rather than the capitalists. From then on, Baku's oil flowed north to Moscow rather than west. And Azerbaijan became just another part of the Soviet Union.

But Moscow never allowed itself to depend on Caspian oil. Siberian oil, after all, was available closer to home and safe from the grasp of greedy neighbors. In World War II, Hitler set his sights on Caspian oil when the Nazis struck toward the Caucasus. The battle of Stalingrad, where the Red Army finally turned the Nazis back, was all about protecting Caspian oil. Even so, for most of Azerbaijan's Soviet history, its oil resources were underdeveloped.

When the Soviet Union collapsed a few years ago, Azerbaijan became independent once again. For three years it fought a border dispute with Armenia, a conflict which has never been truly settled and still flares up in skirmishes every few months. The end result, after several hundred thousand casualties and a lot of ethnic cleansing, is that Armenia has wound up with a considerable portion of what used to be Azerbaijan, and vice versa. Each country also has several hundred thousand refugees it doesn't know what to do with. Armenians are Christians and Azeris are Muslims. Armenia is poor and Azerbaijan just might become very, very rich.

The latest chapter in Baku's history is being written in stone and steel and glass right now. There are new offices and apartment buildings going up all over this city of three-and-a-half million. The newest of them, a twelve-story monstrosity, will house offices, a five-star hotel, and on its ground floor, Baku's first McDonald's. At the airport they are building a new terminal. Swissair has flights to Zurich three times a week. The baggage claim area has advertisements, in English, for Sony, Samsung, Hyundai, Daewoo, Volkswagen, Hertz, and Avis. And all along the highway into Baku there are big billboards advertising American Dream cigarettes (plain and filtered).

On the streets (street signs are still in Russian, since the Azeris have been too busy lately to replace them with Azeri ones) Russian Zhigilis and Volgas share space with new Mercedes (there are now three dealerships here), Isuzus, and Jeep Cherokees. The incessant honking of horns in the inevitable traffic jams is something you'd expect to hear in Cairo.

On most every downtown street corner there's a new gas station. Some of them have even managed to position themselves in peculiar locations at major intersections, so that you literally have to drive through the gas pumps to get to the stoplight. The attendants are all fitted out in jumpsuits of colors that defy any rainbow. And they do windshields, too.

In short, Baku is booming again, and it's all about what in Texas and Oklahoma they call the "Awl Bitnet." The oil business, to you Yankees. The old onshore deposits are pretty well played out, so the action is now 100 miles offshore. The experts think that beneath the unstable seafloor of the Caspian, maybe three or four miles down in the Earth, there are 200 billion barrels of oil. That's a third of all the oil there's supposed to be in the Persian Gulf.

Haidar Aliev, the wily seventy-four-year-old ex-Communist (and member of the Soviet Presidium in the Leonid Brezhnev years) who is now the all-powerful president of Azerbaijan, has rolled out a red carpet for the Western oil companies. And those who've accepted invitations read like an Awl Bitnet Who's Who: Amoco, Chevron, Unocal, Pennzoil, and Exxon. Not to mention British Petroleum and the big Russian state oil company, Lukoil, plus a couple of dozen other oil firms. They are all investing billions of dollars in drilling the Caspian Sea, in the hopes of one day making trillions of dollars.

Money's the subject on a Thursday night at Finnegan's Pub in downtown Baku, where the bar is crowded no matter what night it is. English is the language of choice, and the beer of choice is Guinness on tap. Over in the corner is a British Airways flight crew (daily non-stops to London). In the next booth, a couple of Scots who are selling roomfuls of Swedish modern furniture direct from Stockholm. At the bar, halfway through a Guinness, is Don Churchman, a blond fellow with a crewcut who looks much younger than his thirty-one years, and who sells drinking water. ("In Baku, water is three times as expensive as oil!") Churchman's an American ex-patriot. His dad was a businessman who traveled the Persian Gulf, so he spent eight years growing up in Kuwait, and left just before the Iraqi invasion in 1990. "I joined the National Guard and came back just in time to help lib-erate it," he says. Churchman speaks fluent Arabic and has been here nineteen months. "I can literally walk down the street every day and find something new here, whether it's a bowling alley or a super-market or a pub." Don Churchman loves Baku.

"This is the frontier," he says. "Baku's one of the only places you can get rich. You can't get rich in America anymore. So we're all here. To see a former Soviet country and be able to explain to them what capitalism is, and to bring capitalism to a country that doesn't know it, I mean, that's a real high."

Well, more likely, Don, the Azeris are just returning to form. Their ancestors were wheeling and dealing with the Turks and the Tatars while Don Churchman's (and mine) were still wearing bearskins and trying to figure out how to start a campfire. The Azeris were Capitalists before the economists had a name for it, and the more clever among them are already figuring out how to profit by this new oil bonanza. From the looks of it, though, they'll have to get up pretty early in the morning to get the better of guys like Don Churchman, who remarked, "I wish I could sell one hundred billion barrels of water!"

Churchman's buddy, Tim Holmes, from Syracuse, New York, was just bumming his way around this part of the world when he was offered a job teaching English at the university here. Now he's the most popular professor on the staff, mostly because he's the only native English-speaker on the faculty. Azeris had to learn Russian for seventy years, and they still speak in a mixture of Russian and Azeri, but the demand for English lessons here has mushroomed.

Finnegan's is owned by another American, Charlie Schroeder, a kind of unofficial mayor of Baku's expat community, who speaks with a honeyed Louisiana drawl. Schroeder's in his sixties, with a shock of greying hair and a hearty smile; the perfect maitrê d'. In fact, he's spent most of his life since leaving New Orleans working with the off-shore oil companies around the world. He came here in 1994.

"The town was getting quite a few foreigners, even then," he says. "I really didn't want to open up a restaurant, but my friends in the oil companies wore me down."

Now Schroeder has five restaurants and pubs, with names like Ragin' Cajun (Cajun popcorn, blackened catfish, and eight brands of beer) and Margaritaville (margaritas). And he's seen a lot of change since the dark days of Azerbaijan's struggle with Armenia.

"I'd never seen anyplace as devastated as this. Their whole country had collapsed. The biggest thing I noticed was, nobody smiled. People walked around with their heads down. There was nothing to smile about. But today they're smiling. You see them walking through the parks with their kids, the kids have an ice-cream cone, people are happy again."

The restaurant business is no sure thing, especially if you're trying to run five of them. But Charlie Schroeder figures his business is a lot less of a gamble than the wildcatting the oil companies are currently doing.

"They're takin' a big chance. It's all exploratory work. It's never a guarantee until you punch the hole in the ground and oil comes out. You never know whether you're going to hit it or not. And it's big bucks."

You can see where all the money is going if you take a thirty-five-minute helicopter ride out to Dada Gurgud. It's a floating oil-drilling platform run by the Azerbaijan International Operating Company, an American-owned consortium of twelve oil companies. Kelly Wilson's in charge of the ninety-five-man crew. He looks as if he

Oil rig and worker on the Caspian Sea. (© Bill Gasperini)

ought to be in charge of something. He's six-foot-four with hands the size of meat cleavers and a voice that commands attention. You have the sense that the fellows working on Dada Gurgud do what Kelly Wilson tells them.

The crew is a mixture of Americans like Clint Montford. "I just came aboard. I'm the mud man. The mud man decides what kind of mud you have to feed down the drilling pipes to cool the bit and find out what kind of stuff you're drilling into." There are also Brits, Norwegians, and Azeris. The Azeris comprise about half the crew, and they'll remain here eventually when the expat "roughnecks," as the rig workers call themselves, go off on another job.

"It's a routine," says Wilson. "Twelve hours on, twelve hours off. Twenty-eight days on the rig, twenty-eight days off. It's a work-and-sleep routine and you have to be comfortable with yourself, and entertain yourself. Read a book, play the guitar, watch a video, whatever."

For the expat roughnecks, Baku is no more than an airport. After their twenty-eight days offshore, it's home to Houston or Glasgow or wherever. "But it kinda gets in your blood," says Wilson. "A lot of the guys, you can ask them, they've been home for three weeks and Mama's kind of glad to get you out of her hair for a couple of weeks, ya know. We're gone two hundred days a year."

For Wilson, home is the Bahamas. But he's spent most of his life off more seacoasts than you can count. He was raised in Canada, just north of the Montana border, and started out to be a radio-TV news reporter, believe it or not. But he worked in the Edmonton oil fields one college summer and fell in love with the life.

"After that it was, well, let's see: the Arctic, Saudi Arabia, Kuwait, the North Sea, then Egypt, Nigeria, Cameroon, Congo, Angola, and a couple of other places I forget."

Nobody knows better than Kelly Wilson what it is to wildcat for oil. Right now he's drilling three miles into the Earth in hopes of bringing in a gusher. His last try in the Caspian cost sixteen million dollars and the well came up dry.

"Most of this business is finding out where the oil isn't," he says. "But no question, there's a major, major amount of oil here. You just have to find it, and we will."

The two big questions about the Caspian oil bonanza, if such it turns out to be, are: who's going to wind up with the oil and the profits, and how to get the oil out of the Caspian to the rest of the world? Those questions are, of course, connected.

The Caspian Sea isn't really a sea so much as a kind of great big lake. And it's landlocked. So the oil, once it's extracted, is going to have to be pumped through pipelines somewhere. And that "somewhere" may turn out to be one of the more important and difficult economic and political issues in the whole world in the next decade.

Since Peter the Great, the Russians have always regarded the Caspian as a Russian "lake," rather the way Americans view, say, Lake Superior. Now, though, while Russia still has part of the Caspian coastline, the bulk of the coast is occupied by former Soviet republics like Azerbaijan. At best, the Russians can now only hope to share a portion of what oil is found in the Caspian, along with all the Western oil companies.

That has come as rude shock to the Russian psyche. Imagine if one day Americans woke up and found a consortium of Russian oil companies drilling away in the Gulf of Mexico 100 miles off Brownsville, Texas. You get the idea.

Even so, the Russians have had to come to terms with taking only a small slice of the oil profits from the offshore drilling. They're hoping to make up for it by making a mint from the oil pipelines. What little oil is being pumped out of the Caspian right now goes through a Russian pipeline to the Black Sea at Novorossisk. But the Russians have been charging a king's ransom to pipe it, and the Western oil companies are getting tired of that Russian pipeline monopoly.

Russia's newly independent neighbors on the Caspian, including Azerbaijan, are determined that the pipelines will go their way. But any way at all is problematic. You could pipe the oil west to the Black Sea through Georgia, but it would have to run through the Caucasus Mountain, a hotbed of political unrest. Plus the Turks don't want to risk an oil spill fouling up Istanbul. Or you could pipe it through eastern Turkey, avoiding the Black Sea, to the Mediterranean. But that route is full of restive Kurdish separatists. The easiest and cheapest way to pipe the oil is south, right through Iran to the Persian Gulf. But you know how Washington and Teheran feel about each other.

So in the past few months there has been quite a lot of what you might call "global positioning" on the pipeline route. Last fall, President Aliev himself was invited to Washington for a nice chat with President Clinton and Newt Gingrich and other panjandrums. And when the oil companies brought in their first Caspian well, who was on hand, along with Aliev and the Western oil executives, but then-U.S. Secretary of Transportation Federico Peña? Peña said Washington didn't care where the pipeline went, as long as it didn't go through Russia or Iran. Say again? His Russian counterpart, Boris Nemtsov, replied that it is "100 percent certain" the pipeline will go through Russia.

And what about that route through America's old nemesis, Iran? That's the route the U.S. companies want, although they won't say so publicly. And they are spending a lot of money hiring lobbyists to get what they want, lobbyists with familiar names. Names like Brent Scowcroft, Zbigniew Brezesinski, John Sununu, Lloyd Bentsen, Dick Cheney, James A. Baker III, and Henry Kissinger. Ring any bells?

How much would you like to bet that one of these days in the not-too-distant future, there'll be a sudden rapprochement between Washington and Teheran, that Bill Clinton or his successor will be hailed as the man who "made the opening to Iran," and that any or all of the above will be on hand when they dedicate the new Baku-to-Abadan Iranian oil pipeline?

Well, an outcome of that sort might be good in the long run for the West. It wouldn't hurt for America and Iran to let bygones be bygones. The Teheran hostage crisis was, after all, a long time ago.

But that result would be disastrous for the new Russia and its future. Caspian oil revenues will be essential in helping Russia to break out of a decade of economic depression and become a paid-up member of the capitalist world. Moscow can deal with a bigger NATO on its borders, if it must. But if Washington effectively excludes Russia from fully profiting from the oil in Russia's own "lake," it could do irreparable harm not only to American relations with the second-most-powerful nuclear nation on Earth, but also to Russia's economy and its budding democracy.

This century has seen quite enough of the consequences when a powerful nation feels it has been unjustly aggrieved.

But no matter which way the oil goes, Baku can't lose. The future here is better than bright. Ask Charlie Schroeder.

"I went to Dubai in the mid-sixties, before the oil fields. Then Dubai was just a small thatched-hut village. And if you see Dubai today it's a major modern city comparable to any city in the world. Unlike Dubai, Baku already has the infrastructure. It's a big, functioning city. What Baku needs now is to become the trading center for the Caspian Sea, the way Dubai has become the trading center for the Persian Gulf.

"I keep telling these young Azeri kids, 'Don't think about leaving your country, 'cause this is probably going to be one of the better places in the world in the very near future.' I would say in ten to fifteen years, this place, you won't recognize it."

Charlie Schroeder's a dreamer, of course. You have to be in a place like Baku. But maybe he's a prophet.

We can only hope that history won't repeat itself. Right now, none of that oil money that's got Baku booming, at least on the surface, has trickled down to the average Azeri. One in seven of them is a refugee, and the refugees live in squalid Stalinist apartment buildings at the edge of Baku. If they're lucky, they get by on a pension of $2 a month. Schoolteachers and cops here aren't much better off. They make about $15 a month. Prices have risen 600 percent in the past four years, and it now takes $400 a month to feed a Baku family of four. Obviously, somebody's going hungry. Charlie Schroeder might not be so much of an optimist about Baku if he got out to the projects where the refugees live among the rats and the garbage. These people are not smiling.

Still, out on the Dada Gurgud rig in the Caspian, Kelly Wilson thinks Baku will be better off this time. "I mean, there's been oil here since before the turn of the century, but the trouble was, all the money's gone out before. But I think a lot more of it is going to rub off locally now than in the past."

Well, maybe. Last time, the Rockefellers got rich and the ordinary Azeris got left out. You can only hope that when this Baku oil boom goes bust, as it will, in fifty or sixty years, the ordinary Azeris will have something more to show for it than some rusty old oil derricks and stinking pools of oily water on the shore of the blue waters of the Caspian Sea.

chapter 34

Adieu *MIR*

(June 1998)

O ne of the nice things about my job is that it comes with a complimentary car, courtesy of my office. When I first arrived in Moscow, I was issued a slightly used Opel Frontera, four-wheel drive and all.

The night I moved into our apartment, I drove it home, parked it next to my building, put on the car alarm, stuck an antitheft device on the steering wheel, and went to bed without a worry in the world.

The next morning the car was gone, alarm, antitheft device, and all. Nothing. Stolen. We never saw it again. Presumably, somebody's now happily tooling around in my Frontera in downtown Tashkent or Alma Alta or somewhere. Auto theft is a big business in Moscow, and almost-new four-by-fours are especially prized by car thieves.

So I told the office to give me the oldest car they had. It was a seven-year-old Volvo station wagon, rusting and covered with dents and peeled paint. Absolutely nobody would want to steal that car, and indeed nobody's even tried.

But it runs great, starts on the coldest winter mornings, and has survived three collisions. That's including the drunk who rammed into me and five other cars in his new BMW while we were all stopped at a light. Nobody was hurt, but he totaled his car and the others. But not mine. He bounced off my Volvo like a soccer ball. The Volvo just accumulated a couple of more dents.

I thought about my Volvo this week when America said good-bye to the Russian space station, *MIR*. Like my Volvo, *MIR* is now twelve years old, full of dents, and despite some past problems, has been running great for most of the past year. Like the Energizer Bunny, it just keeps going and going. Incredibly, MIR is still functioning five years past its design life. (Volvos, as we all know, are designed to function forever.)

When the MIR cosmonauts and the U.S. astronauts aboard the space shuttle *Discovery* bid farewell, the cosmonauts gave the astronauts a huge wrench as a going-away gift. It was more than symbolism. MIR's survival has been a testament to Russian ingenuity. Every Russian male, whatever his station in life, is supremely convinced there is nothing ever invented he can't fix, or more likely improve. And MIR's life story has been one big space repair job.

It's why Russians always seem dumbfounded whenever some U.S. congressman views with alarm the deteriorating condition of MIR. When asked by the press last year about the string of mishaps onboard MIR, the mission director, Vladimir Solovyov, answered testily: "Why do these things happen? Do you know why your car breaks down?" (Interfax).

The point that Dr. Solovyov, a car owner himself, was trying to make was: those Americans shouldn't be wringing their hands every time something breaks down on MIR. They should count themselves lucky that the Russians are so innately talented at keeping things running—things like MIR.

Indeed a lot of MIR's problems are institutional and fiscal. The Russians simply haven't spent the money they need to modernize MIR. The computer chips it uses are less powerful than some of those on the cell phone you may be using, much less anything to match Windows 95.

Said Viktor Blagov, one of the Russian space officials, in a rare moment of public pique, "We used to change MIR's computer parts after their technical life expectancy ran out. Now we must use each part until it dies" (Interfax).

The Russian government isn't spending the money it used to, not only on MIR, but on the rest of the Russian space effort. It's hard to justify more money for MIR when millions of Russian workers and pensioners still haven't been paid.

What's more, the Russians are naturally reluctant to invest further in a project that's due to end next year. Cosmonauts will continue to man MIR until the autumn of 1999, and then, if present plans don't change, the space station will be abandoned and MIR will be guided to a lower orbit where it will reenter the atmosphere and burn most of itself up, the remainder splashing (presumably) harmlessly into the ocean, a cosmic funeral pyre for the forerunner of Earth's first international space station.

Despite all the negative publicity, both Moscow and NASA officials in Houston can take some pride for sticking with *MIR*. Over time, in fact, *MIR* has proved to be more a monument to human resourcefulness than human error.

The United States has spent $476 million over the past three years to send seven astronauts to live on *MIR*, and it would be hard to argue that it wasn't money well spent. The last astronaut, Andy Thomas, spent 130 days on *MIR*. Together, those astronauts logged 977 days on *MIR*, and despite all the hand-wringing at NASA and on Capitol Hill, they all came back safely. Before *MIR*, the longest Americans had stayed in space was eighty-four days. Our space shuttle flights last no longer than sixteen days.

So *MIR* has substantially advanced what we on Earth know about living and working in space. We now know vastly more about the physiological and psychological effects of weightlessness, and how to deal with space-induced changes in bones and heart and body fluids (one-word prescription: exercise). We know that humans get lonely in space, thus *MIR* hooked up e-mail and voice channels so that the crew could talk to friends and family from time to time.

We know more now not just about humans in space, but about other living things; how plants like wheat, for example, can be grown over successive generations. It's exactly the kind of knowledge humankind is going to need for longer spaceflights someday, to Mars and beyond.

And though it certainly wasn't planned that way, we Earthlings now know a whole lot more about how to deal with things that go wrong "up there." It is knowledge we'll need when the sixteen-nation international space station is ready for occupancy about 2001. That's going to cost at least $40 billion and will be four times the size of *MIR*. That's four times as many opportunities for something to go wrong

As one NASA official, Jim Van Laak, observes, "What we have not gotten used to in our country is having to sustain a space station on a continuing basis. Any major system like that is going to have failures" (Associated Press and Reuters).

MIR has certainly had its share of failures. But most of them have been fixed with Russian know-how, and with some Yankee ingenuity for good measure. The crises on that new space station, and there will be crises, can be solved in *MIR* fashion. With, among other things, a wrench.

No, it's not comfortable up there on *MIR*, to be sure. American astronauts compare it to camping out in the backseat of an old car. But *MIR* has proved you can live there, and live relatively safely.

The last astronaut on *MIR*, Andy Thomas, even sounded wistful as he ended his tour of duty. "That was kind of a strange experience, to close the hatch for the last time on the station and then to back away. As we pulled farther and farther away and the station got smaller and it turned dark, and it was just flashing lights, that was really kind of a sad moment in a way. To say good-bye and to know that we were never going to be back up there again" (Associated Press and Reuters).

As for the Russian cosmonauts left onboard, they're going to be busier than ever for the next year. When Thomas left, so did the millions of dollars in *MIR* subsidies that Washington has been paying to Moscow. So the Russian government is now desperate to find money to keep *MIR* going. I mean desperate.

The cosmonauts are now required to function as salesmen-in-space for TV commercials from companies all over the world. One day they're demonstrating a new pen that will "write in space" that's for sale on an American home-shopping channel. The next day they're licking Spanish lollipops and drinking Israeli milk. The advertising people have concluded that *MIR* is the ultimate commercial location.

Isn't all that a little, well, tacky? The head of Russia's space agency, Yuri Koptev, makes no apologies. "When we can get tens of millions of dollars, naturally we have to overcome the snobbery of rejecting such [pause to stare at ceiling] projects."

So *MIR* ends up as a kind of cosmic billboard. And the last cosmonauts, when they're not putting out fires and fixing the computers, will be spending their time boldly going where no TV commercial pitchman has gone before. *Dos vadanya, MIR.*

(Postscript: MIR has turned out to have even more staying power than anyone imagined. It's still in space, although the last Russian crew has departed. The Russian government has plans to try to bring it down sometime in 2001, but a consortium of private companies is lobbying to keep it in orbit longer for space research projects. Meanwhile, the bare-bones components of the much-delayed International Space Station, including the problem-plagued Russian module, have finally been put in orbit. Late in 2000, the first ISS crew, an American astronaut and two Russian cosmonauts, moved in, having been sent into orbit from a Russian launch pad in Central Asia by a Russian launch rocket. But that Russian involvement has come at an enormous cost. The United States has had to pay an additional three billion dollars to Moscow to finance completion of the Russian components. Even then, they don't conform to American safety standards, so modifications in orbit will cost even more money. And as they have from the beginning, many

space scientists are still questioning whether the space research that the ISS was designed for couldn't be done much more cheaply and efficiently with mechanical robots.)

chapter 35

Double Trouble

(June 1998)

Well, it would explain a lot. One day you see President Boris Yeltsin out among the masses, glad-handing the local folks, looking fully in charge and in the pink of health. He could be a model for an AARP poster. The next day he's shuffling around the Kremlin, looking ghastly. His hands shake, his words are slurred, and his eyes have that sort of vacant stare, as if he's wondering not only where he is, but who he is.

One minute he's commanding a series of crisis meetings on the economy. The next he's in seclusion at his suburban *dacha*, a recluse for days at a time. One of the Communist deputies in the lower house of the Russian parliament, Aleksander Saliy, thinks he has it all figured out. There are actually two Yeltsins. One of them is a double.

You can find Deputy Saliy in his Kremlin office most any day, pouring over old Yeltsin press photos from the past couple of years, to confirm his conspiracy theory. "Of course there was a real Yeltsin in the beginning," he says. "But I'm wondering about the period during 1996, from the time of the first round of the presidential elections and for the rest of the year. Some specialists in this area have helped me, professionals who have done a computerized analysis of some photographs and video footage of the president. They think that at some times it wasn't really Yeltsin."

You'll remember that in the midst of the 1996 presidential elections, Yeltsin suffered a serious heart attack, a fact the Kremlin managed to keep secret until after he'd won. Later that same year he underwent serious heart surgery, and was hors de combat until well into 1997.

Saliy believes that Yeltsin's daughter and political-consultant-in-residence, Tatyana, found a double for her father to run the country while Yeltsin was indisposed.

"I think it happened around the time of his inauguration," says Saliy. "Look at this picture of him here. The mayor of Moscow is in front and Yeltsin is hidden in back. How come they only show him back there? The real Yeltsin was lying somewhere with an IV in his arm and couldn't move or walk or talk. And then you look at the photos and all of a sudden you have this younger-looking man."

I must say, having seen the photos, whatever Deputy Saliy finds in them escapes me. But he is undeterred, and has called for a formal investigation of all this. Russia doesn't have a provision for special prosecutors, but if it did, I don't doubt that some Russian version of Kenneth Starr would already be handing out subpoenas, with the full support of Saliy's Communist colleagues in the Duma.

As it is, the Kremlin has dismissed Saliy's theory as absurd. But who knows? Josef Stalin, the old Soviet dictator, had a double who stood in for some of his ceremonial chores. And as Saliy likes to say, "In Russia, anything is possible. In your country, they screwed over Nixon for Watergate, and in came another president who pardoned him and it was all very rational. Here, it can drive you crazy."

Mind you, Deputy Saliy is not saying that the Yeltsin double is running Russia these days. The real Yeltsin is back, he believes.

But lately, as you may have noticed, while the real Yeltsin has been in charge, the Russian stock market has tanked; the Russian ruble is in deep doo-doo; and the country's full of protesting miners, teachers, doctors, and state workers.

Maybe it's time to bring back the double.

chapter 36

Road to Retreat

(July 1998)

I got a call the other morning from the folks at the radio desk in New York, wondering if I'd send them a report for their next newscast on an item they'd just seen on the news wires. It seems that one of the Russian army generals had just warned that if the NATO nations went ahead and took military action against the Serbs in the troubled Yugoslav province of Kosovo, it might lead to what the general called a new "Cold War" between Russia and the West. Talk about a Cold War always makes Washington nervous, and that made the general's blustering of some interest.

The radio folks asked if I'd mind keeping my report to twenty-five seconds, as it was a kind of busy day. So I tried to accommodate them as always, being brief. (It takes all of three seconds just to say "Richard Threlkeld, CBS News Moscow.")

There wasn't time to explain, of course, that right now Russia is quite incapable of waging any sort of war, cold or hot, against anybody even half its size. Russia discovered that a couple of years ago, when separatist guerrillas drove the Russian army out of Chechnya. These days, Russia can't even invade itself.

But don't take my word for it. Last winter, the Congressional Research Service (CRS) in Washington put down in black and white, in a report to Congress, what everybody in the Kremlin has known for years. Namely, that Russia is on the verge of "military collapse." Moscow can simply no longer afford the upkeep.

Russian soldier. (© George French)

In the last twelve years, since the days of the Soviet Union, the CRS estimated that troop numbers in the Russian military have dropped by more than two-thirds: from 4.3 million to 1.3 million. Exact figures are impossible to find. The Russian military consists of at least seventeen different armies, including the navy and air force. The Interior Ministry has its own divisions, which fought in Chechnya. There are a quarter-million troops assigned to the Internal Forces that protect President Yeltsin and the rest of the Kremlin hierarchy, and so on. The plain truth is, even the Kremlin doesn't know how many men and women Russia has under arms. By one estimate, it might be as many as three million.

But with few exceptions, they are underpaid, when they are paid at all; underequipped; and undertrained. The military has lost at least two-thirds of its tanks, a third of its artillery and aircraft, and almost half its warships. Training and military exercises have been sharply reduced, new weapons purchases have virtually ceased. In the words of the report, "Few if any of Russia's army divisions are combat-ready."

A case in point: a relic of the Cold War arms buildup, the Russian heavy cruiser *Peter the Great*. It cost the equivalent of a billion dollars to build, and was designed to protect the Russian aircraft carriers competing with the American fleet in the Pacific. But while it was being completed, Moscow sold off the Russian Pacific Fleet's last aircraft carriers to the South Koreans for scrap. So now the *Peter the Great* is in service, assigned to the Northern Fleet, where it has no aircraft carriers to protect.

That's almost comic. What has happened to the soldiers is plain tragedy. There's a notorious scene that was taped a couple of years ago out in the Russian provinces showing soldiers harvesting cabbages, just to get something to eat. It's become a sort of visual symbol of the deterioration of the Russian army.

But you don't have to go out to Siberia to see the same thing. The streets of Moscow abound with furtive groups of young soldiers in uniform, begging passersby for spare change for food or vodka, or even just a cigarette. The usual food allowance for enlisted men is one dollar a day. Few of them now get the coats and boots and other gear they need to withstand the Russian winters. Russian army doctors have testified that fully a third of the soldiers they examined were malnourished.

Ordinary Russians seldom stiff these young men. Almost everybody finds something to give them. Even now, in every opinion poll, the armed forces remain the most trusted institution in the nation, even ahead of the Orthodox Church. Part of the reason is the memory that Russians have, even after half a century, of the sacrifice the Red Army made to defend the motherland against the Nazis. And part of it is the trust that Russians have always had that the military will stay out of politics.

The Russian army has attempted a coup twice in this nation's history, and badly bungled it both times. In the revolution of 1917, the army refused to fire on protestors who occupied the Winter Palace in Petrograd, and finally joined the crowd.

So I've always thought that the nightmare scenarios the planners in the Pentagon and NATO always draw up, about a military coup in today's Russia, are foolish. The time appears long past when the military was strong enough or unified enough to challenge Boris Yeltsin & Co. In fact, the generals and admirals have accepted a brutal downsizing almost without a whimper. A few of them have their eye on Yeltsin's job, but they've chosen to go about trying to get it by using the system. Former Army General Alexander Lebed, who negotiated peace with the Chechens, wants to be the next Russian president. But he's done so by getting himself elected governor of a region in Siberia, which he views as a stepping stone to the Kremlin. In other words, he's opted for democracy.

A more likely scenario is that if conditions in the countryside don't improve, many of the units in Russia's forgotten army will begin to ally themselves with ambitious local politicians, who'll see they get paid and equipped for use against Moscow, in one form or another. Russia's not likely to turn into one big banana republic with revolving military governments. The danger is that it will become balkanized, in which case, Moscow would become irrelevant and wind up replaced with government by warlord, as in China during much of the nineteenth and early twentieth centuries.

In the meantime, the Kremlin soldiers on, trying to plug the gaping holes in its military preparedness with the draft, which has become every bit as unpopular here as it was in the United States during the Vietnam War. Every spring and autumn, there's a call up of about 200,000 eighteen-year-olds. They're required to serve a two-year hitch. As in the United States during the 1960s and 1970s, the vast majority of those who wind up in uniform are the poor and less educated. Here you don't have to flee to Canada if you want to avoid the draft. If you've got the money, you can buy your way out. A bogus military ticket that shows you have already served goes for $5,000. Or you can bribe a doctor to say you're unfit, or bribe your college professor to say you've passed a course exempting you from service. By one estimate, only 13 percent of those called up in 1996 actually went into service.

So who winds up in the army, beyond the luckless and destitute? A quarter of the conscripts have not finished high school. A third are medically or psychologically unfit. A fifth have criminal records. Some army.

If it was just lousy food and living conditions, lousy pay and plain boredom, the draftees might be able to endure it for a couple of years. They wouldn't be the first soldiers in history who detested their hitch in the army. But that's not the worst of it in today's Russian army. It's the violence, and the fear.

In a little warren of offices in a decrepit building around the corner from Lubyanka, the old KGB headquarters in downtown Moscow, you'll find a poignant scene: at desk after desk there are matronly women busily pouring over documents or in earnest conversation with young men in uniform, the soldiers' heads freshly shaved in military style. It's the offices of the Russian Committee of Soldiers' Mothers. The committee was formed a decade ago to try to help mothers of those soldiers who were killed or missing in the war in Chechnya find out what happened to their sons. At least five thousand remain unaccounted for.

Now the committee has signed up ten thousand soldiers' mothers, and it has branched out to help those young men who are drafted to get a legal exemption, and to help those who are already in the army and want to get out for cause, to do so. The committee's one of the few private groups in Russia that monitors human-rights abuses in the military. And it's a daunting task.

Every year, forty thousand Russian recruits desert or go AWOL from their units. In many cases, it's to save their own lives because military hazing in Russia has become a national scandal. The Russian military has always made it rough for its recruits, even in the days of the tsars and the Red Army. It's supposed to toughen a young man and instill discipline and unit control. But in today's army the hazing has been taken to vicious new levels. Beatings and torture are routine. Recruits are kicked and punched and smothered into unconsciousness. It's the sort of "basic training" that would make a U.S. Marine drill instructor blanch.

"It gets worse every year," says Ida Kuklina of the committee. "The recruits are lonely, hungry, and frightened in their barracks. Gangs of soldiers, many of them ex-criminals, run everything. It's an atmosphere that stimulates violence and irresponsibility. It's like a prison really, being in the army, except that in prison people are being punished for their crimes. These young recruits have committed no crime. Also, in prison, the food is generally better."

Why don't they complain? "Well, some of them do," she told me. "They come here. But most are afraid. If their commander or the soldiers who are doing the beatings find out, it'll just be worse for them. Their mail is censored. They have no way of defending themselves. And their commanders, who could stop this but don't because it helps them control their soldiers, go unpunished. Nobody is responsible for anything in the military anymore, especially for human rights."

The committee and its allies among liberal social reformers are demanding a general amnesty for deserters, and that President Yeltsin keep his promises to end the draft and start a professional all-volunteer army. But volunteer armies cost money, and the Communist-dominated lower house of the Russian parliament is cool to the whole idea of ending the draft. The Russian Defense Ministry says it's looking into the hazing practices of some military units, but you don't get the sense that the ministry really has its heart in it.

And so the casualties in Russia's peacetime army mount. Three thousand Russian soldiers die every year of one cause or another. The Soldiers' Mothers Committee estimates that a majority of them are victims of the beatings they get in basic training, or simply commit suicide to end their suffering. Often enough, a "suicide" is the official explanation for some young recruit who took one punch too many.

I met the father of one of those victims this week in the committee's offices. Valery Lavrov is a metalworker in a Moscow suburb. Lavrov is a quiet, dignified man with close-cropped gray hair, and eyes brimming with suffering—and rage.

He carries a picture of his only son, Kostya, who was drafted into the army late last year: a good-looking boy with his father's strong chin, posing proudly in his uniform.

"He didn't try to dodge the draft," says the father. Kostya thought the army was necessary. His grandfather was a military man. We still have his army belt and things, you know, from the Great Patriotic War. I don't like to look at them now because it's impossible to compare this army with the army that was back then. It's no longer an army now.

"Kostya liked the army at first. He said so in his letters. But then the letters stopped coming. You can't say anything bad in the letters because the censors will take it out. We didn't see him in person until the day after he took his oath of service. He was very troubled. We asked him what was wrong, and he just said that the lower part of his stomach was hurting. But when I asked if he had been beaten, he wouldn't say. I asked again and again and he cried, but this child of mine would never tell. He was honest, and if everyone else was going to endure, he would endure. He didn't want to go back to his unit, but I said, finally, 'Kostya, it's time to go.'"

It was the last time the Lavrovs saw their son alive. In February, he was transferred to a different unit, which, they learned later, had a history of particularly vicious hazing practices, and it wasn't long before they got a phone call.

"I went to a sauna that day," says the father. "I just got back and a neighbor phoned and said there was a call from the regional military commission. We called back and the brigade commander told us, 'Your son has hung himself.' "

A few days later, the Lavrovs received a letter from Kostya, written just before he died and smuggled out of the barracks. It said that in this new unit they'd beat him badly, smashed his head against a nightstand, and smothered him. It went on for three hours. At the bottom of the letter was a big "SOS."

"We went to his unit, but the commander wouldn't tell us anything. All of the enlisted men were afraid to talk. Then, before the funeral, Kostya's grandmother started to wipe his body with holy water, and we noticed the wounds on his body. We looked at his legs. They were covered with bruises from the beatings. His knees were all torn up. They'd made him crawl. And there was blood coming from a wound in the back of his head. My son didn't commit suicide. My son was murdered."

Valery Lavrov doesn't have much money, but he's spending what he's got to file a complaint with the military authorities and demand an investigation. Valery Lavrov is determined to find out what really happened to his son. He's prepared to make trouble, and damn the consequences.

There may be some consequences. "A week ago," he says, "I was going to work and waiting for the streetcar. A big guy in a black jean jacket and tattoos up to his elbows sidled up to me on the platform. I could tell he was a criminal. He told me if I don't calm down and stop all this, I will go where my son went. Then he turned around and left. So that's when I sent Kostya's mother off to stay with relatives. Me? They can scare me, but they won't stop me."

Just outside the Kremlin wall is one of Russia's most sacred places. It's the Tomb of the Unknown Soldier, with an eternal flame and guarded by two handsome sentries in splendid uniforms. It's where brides and bridegrooms go these days to have their pictures taken after the wedding. It is, of course, a memorial to the millions of brave Russian soldiers who died defending their country in World War II.

There will be no such memorial for Kostya Lavrov, aged eighteen, or the thousands of other Russian military recruits who are dying at the hands of their fellow soldiers, brutally, needlessly, senselessly, every day.

chapter 37

Cops
(July 1998)

Stanley Williams is a pleasant, thoughtful fellow with a quick smile and a ready laugh, even today. He looks a lot younger than his thirty-seven years, although considering what he's been through, perhaps he's done his aging inside.

Williams is black, and he grew up in a rough neighborhood on Newark, New Jersey's south side.

"I always had a good feeling about cops," he told me. In Newark, most of them are black, like me. And you figure they're there to protect you. There are places in Newark where you need some protection."

He didn't reckon on the cops in Moscow. Williams moved here a couple of years ago and wound up as a disc jockey at a Moscow club named The Hungry Duck. It's a raunchy sort of place, featuring male strippers and bar fights. "But I wanted to make a career of music," he says, "so I thought, what the heck? Moscow? Sure."

He hadn't been in Moscow long the night he walked out of the Club Relax, where they were setting up an African students' night. Williams was hoping to get a DJ gig there. A couple of policemen stopped him on the street.

"I didn't speak much Russian," he explains. "But I made out that they wanted to check my ID. So I showed them my American passport, which contained my local address. The next thing I knew, they'd handcuffed me, thrown a hood over my head, and bundled me into a car. We drove and drove and when we stopped they took off my hood and I realized we were at my apartment."

By this time there were about a dozen cops at the scene. They'd brought a battering ram to knock down his door. Williams produced his keys instead and they all went inside.

Williams remembers, "I wanted to ask them, where was their search warrant? But I didn't know how to say that in Russian, and besides, I figured that wasn't a question they wanted to hear at the moment."

The police spent an hour searching and trashing his apartment and produced a small sack of marijuana. Williams insists it wasn't his, but he's not accusing the cops of planting it, either. "I'd had some parties at my place, and we'd smoked some marijuana, and maybe somebody left it there. At that point, it really didn't matter."

Stanley Williams went off to a jail in a police precinct far across the city. For nine days he slept on a wooden board in his cell, breakfasted on a cup a tea, had a bowl of soup for lunch, and two slices of black bread for dinner. He didn't get to make a phone call, he didn't get a lawyer, he didn't get his rights read to him, and he never was told what the charges were.

Eventually he smuggled a note out with a prisoner who was being released, somebody contacted the American embassy, and an embassy official came to see him. He wasn't much help. The official told Williams he'd been charged with possession of marijuana and under Russian law he could be kept up to thirty days, while authorities investigated, before he was either released or transferred.

Stanley Williams probably never saw a public opinion poll of some residents of Moscow, the subject of which was cops and crime. Forty-three percent of those asked said they'd never open the door to the police under any circumstances. Thirty-seven percent said they were just as scared of the police as the criminals.

He didn't know that in Russia the cops don't need a search warrant to break down somebody's door if they suspect funny business. All they need is to round up a couple of neighbors as witnesses.

And of course Williams had never seen the annual reports from Amnesty International, which regularly denounces Russian law-enforcement practices for systematic violations of civil liberties. Last year, Amnesty found that "Under the guise of fighting crime, the Russian Federation has expanded the powers of security and law-enforcement agencies to the detriment of constitutional rights, and members of ethnic minorities are particularly vulnerable" (Amnesty International report, *Torture in Russia*, April 3, 1997).

What Williams was quickly discovering is that Russia isn't Newark. There are almost three hundred thousand suspects now awaiting trial in Russia's jails and prisons. The average stay is

Before the storm: Police await crowd-control duty.
(© 1996 Jonathan Sanders)

upward of a year. A good portion of the inmates have no idea what crime they've committed, and aren't told. Habeas corpus is a joke.

Bail is legal, theoretically, but it's really only available to the 1 percent of defendants, usually mobsters, who can afford to bribe a judge. It's legal to hold a suspect up to three days for no reason at all. You're not allowed a phone call from jail if the cops think the call could "interfere" with their case. Ergo, no phone calls.

As Stanley Williams remembers, "I didn't get a lawyer, I didn't get a translator. I was just put in a bucket with no hope of climbing out."

At least not anytime soon. Russia's criminal court system is a mess. Prosecutors must finish their investigation within two years, but there's nothing that says a trial judge can't keep the prisoner indefinitely. And that's usually what happens. Russian law is modeled on the European system, which puts the burden on the judge, not a jury, to find a defendant guilty or innocent. It's up to the judge to get additional information, obtain testimony, and clean up after sloppy police work. No judge has time for all that. No wonder there are a 1.6 million people now behind bars in Russia, and that's more than a decade after they closed down the Communist gulags.

It's true that for the first time since the Communist revolution, jury trials are now in operation in a small percentage of Russia's regions. But because of the national case overload, less than 1 percent of criminal cases ever end in an acquittal.

If the judges are too often something less than Solomonic, the cops are something right out of purgatory. A policeman earns on the order of $100 a month. So the good ones have quit to join private security firms or the private armies of the tycoons and mafia dons, where the pay and benefits are significantly better.

The main thing for most cops is to get a confession right away, clean up the books, and look good to the boss. The easiest way to do that is to torture a confession out of the suspect.

Stanley Williams says he went through some of that in his first few days behind bars. "They roughed me up some, tried some judo holds on my neck, that sort of thing. But I wouldn't confess to anything. After a while they quit. Maybe they didn't want to really get rough with an American citizen, I don't know."

Williams was actually very lucky. "Once you're in the hands of the police, they can do with you whatever they want," says Diederik Lohman, who runs the Moscow office for Human Rights Watch/Helsinki.

"Police will torture you in ways that don't leave a mark. People will be beaten on their vital organs. Or police will put books on someone's head and strike the books, so there's no marks, but you'll have a ferocious headache. Or they'll cover someone's head with a plastic bag or an old-fashioned gas mask. This method is called the 'elephant.' It cuts off the oxygen supply so that gradually the suspect loses consciousness. This is repeated until the person confesses. Then there's always electric shock. It's incredible, but people are even tortured for little crimes, like stealing a jacket. Women and children are tortured. It happens very often. I know a Moscow judge, one of the very few progressives, who sits on a city criminal court. He says that four out of five defendants who appear before him say they have been tortured in some way."

The Russian government is not unaware of this hangover from the days of the Communist terror. Over the years, Russia has signed all sorts of international conventions against the use of torture, most recently the one framed by the Council of Europe, which permits the council to make surprise visits to Russia to check up on the practice. And last year, a presidential commission here uncovered what it said was widespread evidence of torture and forced confessions. The commission recommended changes in the law to the Russian parliament, but nothing's happened. In fact, the current Russian constitution doesn't even mention the word "torture." The new Interior Minister, Sergei Stepashin, remarked not long ago that he approved of "so-called human rights violations" if the suspect in question was a "criminal." This is not a hopeful sign for future reform.

All of this might be explained, but certainly not justified, if Russia's cops were doing what they're supposed to do: stopping crime. But they're making a mess of that, too. Even the new prime minister, Sergei Kiriyenko, felt obliged to call the cops on the carpet last spring, accusing them of telling "shameless lies" to cover up their ineptitude, or worse. "Law enforcement has failed to change the crime rate in this country," said Kiriyenko (quoted by Interfax).

No kidding. According to Itar-Tass, the number of recorded crimes in Russia rose 6 percent to about 620,000 in just the first three months of this year. Mr. Kiriyenko did not indicate what he planned to do about all this. Higher police salaries, maybe, to attract better cops? No, he said, salaries can't be raised until the government gets more money from the taxpayers.

Meanwhile, here is the sort of thing the police are doing: This month, Moscow is host to something called the World Youth Games, an event which Mayor Yuri Luzhkov is planning to use as a launch vehicle to make Moscow the site of the Olympic Games in 2012. So the Moscow police are making sure there won't be any noticeable "undesirables" in town when the young athletes from all over the world show up. "Undesirables" like the thousands of homeless here. A couple of weeks ago, the cops summarily closed down two charity programs that provide food and medical care for these street people.

And the police are enforcing a city ordinance that allows them to pick up anybody without proper documents, including an internal passport, a hangover from Soviet days, giving people permission to be in Moscow. The miscreants are then bought one-way train tickets out of town and told not to come back. An estimated seven thousand undocumented persons have already been shown the gate in that fashion just this year, and thousands more will likely follow them in the coming days. Russia's Constitutional Court has ruled that ejecting people this way is unconstitutional, but Mayor Luzhkov insists that the court's ruling "doesn't apply" to Moscow.

Mayor Luzhkov is a prime contender to succeed Boris Yeltsin as president of the Russian Federation the year after next. If he does, where's he going to send all the millions of homeless in the rest of Russia, when he occasionally wants to gussy up the place for foreigners. Mongolia?

Stanley Williams wasn't homeless, of course. He was just in the wrong place at the wrong time that night. And he was the wrong color. As a result, he spent twenty-two months in a succession of Russian prisons. Eventually, his health began to fail. And that worried the U.S. embassy, which began to pressure the Russians for his release. Eventually, he got to trial. The judge acquitted him, and last winter, he was finally set free. Stanley Williams was one of the miniscule percentage of defendants who took on Russia's criminal justice system and won. Williams was fortunate. He's an American, and he had the support of the U.S. embassy.

On the other hand, Stanley Williams is black. Almost certainly, if he'd been white, he'd never have been picked up by the Moscow police that night. Blacks and Asians in this country are all fair game for the cops. You can see the police hassling the Kazakhs and Azeris and the Chechens every day in the Metro stations. If you get up early enough and pick the right street market, you can watch the cops working out their truncheons on the heads of Uzbek street sellers, who haven't paid off the right guy for permission to put up a stall. Anybody whose skin is a little darker, whose eyes are not so round, who doesn't, in short, resemble an ethnic Russian, is a "blackass" to the cop on the beat.

You'd have thought Stanley Williams would have been on the next plane to Newark when they let him out of prison, but he's still here. He's still working nights at the Hungry Duck and teaching music. "I didn't want them to scare me off," he says. "I want to take something back from this experience. I want to find out that there's another Russia, not the one I've seen for the last two years. And, heck, it wasn't a total waste. I can speak Russian now."

Stanley Williams is a braver man than I'll ever be. If I were a black man, or brown, or Asian, I wouldn't live in this country. Not for a minute.

chapter 38

The
Romanovs'
Last Rites
(July 1998)

It took eighty years to the day, but the Romanov dynasty, which ruled Russia for 304 years, has now been properly put to rest.

The remains of the last of the Romanovs, Tsar Nicholas II; his wife, the Empress Alexandra; three of their children; and four of their servants are now interred in a vault in a side chapel of the Cathedral of St. Peter and St. Paul in St. Petersburg, with the other Romanov tsars.

You've got to give the Russians credit, they certainly know how to put on a memorial service. The ceremonies were beautiful and quite touching, but also a little weird, reflecting the confusion with which Russia today regards its history.

For example: St. Petersburg, the old tsarist capital founded by Peter the Great, changed its name to Petersburg early in this century. But then, when the Russians went to war with Germany in 1914, the Russians decided that "Petersburg" sounded too Germanic, so they changed it again to Petrograd, and that lasted until the 1917 revolution. The Bolsheviks changed it to Leningrad after Lenin's death in 1922, and now in post–Communist Russia, it's St. Petersburg again.

For example: The Cathedral of St. Peter and St. Paul, on an island in the River Neva, was the place the Bolsheviks used to launch their final attack on the Winter Palace in 1917, the start of the Russian Revolution and a chain of events that led to the abdication of the tsar. As a result, he got only a nineteen-gun salute at this ceremony, not

233

Honor guards stand near coffins containing the remains of the last Russian Czar Nicholas II, his wife, Alexandra, three of their five children, the family doctor, and three servants in the St. Peter and Paul Cathedral of the St. Peter and Paul Fortress in St. Petersburg, Thursday, July 16, 1998. The two coffins draped in the royal flag are of Nicholas II and his wife, Alexandra. (AP Photo/Dmitry Lovetsky)

the traditional twenty-one guns. Even so, the noise set off car alarms all over St. Petersburg.

For example: They were going to play the tune "God Save the Tsar" at the service, but they cancelled that because it used to be the tsarist national anthem. Instead, as the coffins were carried into the cathedral, the funeral lament was played by a pipe major of the Royal Scots Dragoon Guards, of all things. They also killed plans to have a corps of Russian cadets lower their regimental flags as the tsar's remains passed by. As it happens, Russia's regimental flags still have a portrait of Lenin on them. So they made do with the new Russian national flag, which has no portraits of anybody.

There was a gaggle of protestors among the five hundred onlookers outside the cathedral, complaining of the expense involved in putting the Romanovs to rest when millions of Russian workers were going unpaid. In fact, though, this was a bare-bones memorial, for which the government had budgeted only $830,000 including coffins, flowers, musicians, transportation, and cathedral paint-up-fix-up.

The ceremonies were carried nationwide on Russian TV, and one of the channels even draped its news announcers in black and accompanied its newscasts with pictures of the tsar's family. For those who had a chance to watch, it was certainly a TV moment. Church bells tolled; the deep bass voices of the twelve officiating clergy, dressed in gold and white robes, reverberated about the cathedral, mixed with the voices of the choir. And you could almost smell the clouds of incense.

But the fact is, most Russians didn't watch. They didn't have time. Today was not a holiday, just business as usual. And beyond a certain curiosity, most Russians probably didn't think much about the goings on at St. Petersburg.

The cathedral, though, was fully packed with, among others, fifty-two members of the Romanov family, descendants of the tsars. They included Prince Rostislav, a Yale graduate and now a banker in London. And Paul Ilyinsky, the mayor of Palm Beach, Florida. Not to mention Britain's Prince Michael, a grandson of King George V and therefore a first cousin of the tsar's, who is a fluent Russian-speaker and has business interests in Moscow. (It was King George's refusal to provide sanctuary in Britain for the tsar and his family after the revolution that sealed the tsar's fate.) The audience also included various other luminaries in today's Russia, and representatives from 120 different countries (although nobody of high official rank, since this was not regarded as a state occasion). And there were some others, including Alexander Lebed, the former general who's now a regional governor in Siberia and potential presidential candidate. He signed some autographs but was relegated to the back pews.

There were also some no-shows, including another presidential pretender, Moscow mayor Yuri Luzhkov. He lobbied to have the tsar's remains interred in Moscow. When that didn't happen, Luzhkov organized his own service, at a monastery outside Moscow, in which the patriarch of the Russian Orthodox Church, Alexei II, officiated.

Patriarch Alexei boycotted the St. Petersburg affair on the grounds that he's not certain that the remains in question are really those of the Romanovs and their retainers. But as usual with affairs in Russia, there's more here than meets the eye.

The tsar and his family were detained in Yekaterinburg by the Bolsheviks after the revolution. In the summer of 1918, under orders from Lenin himself and with the royalist White Russian troops at the gates of Yekaterinburg, the tsar's captors lined the family up as if to take a photo, then shot and bayoneted all of them. Afterward, they butchered the bodies and attempted to burn them, and buried the remains in a rude grave.

The grave was uncovered in 1991, and seven years of DNA and other analysis has established to virtually everyone's satisfaction that the remains interred today are in fact genuine. The remains of the tsar's son, Alexei, and another daughter, Marie, have never been found.

The trouble is, there are some other Romanov remains at issue. It happens that two days after the tsar's murder, royalist troops were said to have discovered the grave, and an investigator dug up forty-eight bone and flesh fragments from the remains which are now encased in a leather jewelry box sealed in a wall at St. Job's Russian Church in Brussels, Belgium. The church belongs to the Russian Church Abroad, a rival Orthodox group of Russian exiles, who held their own funeral for the tsar at St. Job's in 1968, and later canonized him. The Russian Church Abroad regards Patriarch Alexei and his fellow clergy in Russia as old Soviet KGB appointees who are simply leftovers from Communist days, which in fact they are. Alexei hopes eventually to effect a reconciliation, and apparently felt that lending his presence to the doings at St. Petersburg would have made that more difficult.

Out of respect for the patriarch's position, President Yeltsin would have been a no-show as well. But his political instincts got the better of him, and a day before the service, he decided to go to St. Petersburg after all.

So it was that ex-Communist Boris Yeltsin and his wife, Naina, both dressed in mourners' black, were at the center of the services, holding memorial candles and bowing in respect before the flag-draped coffins. Yeltsin looked tired, but he proved he can still hit the curveball. His eulogy, covered by CBS news, was eloquent and moving, and brought many in the audience to tears. Judge for yourself:

"We have long been silent about this monstrous crime," Yeltsin said. "We must say the truth. The Yekaterinburg massacre has become one of the most shameful pages of our history. By burying the remains of innocent victims, we want to expiate the sins of our ancestors. Guilty are those who committed this heinous crime and those who have been justifying it for decades, all of us. The burial of the victims' remains is an act of human justice and expiation of common guilt. I bow my head before the victims of this merciless slaying. While building a new Russia we must rely on its historical experience. Many glorious pages of our history are linked with the Romanovs. But also connected with their name is one of the most bitter lessons: the attempts to change life by violence are doomed.

Let us remember those innocent victims who have fallen to hatred and violence. May they rest in peace."

Yeltsin tactfully left out any mention of his own part in the Romanov story; as Communist boss in Yekaterinburg a few years ago, he carried out party orders to destroy the house where the tsar and his family were murdered, to prevent it from becoming a monarchist shrine.

And of course there's some question whether the tsar will be regarded by historians as all that "innocent." About the best you can say of Nicholas was that he was a good family man. He was also an ineffectual leader, an incompetent military commander, a virulent anti-Semite, and a disastrous statesman who unnecessarily involved his countrymen in wars with Japan and Germany. Those conflicts ultimately led to the Russian Revolution, and seventy years of calamity far worse than anything the Romanovs had ever inflicted on Russia.

The day of his coronation, one thousand onlookers in the crowd were trampled to death in the confusion, but Nicholas was nonetheless the life of the party at the coronation ball that night. The depth of the tsar's detachment is evident in his diary entry upon hearing the news of the Russian navy's catastrophic defeat by the Japanese at Tsushima in 1905: "Took a walk in the park. Killed a crow." Most certainly Nicholas would have done to Lenin, Trotsky, and other revolutionaries what Lenin did to the tsar and his family, had Nicholas been in a position to do so.

Which may explain why, as one journalist noted of the ceremony, "They came to bury Russia's last tsar, not to praise him." In fact, Nicholas's name was never mentioned during the proceedings. Instead, the officiating priest, Father Boris Glebov, prayed only for those "Whose names are known only to God, and for all those tortured and killed in the years of bitter persecution for the faith of Christ."

As for Yeltsin, his remarks at St. Petersburg were an attempt to put the Russian nation on the couch, so to speak, and to knit the past and the present and the future together. "On the eve of the third millennium," he said, "we must do it for the sake of our generation and those to come." For my money, it was Boris Yeltsin's best public performance since the day he stood on that tank in Moscow in 1991 and defended his countrymen against a military coup.

It makes you wonder what Russian history would have been like if somebody like Boris Yeltsin had been that last Romanov.

chapter 39

Crash

(September 1998)

Maybe the Rolling Stones had something to do
with it. For thirty-one years, Mick Jagger and his fellow Stones
had been trying to play Moscow, about the only world capital they
hadn't visited.

They'd first tried in 1967, but the then-Soviet leadership concluded they were too decadent. Nonetheless, the young Russian proletariat, who wanted nothing more than a chance to be a little decadent, bought the Stones' records and worshiped their music.

Now, the Rolling Stones, well into middle age, were in Moscow at
last, at the city's biggest sports stadium, for a one-nighter. They
played to seventy thousand Russian Stoneheads who'd come from as
far away as Siberia to see the strobes and lasers and the Jagger strut,
and to listen to the Stones' golden oldies, beginning, of course, with
"Satisfaction."

It didn't matter that there was a cold rain, or that the Stones were
getting a little long in the tooth (back in Britain, the kids had cruelly
nicknamed them "The Strolling Oldies"). They could have danced
and sung all night.

That was August 11. True, most of the Stones' fans at the stadium
that evening didn't have stock portfolios, so they probably didn't
know or care that the Russian stock market had fallen almost 10 percent that day, and that this was probably the last carefree evening
they'd spend for a long, long time.

Two days later, Russian stocks fell another 15 percent. Black

Thursday they called it. The Russian exchange index in October of 1997 was 571. Now, it was flirting with 100 and still dropping, a loss of nearly 80 percent of share value. That wasn't supposed to happen.

This was, after all, one of the first years since Russia went capitalist in 1991 that the economy was actually growing, an anemic rise to be sure, but growing instead of shrinking. The International Monetary Fund, after much grumbling, had just granted Russia yet another loan package, this one more than $22 billion, and even agreed to release the first $5 billion of it to help shore up the value of the ruble.

There was more new construction in downtown Moscow this summer than in downtown Tokyo. Traffic on the boulevards was thicker than ever, and a whole new class of young Russian capitalists or capitalist wanna-bes crowded the tree-shaded patios of the new cafés and restaurants, nibbling on Norwegian salmon washed down with Irish ale.

But the foreign investors who'd financed the Russian debt all those years, knew otherwise. So did the currency speculators who bet on whether the ruble was going up or down. They'd watched last year, when Asian investors pulled their money out of Russia to prop up their own sagging finances back home. They'd watched this year when world prices for crude oil, Russia's only truly lucrative export and main source of foreign exchange, fell by half, costing Russia more than $10 billion. And they knew that even with the IMF loan, the Russian government still had no way of paying $20 billion in back wages to its people, or its other domestic debts.

Finally, the currency speculators knew there was no hope. In late July, the Communist majority in the Duma had effectively gutted the government's economic reform program, which the IMF had prescribed as a condition for its new loan. The financier George Soros, even helped trigger Black Thursday by rendering a public judgment that "The meltdown in Russian financial markets has reached a terminal phase."

Soros urged a quick devaluation of the ruble, which for the past couple of years has stayed remarkably stable, at about six to the dollar. Soros said it ought to be eight to the dollar, or more, or there would be a fiscal catastrophe.

The next day, Friday, President Yeltsin made two things very clear. There would be no devaluation of the ruble, and he didn't consider the stock market goings-on important enough to interrupt his vacation.

Maybe that was okay for him. But the lights burned late all that weekend in the Kremlin and the Russian White House. At issue were three big words: *Gosudarstvennie Kratkosrochnie Obligatsii*—GKOs for short. They're short-term treasury bills which, since 1993 and with the advice and consent of Western economic advisors, the Russian government has been selling to finance its debts. The Western economists figured that was better than simply printing more money and retriggering the hyperinflation of the early nineties.

The trouble was, GKOs became a bad habit for the Russian government. Instead of making the tough economic-reform decisions and raising taxes (or even trying harder to collect them), the Kremlin just kept selling more GKOs, tens of billions of dollars worth of new debt. But foreign investors, who became more and more nervous as Russia's finances got shakier and shakier, kept demanding higher returns. Eventually, this summer the Russian treasury was paying 170 percent interest on its GKOs. That meant the government had to keep borrowing more and more to pay that huge amount of interest. For Russia, the GKOs became the monetary equivalent of crack cocaine.

That made the currency speculators nervous, and they started selling off rubles to buy dollars and other stable currencies. And the Russian treasury had to step in with its dwindling supply of reserves to buy back rubles to keep the currency price stable.

So all that long weekend, Russia's economic reformers, the older ones—Yegor Gaidar and Anatoly Chubais—and the younger ones—Prime Minister Sergei Kiriyenko and his aides—were closeted with Russia's business barons and the IMF representatives, grasping for a way to prevent an economic crash and the consequent destruction of eight years of work on the edifice of Russian capitalism, rickety as it was. They failed.

On Monday morning, August 17, the Kremlin announced it was defaulting on $40 billion in GKOs *and*, Boris Yeltsin's assurances notwithstanding, devaluing the ruble from six-to-the-dollar to nine-and-a-half. In a twinkling, the Kremlin had stiffed investors, most of them from overseas, on billions of dollars' worth of Russia bonds, and robbed the ruble of a third of its value. Screw the foreigners and screw your own citizens, too. Quite a day's work.

The world has seen its share of international deadbeats in the last couple of decades—Mexico, Venezuela, and others who have flirted with bankruptcy—but nothing like this. No nation had dared to repudiate its foreign debt *and* devalue its currency simultaneously since, well, since the Russians did it in 1917, when the Communists first came to power. The Bolsheviks defaulted on millions of gold rubles that had been sold by the tsarist government to finance its part in World War I. Russia still hasn't paid off the $400 million it owes its creditors for that.

So, that was Monday. By Tuesday, a lot of Russia's fifteen hundred private banks were on the verge of going bankrupt, just like the government. Most Russian banks really aren't "banks" the way we Americans think of them. They don't loan you money so you can start a business or buy a house. The Russians call them "pocket banks," a wry reference to the fact that they're owned by the big-business barons who use them to launder their "pocket" money and get it out of the country. In addition, a lot of the banks found it much more profitable to speculate in the ruble or buy those high-interest GKOs. When the ruble tanked and the GKOs became wastepaper, the banks got in trouble, too.

So to prevent a wholesale collapse of the banking system, the government simply slapped a two-month freeze on withdrawals from the biggest private banks. What that meant, as a practical matter, was that if you had your savings in a private Russian bank you could kiss those rubles good-bye. Fortunately, most Russians who have a savings account have it in the state savings bank, Sberbank. With luck, they might see some of their savings, someday.

But most Russians don't have their money in a bank, and with good reason. What rubles they have saved for a rainy day they keep under their mattresses or in the root cellar. The value of this kind of home savings has been estimated at upward of $75 billion.

So the Russians who have some money in the banks either lost it, or can't get at it, while the value of the ruble steadily slips. And the Russians who have their savings stashed at home have found their nest egg is suddenly halfway to worthless. The only Russians who don't have to worry about any of the above are those who are flat broke, and there are not a few of them, either.

In the days following that enforced bank "holiday," the streets of Moscow and every other Russian city were dotted with pitiful little clutches of people outside the shuttered doors of the banks, vainly hoping for some sort of word on what happened to their rubles. They didn't seem angry, these people. They seemed almost resigned, as if they expected something like this to happen. And of course it has.

In 1947, Stalin proclaimed a currency "reform" that robbed millions of Russians who were just starting to recover from the war years. What little money they had left was effectively confiscated in a "voluntary" campaign to buy government bonds. There was another currency reform in the Krushchev years which prompted such serious inflation that there were price riots in some of the provincial cities. Even after Communism crumbled, currency changes in 1992 and 1993 fueled a price rise of more than 250 percent and prompted a couple of currency panics. No wonder most

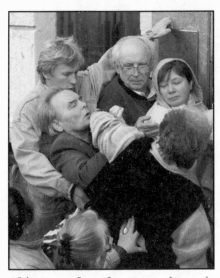

Clients of a downtown branch of the SBS-Agro, a leading Russian commercial bank, jostle as they enter the bank hoping to withdraw their deposits in Moscow in early August 27, 1998. Many Russian banks found themselves on the verge of collapse following the ruble's devaluation and had suspended withdrawals. (AP Photo/Misha Japardize)

Russians keep their rubles where they can see them.

Now, with the ruble dropping from nine-to-a-dollar, to fifteen-to-a-dollar, and even lower as the days went by, people were fishing out their rubles and spending them while they were still worth something, a natural consumers' response to instant inflation. This was most evident in Moscow, which has been the principal beneficiary and showpiece of this brief economic bubble.

The electronic stores on the Moscow Garden Ring were almost as crowded with people as the beleaguered banks. Shoppers, like Igor, who'd been waiting in line for an hour, were buying tangibles, something to hang on to no matter what happened to the ruble. "My TV set's getting old anyway," said Igor, "and next year foreign-made TVs will probably cost so many rubles I won't be able to afford one. So I bought two, just in case."

Igor was lucky. A few days later, there weren't any foreign-made TVs left for sale in Moscow, and not much of anything else either. Moscow depends on imports from hard-currency Western countries for about a third of its foodstuffs and about three-fourths of everything else, including clothing, appliances, and medicines.

With the collapse of Communism, Russians and the citizens of the old Soviet republics and Warsaw Pact nations didn't have to buy Russian products anymore, which are regarded as *barakhlo*, or junk, by consumers here. So those Russians who could afford it started buying virtually everything from abroad, from autos to stereo sets to clothing and even foodstuffs. Russian collective farms slaughtered most of their cattle and poultry and started importing tens of billions of dollars every year in vegetable oil, sugar, meat, and dairy products from places like Germany, Sweden, and even the United States.

The freezers in Moscow supermarkets were customarily filled with hundreds of pounds of Tyson's chicken parts. The Russians call them "Bush's legs" because it was President George Bush who helped broker the trade deal that brought the Tyson's legs, thighs, breasts, etc. to Moscow. Had Russians known that the Tyson people, who are among the biggest movers and shakers in Arkansas, helped finance Bill Clinton's campaign for the White House, perhaps they'd have called them "Clinton's legs."

The result of the Kremlin's simultaneous default and devaluation prompted most foreign exporters to simply stop shipping anything to Russia until they could be sure they'd get paid in hard currency. Russian banks couldn't help because they were barely staying afloat. In a few days, Russian food imports had fallen by 80 percent. And prices for imported food had risen 500 percent. The familiar little neighborhood kiosks on Moscow streets were suddenly shuttered. The proprietors couldn't get Danish ham or Dutch cheese. In the days that followed, fully one-third of Russia's small businesses shut down or went bankrupt.

The markets and shops in Moscow began to take on the gray, decrepit look I remembered from the Soviet days. The touts on the Old Arbat who'd always change your rubles for dollars or deutsche marks were gone, replaced by "No hard currency for sale" signs.

The supermarket shelves gradually emptied of most everything except those few items still made in Russia: sausage, candy, salt, flour, bread, cigarettes, and of course, vodka. Oh, and caviar. In one market we actually found that a small tin of Russian caviar was cheaper than a jumbo-sized package of toilet paper! And the prices! Within days of the devaluation, the Russian minimum wage, the equivalent of four dollars a month, would buy just two tins of meat preserves, a single loaf of bread, and a quart of cooking oil. That wasn't news to Maria O., the pensioner we encountered in the supermarket with the overpriced toilet paper. Her pension wasn't anywhere near four dollars a month, and in any event she hadn't been paid since the spring. "My granddaughters are begging for milk, and I can't afford it," she said. "Even a little. This is all the politicians' fault. They should be chucked out."

In no time at all, Maria and tens of millions of her fellow Russians had become crash victims. Yet, as they always seem to do in times of crisis, they muttered, raged, and then stolidly persevered. For example, no fiscal catastrophe was going to interfere with the most important Russian ritual of the late summer: the first day of school.

The previous day, we found Natalia Levochkina, and her daughter, Yulia, and son, Kolia, fighting the crowds in the aisles of

Moscow's *Detsky Mir*, or Children's World. Natalia is an electronics engineer who had to quit when her firm couldn't afford to meet its payroll. Now she's barely earning a living as a social worker. But she and her husband weren't going to scrimp when it came to dressing up the kids for school.

"We've spent about a thousand rubles each for Yulia and Kolia," she said. "That's about a hundred dollars for blue jeans, a pair of shirts, a warm jacket, and school supplies. It has cost the two of us our monthly salaries."

Kolia was especially excited. "It's the most important day of the year. You'll see. All us kids get dressed up. The boys will wear suits, and the girls will have ribbons in their hair."

The flowers were the last thing on Natalia's list. "You have to have flowers. Every child brings flowers to the teacher. It's the custom. Ten dollars for two small bunches of French carnations. They're the most expensive part," Natalia explained. "You can't buy carnations in advance."

When Yulia and Kolia went to school the next day, we tagged along. Kolia had on a new suit and Yulia had a new dress and a pink flower in her hair. And carnations for her teacher. There were thirty-five kids in her class and each and every one of them brought flowers. You wondered what the teacher, who hadn't been paid in months, was going to do with all those fresh flowers.

The last we saw of Yulia Levochkina, she was just starting third grade. The Russian economy is currently in critical condition, but it was a pleasure to report at least that on the first day of classes at Moscow Primary School Number 554, everything was, as the Russians say, "Normalna." Everything's okay.

Everything was not okay this month, however, in the capitalist boardrooms around the world. A great deal of overseas money had bought into the Russian boom of the past year, and had in fact mostly financed it. Now, in New York and Frankfurt and Tokyo, the bills were coming due. And they added up to at least $100 billion. That's the amount that Western banks and other lenders and investors are estimated to have lost in Russia's virtual bankruptcy. George Soros's Quantum Fund lost $2 billion all by itself. Credit Suisse First Boston was out a quarter-billion. And so on. A lot of these clever lenders turned out to be pretty dumb after all.

Meantime, Russia's business barons were, as usual, looking out for number one. The Russian Central Bank claimed it used the first $5 billion tranche of that IMF loan, in July, in a failed attempt to shore up the hard-pressed ruble. But at least half a billion dollars in rubles were released to those beleaguered pocket banks, who were supposed to use the money to pay creditors and frantic depositors. Instead, the banks cynically dumped their rubles for dollars on the foreign-exchange markets, pocketing a handsome profit. The creditors and depositors got nothing. And by month's end, Interfax reported that the Russian government's chief auditor discovered that at least a billion dollars of that IMF emergency loan had been "diverted, misused, or simply stolen."

By the time of the August Crash, the September 23, 1998 *Wall Street Journal* reported, the IMF had, since 1991, poured a total of $31 billion's worth of economic aid into Russia, with virtually nothing to show for it except the contempt of the recipients. Soon after the crash, Russia's economic Mr. Fixit, Anatoly Chubais, conceded in an interview with the *Kommersant Daily* that Russia had "tricked" foreign lenders into granting that $22 billion bailout this summer. Chubais, who had been instrumental in arranging the financial deal, used the Russian slang word *kinuli*, which means "cheated" or "conned," and he claimed later that he didn't mean it to sound dishonest. But he also said that if Russia had been truthful with the West about its financial condition, the economy would have collapsed months ago, and the West "would have stopped dealing with us forever."

Which, by month's end, seemed like a pretty good bet. Russia had defaulted, devalued, and accumulated an estimated $158 billion of debt, with no prospect of ever repaying it. Tsar Boris has spent the past eight years importing Western capitalism, the way another tsar, Peter the Great, had imported a Western military machine centuries before. The difference is, Tsar Boris now has not much to show for it except Moscow's rapidly fading glitzy facade.

One of Tsar Boris's economic aides, when asked recently how Russia hopes to pay off its debts, cheerfully replied, "Emissions, of course, emissions!" "Emissions" is the word the Kremlin uses for printing money.

chapter 40

Politics
Unusual
(September 1998)

There's something to be said for a parliamentary system of government, even one as ramshackle as Russia's.

When the stocks crashed on Wall Street in 1929 and America spiraled into deep depression, you'll recall, President Herbert Hoover had barely moved into the White House. So for the better part of four years, the Hoover administration fumbled and bumbled as the economy crumbled. It wasn't until early 1933 that a new government under Franklin Roosevelt, armed with a powerful new voter mandate, could begin to sort things out.

American governments are slaves to the calendar. Americans elect their officeholders for specific terms, irrespective of what sort of job they're doing or changing circumstances. Parliamentary governments, however, are predicated upon confidence. If enough voters lose confidence in the people they elect, they get to schedule a new election right then and there, so they can throw the bums out, if they choose, and elect some replacements.

So it didn't take long for Russia's economic catastrophe of August 17 to cause some serious political alterations. If President Yeltsin had been reading the political polls that week, he'd have learned that his approval rating had fallen to 11 percent. That was several points lower than the level at which Richard Nixon bottomed out in America a generation ago, just before he resigned his presidency.

And just in case Yeltsin missed the poll figures, the Duma had a message for him. On August 21, the Duma voted to ask President

Russian Parliament Building. (© George French)

Yeltsin to resign. The vote was 245 to 32. That news was finally enough to bring Boris Yeltsin back from vacation.

It also brought some other people to the Kremlin. The guys the Russians in the street call the *semibankirshchina*, or the "seven bankers." It's a wry play on words, referring to the *semiboyarshchina*, the "seven nobles" who ran roughshod over Russia in the seventeenth century, culminating in the brief reign, and eventual dispatch, of the tsar pretender, Boris Gudonov. Boris Gudonov. Boris Yeltsin. Two Tsars Boris. Get it?

The *semibankirshchina* are the tycoons who financed Yeltsin's reelection a couple of years ago. There are actually more than seven. There are perhaps three dozen oligarchs in Russia who control at least half of the economy. Five of them are thought to be billionaires. Their influence with the Kremlin has waxed and waned in Yeltsin's most recent term. Mainly it has waxed.

They are for the most part members of the old Soviet elite who made a quick change when capitalism came along. Typically, they started out their careers in the Komsomol, the Young Communist league, and moved into academia, the arts, the media, and other promising careers. When the Soviet Union vanished, they used their connections to loot the country's industrial structure and build their own business and banking empires.

They're not unique in Russian history, these boyar-bankers. Under the tsars in the mid-nineteenth century, Moscow had a score of millionaires, almost as many as New York City. Their numbers grew as the twentieth century dawned, and Russia's venture capitalism began to blossom. And the ordinary Russians hated them then as much as they despise the boyar-bankers of today. *Byziness* has always been a dirty word in Russia. Anton Chekhov, the Russian playwright, summed it up back in 1904 when he wrote *The Cherry Orchard*. Trofimov, the student, says to Lopahin, the *byzinessman*, "You're a wealthy man, and before long you'll be a millionaire. And insofar as a wild beast is necessary because it devours everything in its path and so converts one kind of matter into another, you are necessary also." Few Russians shed any tears when those tsarist millionaires were eradicated by the Bolsheviks.

And not a few observers have compared today's Russian tycoons to the South Korean "Chaebols," the family-controlled business conglomerates whose excesses prompted the recent South Korean economic collapse. But, as Russian critics note, at least those "Chaebols" have left the South Koreans something to show for it: highways, factories, brand-new cities, and, for a time, prosperity. Russia's boyar-bankers have kept it all for themselves.

Boris Nemstov, a former provincial governor and one of the leaders of the economic reformers Yeltsin brought into his government, told Reuters that today's tycoons practice a "Demented, warped, irresponsible capitalism. They don't pay their workers and they don't pay their taxes."

Nemstov and his protégé, Prime Minister Sergei Kiriyenko, whom Yeltsin had suddenly appointed last March, spent the spring and summer battling the barons. Kiriyenko took his orders from Yeltsin seriously. Reform the economy, without fear or favor. Kiriyenko wouldn't even meet with the barons at the outset. Eventually, when he did, the discussions dissolved into bitter invective over Kiriyenko's insistence that the barons pay their taxes, billions and billions of dollars in back taxes.

When Kiriyenko first took office, I was one of the chorus of instant analysts who figured young Sergei, a relatively unknown banker and businessman, was in way over his head. He looked like Wally Cox playing Mr. Peepers on that old TV show, and we imagined he'd be just about as effective. We were wrong. Kiriyenko turned out to be the most diligent and dedicated reformer in the Kremlin. The trouble was, his only patron was Yeltsin himself.

In the days after the August 17 crash, Kiriyenko and his staff began preparing a series of measures that would have bankrupted many of the barons' banks and industrial conglomerates. That was too much for the barons, and one baron in particular, Boris Berezovsky. At age fifty-two, Berezovsky has already led several lives: Young Communist, respected mathematician, automobile magnate, political power broker, and murder suspect. These days, Berezovsky owns or controls Russia's biggest car dealership, a bank (of course), an oil company, the biggest national airline (Aeroflot), a newspaper, the country's main television network, and perhaps the Kremlin itself. He's a billionaire at least a couple of times over.

When I see Berezovsky in person, I'm always surprised at how diminutive and delicate he is, with tiny hands and feet, and always impeccably dressed in a dark suit and cautious neckties. He seems incapable of sitting still or even listening without doodling something on a piece of paper, and in conversation, his dark, deep-set eyes seem to burn holes into his listeners.

Berezovsky's a man with a dark past, and maybe a dark present as well. In 1994, somebody set off a bomb in his car and decapitated his bodyguard. Berezovsky wasn't hurt, but the three Russians who were said to be the assassins were later found executed. A year later, Berezovsky got into an argument with Vlad Listev, a famous talk-show host on Berezovsky's network. Listev didn't want commercials on the network. Berezovsky did. One night somebody shot and killed Listev. The police brought Berezovsky in for questioning, but released him for lack of evidence. Berezovsky professes himself mystified by the murder.

But he doesn't take chances. These days, he tools around Moscow in a bulletproof Mercedes 600, surrounded by a caravan of limos and SUVs, carrying part of his one-hundred-fifty-man security force. He shuttles between his three Moscow apartments and his *dacha* on the edge of Moscow, plus his mansions in Switzerland and Spain. At one point, Berezovsky even applied for an Israeli passport, just in case things got too dangerous. Like many of the Russian barons, Berezovsky is Jewish. In a country with a past and present full of virulent anti-Semitism, that's one more reason for many Russians to hate and loathe him and the others.

His admirers, and there aren't many, say Boris Berezovsky is the son Boris Yeltsin never had. His critics simply call him (behind his back of course) "Rasputin." Certainly he's the ultimate political climber. He made a nuisance of himself around the Kremlin, but eventually charmed his way into Yeltsin's inner circle. He befriended Yeltsin's chief of staff, Anatoly Chubais, and used that connection to finance the publication of Yeltsin's memoirs.

It was Chubais who helped manage the TV ad campaign that turned the presidential election around for Yeltsin in 1996. And it was Berezovsky who convinced the rest of the boyar-bankers to bankroll it. Their reward from Yeltsin was two more years of the economic stewardship of another of the barons, Prime Minister Viktor Chernomyrdin, during which they and the rest of Russia's rich got richer and the poor got poorer. Berezovsky and his fellow barons were nettled, to say the least, when Yeltsin and Chubais turned on them last March, sacked Chernomyrdin, and defiantly brought in young Kiriyenko. By that time, Berezovsky and Chubais were bitter enemies.

So now it's a Friday, four days after the ruble has crashed, Yeltsin is at rock bottom in the polls, the parliament's calling on him to resign, and you're Boris Berezovsky. What do you do?

You sense an opportunity. As closely as it can be reconstructed from a few facts, a few more suppositions, and a lot of rumor, Berezovsky spent the next day, Saturday, working on his two principal allies in the Kremlin, Yeltsin's chief of staff Valentin Yumashev, and Yeltsin's daugher, Tatyana Dyachenko, who has become, among other things, Yeltsin's primary media advisor. (She thought up the idea of getting Yeltsin to dance a jig in public whenever the band played at his campaign stops in 1996, a photo-op strategy that may well have led to her father's subsequent heart attack.) And when he wasn't leaning on them, Berezovsky was finding common cause with the other boyar-bankers. The object was simple: Kiriyenko out. Viktor Chernomyrdin back in.

On Sunday, August 23, Kiriyenko, aware of Berezovsky's maneuvering, went to see Yeltsin, who wanted to know if Kiriyenko would stay on if some "changes" were made in the government. Kiriyenko claims he told Yeltsin he wanted to "take a break." He'd seen the handwriting.

That afternoon, Yeltsin did as Berezovsky and the barons wanted. He replaced Kiriyenko with Chernomyrdin as prime-minister-designate, and sacked Boris Nemstov for good measure.

That evening, Kiriyenko told the Moscow newspaper *Kommersant* that he and his mentor, Nemstov, left their offices in the Russian White House for the last time.

They walked a few yards to a little part of Moscow that Betsy and I had come to know well in the previous weeks. Our apartment is just north of the Russian White House, with a view of a little bridge and green park at the side of the building. There, since the spring, a few dozen coal miners had encamped, hoping their quiet, live-in protest demonstration would shame the government into paying millions of Russian coal miners their back wages. Some of the demonstrators had come all the way from Siberia, Heaven knows how! Betsy and I would check on them every morning when we went to work and every evening when we went home. We could hear them from our living room, day and night, periodically pounding their work helmets on the pavement to get attention. All the newspaper and broadcast folks, including us, did stories about the miners and their squatters' camp, and the authorities were wise enough to let the miners alone as long as they stayed nonviolent.

The city even sent them some food and drink from time to time. But the government never did much of anything about their back wages. Eventually, their story got old and tired and we reporters moved on. But the miners stayed, rain or shine, and eventually seemed to become just an odd part of the local scenery.

Now Sergei Kiriyenko and Boris Nemtsov were without paying jobs too. The two of them kept their bodyguards at a distance while they spent an hour chatting with the miners, and sharing a bottle of vodka they'd brought along. Their astonished audience didn't quite know what to make of them. One of the miners, Sasha, said that the two officials seemed sad and resigned. "I didn't realize they were such little fellows," said Sasha. "They said they tried to make things better for us and the rest of the Russian people, but the bigwigs wouldn't let them. We asked them, where was our money? They said the bigwigs got it." It wasn't clear whether the "bigwigs" were Yeltsin, Berezovsky, or both.

The next day, Monday, Yeltsin submitted Chernomyrdin's name to the Duma for approval. As everyone had now learned as a result of the past leadership crises under Yeltsin, the Duma would have three opportunities to confirm the prime-minister-designate. If it didn't, the parliament would be dissolved and there would have to be new elections.

Nobody wanted that this time, not even the voters. The prospect of a political apocalypse on top of an economic one was just too scary. In a new poll, two-thirds of those Russians who were asked were convinced that military force was going to be used before this crisis was over. And half of them thought Yeltsin ought to resign. As for Chernomyrdin, fewer than one in twenty Russians, according to the polls, thought he was honest. And only 2 percent thought he even knew what he was doing.

Yeltsin told the nation he was nominating Chernomyrdin because Russia needed a "heavyweight" at the helm. The Duma had a different view. Not only the Communist delegates, who controlled the Duma, but the Democrats, the leftists, the radicals, and others all regarded Chernomyrdin as used goods, and damaged at that. As the

Communist leader, Gennady Zyuganov, told me, "If the man's not capable of saving a sinking ship, why should I vote for him and get into the wreck myself?" On the initial ballot, the Duma rejected Chernomyrdin, 253 to 94. It didn't help that when Chernomyrdin addressed the skeptical Duma, his economic proposals were vague and unfocused.

Yeltsin immediately renominated Chernomyrdin, confident that the Duma, which had always knuckled under before, would do so this time. But this time was different. There was a tension in the Moscow air I'd never felt before. The coal miners in the little White House park near our apartment had taken to besieging the halls of the Duma downtown and harassing the deputies. Their protesting colleagues were once again blocking the railroad tracks thousands of miles away in Siberia. Mail, food, and manufacturing supplies had stopped.

The city was rife with nasty rumors. The internal security troops were said to be in training for a declaration of martial law. Almost every day we climbed into our cars to chase down a troop scare somewhere. "They say there are tanks on the Kiev Bridge!" "Armored personnel carriers are passing the airport!" None of the alarms was ever genuine, but it made all of us a little jumpy, including no doubt the ordinary Muscovites, who were hearing the same rumors.

It didn't help to hear that the former army general, Alexander Lebed ("Russia's Patton Wanna-be," a diplomat at the U.S. embassy here liked to call him), was saying that the Russian army, much of which hasn't been paid since last May, was in a "revolutionary mood."

At this moment, Lebed is arguably the most respected man in Russia, and without trying to make it too obvious, he's been running hard to win the race to replace Yeltsin in the 2000 elections. Thanks to tens of millions of dollars in campaign contributions from Boris Berezovsky (there's that man again!), Lebed was able to blitz the vast mineral-rich Siberian region of Krasnoyarsk with enough TV commercials to get himself elected governor this spring. That entitles him to a seat in the upper house of the Russian parliament and gets him to Moscow often enough to stay noticed.

And sometimes Lebed can cause enough consternation just by staying home in Krasnoyarsk, as he did earlier this summer, when he sent an open letter to the Kremlin demanding that unless the servicemen who operate the nuclear ICBMs in his region got their back wages, he would consider "establishing territorial jurisdiction" over the weapons. "We in Krasnoyarsk could become a headache for the world community, just like India and Pakistan," wrote Lebed. Loose-Nukes Lebed.

For anyone handicapping the Kremlin sweepstakes in 2000,

you've got to take Alexander Lebed seriously. And don't make any remarks within earshot about his last name, which in Russian means "swan." The Swan has a legendary temper. He's a former airborne commander who served his duty in Afghanistan and in the Caucasus, where he gained the respect, admiration, and affection of his troops for battling his superiors for better pay and living conditions. He supported Yeltsin in the 1991 coup, but ran against him in the early 1996 elections. It was Berezovsky who convinced Lebed to finally give up his candidacy and support Yeltsin in the final round of voting, which ensured a Yeltsin victory. Lebed's reward was a big job in the Yeltsin government. And he managed to settle the war in Chechnya in the four months he remained in the Kremlin, before Yeltsin washed his hands of him. Alexander Lebed had become too popular.

Russians are fond of Lebed (he got well over 10 percent of the vote for president when he ran) because he seems to be honest and sincerely despises the corruption he and every honest Russian (most of them are!) see around them. Lebed is the ultimate law-and-order candidate. But he's not a deep thinker or an ideologue, and those who've known him well think he can be easily manipulated. And as for his preferred style of government, well, authoritarian is too gentle a word.

Alexander Lebed's one of the few people I've ever met who are just as impressive (unnerving?) in person as they seem to be on the TV. During my chat with him, I noticed he was wearing what appeared to be a Saville Row suit. But he's built like a fireplug, so though he seems shorter than his six feet, he seems almost that wide, and he's all muscle. As a result, his fancy suit hung on him like a pair of pajamas. His voice, when he speaks, which isn't often or for very long, sounds rather like a cement mixer turning on low. It is devoid, so far as I could hear, of any treble whatsoever.

Lebed is all military. He crushed my hand in greeting even though I'd tried to prepare for that and kept my fingers as fistlike as possible. Forget it. My hand was still aching an hour later. And when he talks with you, he gives you the soldier stare. I think they must teach it at command school in every army everywhere. He looks you straight in the eye, seemingly without blinking, and never averts his eyes. Not once. He's pretty good at it. I don't think he even blinked for half an hour. But he's got a ways to go to beat Gen. William Westmoreland. "Westy" was a legend in the Pentagon for giving great briefings, soldier stare and all. It was how he got to run the war in Vietnam. Back then, every time I'd interview Gen. Westmoreland, he'd stare right into me with those clear blue eyes as he talked. It was all very direct and very compelling and designed to erase any doubt you might have that "we were doing the right thing." Maybe that's what Westmoreland really thought, but it took me a long time to realize that there was a lot less there than met the eye, so to speak.

Lebed was obviously still furious with Yeltsin—and disgusted. "Nobody has ever humiliated the army like Yeltsin has," he fumed. "The tsar's armies were well fed and received their pay. Today, the army is starving. Yeltsin thinks he's the tsar. He lives in a fantasy world. In the parliament, the Communists and Democrats shout at each other and nothing happens. The people are no longer simply angry anymore. They are deeply and silently furious!"

Isn't there a peaceful way out of this crisis, I asked?

"Of course. But we need a powerful and strong-willed person leading the country."

"What if that's you?" I asked. "Should America and the West be afraid of a powerful and strong-willed former army general running Russia?"

"No," Lebed said. There was a flicker of a smile at the edge of his lips but his eyes weren't smiling. "After all, General Eisenhower led America, didn't he?"

I liked Ike. I don't like Lebed.

Before long, Chernomyrdin himself was sounding Lebed-like. In another appeal to the Duma for confirmation that week, Chernomyrdin announced he was planning an "economic dictatorship." What that seemed to mean is that he would print millions and millions of new rubles right now to pay everybody's back wages and worry about it later. Consequently the ruble, which was worth seventeen cents a couple of weeks previously and was worth just a nickel at the moment, would be virtually worthless by the time everyone got his money. Nobody was buying Chernomyrdin's "dictatorship," least of all the Duma delegates, who voted him down a second time, almost two-to-one. One ballot to go before chaos. I reminded news watchers on my network that night of the old anecdote about the Russian pessimist and the Russian optimist. The pessimist says, "Things are so bad in Russia they can't possibly get any worse." The optimist happily begs to differ. "Oh yes they can!"

Maybe the optimist was premature. This time, Boris Yeltsin didn't defiantly resubmit Chernomyrdin's name for a final vote. There was a lot of bargaining apparently going at Yeltsin's retreat outside Moscow, and this time, it apparently did *not* include Berezovsky and the other boyar-barons.

Yeltsin and his entourage had finally concluded that Chernomyrdin could not be stuffed down the Duma's throat. So if not him, who for prime minister? Well, it had to be somebody who wouldn't upstage President Yeltsin, who would be palatable to the Duma's Communists, and who had no evident desire to ever become president of Russia. It took a day and a night of bargaining to get a deal. It would have gone a lot quicker, except the candidate they settled on didn't want the job (and who could blame him?). Both the Kremlin and the Duma had to beg him before Yevgeny Primakov finally said yes.

At age sixty-eight, a year older than Yeltsin and in delicate health himself, Primakov was nonetheless right where he'd always wanted to be: running Russia's foreign policy. He's been foreign minister for better than two years, and he's won grudging respect even from his counterparts in the West, with whom he often clashes. Primakov has played a weak hand masterfully. He's developed a public friendship with Secretary of State Madeleine Albright, although they don't usually see eye-to-eye on matters involving, say, Iraq or the Balkans.

Prime Minister Primakov is enough to make not a few folks in Washington nervous. Ten years ago, in the waning days of Soviet Russia, Primakov was a member of both the Communist Party Central Committee and the ruling Politburo. He counts Saddam Hussein of Iraq and Hafez Assad of Syria among his friends, and he literally speaks their language. He is fluent in Arabic. And he spent a few years running Russia's secret service, the successor to the old Soviet KGB. If that alarms some of the Washington pundits, they'll now know how the Russians felt when that old spymaster George Bush, former head of the CIA, became president of the United States.

Primakov does have a doctorate in economics from Moscow State, but that's an old Soviet-era sheepskin, and it's unlikely his Soviet-era economic studies will serve him all that well as he wrestles with Russia's robber-baron capitalism of today. All that's certain about his political views is that he's what the Russians call a *gosudarstvennik*, somebody who believes firmly in a powerful, centralized state role in Russia's economic, political, and foreign affairs.

From the standpoint of the Kremlin and the Duma, Primakov had two assets: he was not a threat to anybody, and he was, reluctantly, available. It was a measure of the desperation among the politicians that his candidacy was promoted by the strangest of political bedfellows here: Grigory Yavlinsky, leader of the Democrat bloc in the Duma, *and* his bitter enemy, Gennady Zyuganov, the head of the dominant Communist faction. "It's a way out of the crisis," said Yavlinsky. "This will be good for Russia," Zyuganov enthused. Even former Soviet premier Mikhail Gorbachev, now despised by most everybody in Russian politics, chimed in, "Primakov will work to get rid of the radical liberal economic extremists."

It was with an almost audible sigh of relief that the Duma overwhelmingly confirmed Primakov the next afternoon. "I'll tell you in advance," Primakov told the deputies, "I'm no magician."

But he is determined to drive a stake into the heart of Yeltsin's now-discredited economic reform program, and get back to things the way they were. To run the Central Bank, the Russian equivalent of Treasury Secretary, he's brought back Viktor Gerashchenko, who used to run the Soviet State Bank in the Communist days. Gerashchenko was the central banker early on in Yeltsin's first term, too, but his habit of printing money to pay off Russia's debts caused the ruble to crash and he was fired. Harvard's Jeffrey Sachs, one of the Kremlin's former economic advisers, once famously referred to Gerashchenko as "the worst central bank governor in history." There's no indication Gerashchenko has altered his profligate habits or his outlook. The other day he referred to Western investors who are clamoring to get their money out of those now-worthless Russian treasury bonds as "greedy and stupid."

The man Primakov's chosen to actually run the economy is Yuri Maslyukov, another Communist. Maslyukov is also the former head of Gosplan, the huge bureaucracy that ran the Soviet Union's planned economy. Five-year plan after five-year plan, Maslyukov ran it right into the ground. Mr. Maslyukov now says he thinks America and the West are responsible for Russia's economic crisis, and should be made to pay whatever it costs to make things right here.

And those few remaining holdover reformers who were on the Communists' hit list are either going or gone: Boris Fyodorov, the diligent tax collector who ruffled too many feathers; Alexander Shohkin, a centrist economic expert; and Dmitry Vasilev, head of the Securities Commission.

All of this ought to make the Communists delighted, but the Communists are suffering through an identity crisis. Although the party effectively controls the parliament, with about 30 percent of the delegates, it's not very likely to improve its standing. And nobody seriously believes the Communists can ever again win a majority in a presidential election. Seventy-odd years of tyrannical rule have left too many bad memories lingering in the minds of most Russians.

So the paradox is that even though the Communists are the largest political party in Russia, with the strongest national political organization, the Communists can't take power. And even if they could, they're no longer entirely certain who they are. Among the Communist delegates in the Duma these days are the requisite number of party hacks, a couple of former cosmonauts, a movie actor, and a millionaire banker-businessman. Communist leaders get very nervous when you start asking them whether they'd like to renationalize all the property that's been privatized in the last decade. In fact, 70 percent of the Russian economy has now been effectively privatized. And Zyuganov actually remarked the other day that maybe Russia could take some lessons from what President Franklin Roosevelt did to try to pull America out of its depression in the 1930s. Gennady Zyuganov a New Dealer? There's an identity crisis for you.

And of course things haven't worked out well at all for Boris Berezovsky and the boyar-barons. Their man was Chernomyrdin, and they couldn't get him past the Duma.

Primakov is an ex-Communist, but in recent years he's steered clear of party politics. And he's no friend of Berezovsky and his friends. Nor are the former and present Communists who now make up the Primakov entourage. Berezovsky and the boyar-barons may wind up wishing for the good old days of Sergei Kiriyenko. At least he was the devil they knew.

And ordinary Russians? Well, by the government's own estimate, inflation will soar to 230 percent by year's end. Maybe more than that. The Primakov regime has just conceded that it has already printed up about a billion dollars in new rubles to pay the army's back wages. Wait until the soldiers discover how little those inflated rubles will buy! Tax collection has virtually stopped.

And according to Kremlin auditors, Russia's economy, which until August had been growing slightly, will decline by at least 8 percent for the year. That's not just a depression. That's a disaster.

I spent one September morning in one of the Moscow neighborhoods, at a job fair. With Western firms pulling out, with Moscow's smart shops and elegant restaurants closing down, with many banks already closed, I figured there would be a lot of the new young Russian bourgeoisie, who'd prospered during the Russian bubble, out here now looking for work. I had no idea. There were thousands of them. The line of applicants stretched for blocks and blocks even though the jobs available were menial ones. The people in the lines were supposed to get unemployment and welfare benefits. But the government hasn't got the money, so for them and millions of others, Russia's social safety net has vanished.

Halfway down the line I encountered Irina A., a slender, studious, no-nonsense design engineer who lost her job last month. "I've got two kids at home," she said. "I'm wearing my last decent dress. I can't afford to buy us anything but bread and milk. The only shopping I can do anymore is window shopping."

Maybe Yevgeny Primakov's Communist economists can spare Irina some of their new rubles, hot off the press.

chapter 41

September Song
(October 1998)

I know that someday, when the roll is called in that
newsroom Way Up Yonder and I'm called upon to recite what
I did or didn't do for the betterment of humankind, I'll have to mention the day I caused the Dow Jones Industrial Average to fall 360
points. That'll take some explaining.

In the early afternoon of August 27, I stood before a live TV
camera in our network news studio in Moscow and announced to
our audience what we had learned:

> Russian President Boris Yeltsin has signed an order resigning from
> office. The resignation is not dated, and will await the confirmation
> of his prime-minister-designate, Viktor Chernomyrdin, which is
> expected to be sometime next week. Under the arrangement, we are
> told, Yeltsin would then formally resign and the prime minister
> would become interim president of Russia. Negotiations are now
> underway which would stipulate Yeltsin's salary and housing and
> other details, after Yeltsin leaves office. At the same time, a special
> government commission is preparing legislation making Yeltsin
> immune from prosecution after he leaves office, in the event his
> enemies attempt a political vendetta. In other words, a pardon in
> advance. Sources emphasized that Yeltsin's resignation will not be
> final until he authorizes it, and that in coming days, Yeltsin could
> change his mind and unsign what he has just signed.

The story was ours exclusively and the effect was as if we'd thrown a live hornet's nest into the world media maw. It quickly bounced all over the satellites into every newspaper, news wire, broadcast network, and stock ticker around the globe. The qualifications we wrote into our piece got lost, as they always do, in the telling and retelling. What stuck in everyone's mind were two words: "Yeltsin" and "Resign."

The Kremlin press office was quick to deny our story, calling it "stupid." But since the Kremlin press office isn't exactly brimming with credibility, nobody gave the denial any credence. And since Moscow was eight hours ahead of New York, about the time we went on the air with our story, Wall Street was just waking up. And Wall Street was still suffering a headache from Russia's decision ten days previously to default on its Western creditors and devalue its currency. Yeltsin represented Wall Street's, and the West's, last best hope of preventing Russia from completely collapsing, not to mention getting its money back. And Yeltsin was resigning? By the end of the trading day, the Dow Jones had dropped 360 points. I'd done that. Me.

Not without good reason. We'd been digging into the story for weeks, and we'd just that day confirmed all the main points in the report from two independent sources: one close to the Yeltsin family, the other within the Kremlin. They'd agreed to speak to us on condition we keep their names secret, just as Woodward and Bernstein had done with "Deep Throat" during their investigation of Watergate. Except that in this case, we had a "Deep Throat" and a "Sore Throat," as we called them. (Eventually, we found two other secret sources within the government who, like the others, had also actually seen the resignation letter. We dubbed them "Strep Throat" and "Full Throat.")

By the next evening, the resignation report had created such a stir, with distressed phone calls now fluttering back and forth between the Kremlin and the White House, Number Ten Downing Street, etc., that Yeltsin himself actually went on Russian TV to insist he was not going to resign. In a carefully scripted and edited "interview" with a Russian TV journalist, Yeltsin said, "I'm not going anywhere. I am going to work." And he vowed he would finish out his term, which ends in less than two years, and then retire.

But the resignation talk wasn't just coming from me. The Communists who control the Russian parliament had been demanding his resignation for weeks. Yeltsin's Kremlin predecessor and bête noire, Mikhail Gorbachev, had that day urged Yeltsin to step down. "He's obviously become weak," Gorbachev said. "Not only physically, but intellectually." The conventional wisdom among analysts in the media and in academia has been along the same lines. Viktor Kremenyuk, a veteran Kremlin-watcher from the USA-Canada Institute in Moscow, told me: "I think there is a high percentage-possibility, a probability, that he [Yeltsin] will have to resign."

One of the reasons for all the pessimism about Yeltsin's future among the Kremlin-watchers is that there hasn't been much of Boris Yeltsin to watch the past few months. He's either been on vacation, at his *dacha* just outside Moscow, or at a spa called Gorky-9 which, since Yeltsin's heart surgery, has been converted into a complete cardiac center. It has just one patient. On the few occasions he's been to his Kremlin office, Yeltsin's usually spent no more than an hour or two, signing some papers and posing for photographers.

What we do know of Yeltsin's condition, from our own sources and from the investigations by the Russian media, is not encouraging: He's fired his two most competent doctors, including Renat Akchurin, who performed Yeltsin's heart surgery. His new attending physician is Dr. Andrey Fesenko. He is Yeltsin's grandchildren's pediatrician. Dr. Fesenko allows Yeltsin to drink vodka. Our sources insist Yeltsin's never stopped drinking, although he's cut down from a pint of vodka in an evening to half a pint. He's said to suffer from low blood pressure and hardening of the arteries, and there's some concern whether his brain and other vital organs are getting enough oxygen. He's in pain much of the time, and takes mild narcotics to relieve it. It explains why he walks so stiffly and gingerly in public. He hurts. He's also getting hard of hearing and somewhat nearsighted (he now wears glasses in private to read documents). Our sources even claim that before a major public appearance, his medical staff pumps several pints of whole blood into Yeltsin, to help achieve that healthy bloom in his cheeks. Absent the transfusions, he looks a sixty-seven-year-old man in the body of an eighty-year-old.

So is Boris Yeltsin, you know, okay? Is he still in charge in the Kremlin? And if he isn't, who is? Only three people, I suspect, know the real answer to that: Yeltsin himself; his forty-year-old chief of staff, Valentin Yumashev; and his youngest daughter, Tatyana Dyachenko. At thirty-eight, she's married and the mother of two sons. And since her father's last presidential campaign, Tatyana has been his official image-maker.

Beyond that, as with so much of the Kremlin's palace intrigues over the centuries, it's all rumor, speculation, and gossip, laced with a lot of envy. It's Yumashev's job to keep the paperwork flowing and make sure his boss signs off on the big decisions. That's what a chief of staff is for, especially when the boss is under the weather a lot. Is Yumashev using Yeltsin's ill health to advance his own agenda? Does he give Yeltsin honest advice? Is Yeltsin even aware of what he's supposed to be deciding? Yeltsin's critics, of course, take the dark view. In truth, nobody except the above-mentioned trio truly knows.

We do know that Tatyana is clever and energetic. She is also spoiled and impatient and inflexible. If she were in third grade, the teacher would write on her report card, "Has difficulties with others." The Kremlin staff refers to her (behind her back) as "Tsarevna." On more than one occasion, she's flown into a rage while editing one of Yeltsin's TV appearances. (Although, in her defense, I've known more than a few TV news producers who fly into irrational rages in the editing room all the time.) There are those in the Kremlin who say Tatyana's making all sorts of economic, political, and foreign policy decisions on behalf of her father, decisions which are far beyond her competence (although I can remember how those smart fellows in the White House and the State Department used to lament to us reporters, on background of course, what a shame it was that Nancy Reagan was giving Ronnie all that advice about how to handle the Russians, the Libyans, and the Sandinistas, before the president went to sleep every night).

Tatyana's always been her father's favorite. Consequently, she's the only one in his entourage who can tell him the unpleasant truth, which, her critics complain is almost never. Certainly Tatyana's been fiercely loyal to her father. When she thought it best served her father's interest, she has cynically made and broken political friendships with, among others, Anatoly Chubais, the Kremlin economic reformer, and Chubais's archenemy, Boris Berezovsky, the business tycoon.

That may be why she has thus far resisted advising Yeltsin to resign, even though it might be better for her father's physical health. Or perhaps Tatyana's waiting for the right deal. No revenge from a new parliament or a new president? No loss of ex-presidential privileges? Safe and comfortable passage to somewhere nice, somewhere else in the world? As the Russian serfs used to say when they contemplated the Kremlin, "Only God and the tsar know."

God knows, you'd be hard put to pick a worse time than right now for a Moscow summit with the president of the United States, but state visits are hard to cancel once they're scheduled. Unless you can think of a very good reason, it's a lot worse to snub your host by cancelling than going through the motions. And that's certainly what both Bill Clinton and Boris Yeltsin were doing in Moscow the first two days of September; going through the motions.

A Moscow newspaper headlined it, "The Summit of the Two Unfortunates." Indeed. President Yeltsin was, to put it kindly, disengaged. And he was also embroiled in another leadership crisis. President Clinton was all too engaged with the Monica Lewinsky affair.

Russian president Boris Yeltsin, right, and President Clinton, left, smile as U.S. Secretary of State Madeleine Albright and Russian acting foreign minister Yevgeny Primakov, far right, exchange just-signed documents in Moscow's Kremlin, September 2, 1998. Yeltsin assured Clinton that he wouldn't abandon democratic and market reforms. (AP Photo/J. Scott Applewhite)

He and Mrs. Clinton arrived in Moscow in a cold rain, looking about as dismal as the weather.

The next and last day of the summit was plainly awful, for both presidents. There was the postsummit news conference, live on TV all around the world. For Clinton, it was the first time he'd had to face the media in the two weeks since he'd admitted, in a live TV broadcast to the nation, that he'd had sexual relations with Ms. Lewinsky. The media didn't want to know about Russia. They wanted to know why he hadn't said he was sorry.

"I've acknowledged that I made a mistake, said I regretted it, and asked to be forgiven," Clinton said glumly.

Yeltsin hadn't faced the media live in months. You can get away with that in Russia. He looked all right, even perky, with that familiar rosy glow in his cheeks. What few questions he was asked he answered briefly, his responses slow and halting. The news conference was about over. Yeltsin was almost home free. Then somebody asked him something hard. How are you going to form a new government?

"I must say that . . . ," Yeltsin began. Then he stopped. His eyes stared off into space, as if made of glass. He paused. Five seconds. Ten. Fifteen. Clinton stared straight ahead. Then stared at Yeltsin. Then stared at the ceiling. Yeltsin said something. "That rather many events will take place in order for us to achieve those results." He stopped. Another seemingly interminable pause. Even the reporters were looking away, as if they were witnessing a traffic accident. Finally, Yeltsin uttered, "*Vsyo!*" "That's all!"

Clinton tried to help. With a little forced chuckle, he added, "That ought to be my answer, too, that was pretty good!" Nobody laughed. The next question was addressed to Clinton. It was about Monica Lewinsky.

The Russian TV viewers who'd happened to tune in to the live TV coverage of the news conference saw, for a few seconds at least, that their president had been transformed into a befuddled, pathetic old man. Those who looked at the news reports on all the Russian TV stations and networks that night saw something quite different. Yeltsin's gaffe had been carefully edited out. Everywhere. You can get away with that in Russia.

Clinton's day wasn't over. The only concrete thing to come out of this "summit" was agreement on a couple of measures to slightly reduce the threat of accidental nuclear attack, something that might be more reassuring if it were clear the Russian government knows exactly where all of its nuclear weapons are.

Then Clinton went over to the U.S. ambassador's residence where, as reported by CBS News, for two hours he got an earful about Boris Yeltsin from his critics in the Russian parliament. Gennady Zyuganov, the Communist leader: "The Kremlin is half-dead. The government is paralyzed." Alexander Lebed, the former army general who could be the next president: "The situation here now is worse than in 1917. The people cannot tolerate it anymore. And the existence of a huge stock of unguarded nuclear weapons just adds to the tension."

Then the Clintons got on Air Force One to go back home, and face more Monica.

Soon after the summit fiasco, Yeltsin's longtime press spokesman, Sergei Yastrzhembsky, lost his job. The rumor was that Yastrzhembsky had advised Yeltsin to drop his nomination of Chernomyrdin for prime minister, pretty good advice as it turned out. But his boss, Yumashev, regarded that as an act of betrayal. All of us journalists had come to know Yastrzhembsky, a former diplomat who speaks four languages fluently. We didn't like him much. He's arrogant and devious, just what you'd expect in a press spokesman. But he was very good at his job; as adept, in his way, as Mike McCurry is for President Clinton. They replaced Yastrzhembsky with a hack who worked for one of the local TV production companies. It served the Kremlin right. What happened to Boris Yeltsin the next month in Uzbekistan never would have occurred on Yastrzhembsky's watch.

Yumashev and Yeltsin's new handlers had decided the president was well enough to take a tour of some of the old Soviet republics in Central Asia. They were wrong. Yeltsin arrived in Tashkent, where Uzbek president Islam Karimov met him with full military honors. Then Karimov decided Yeltsin should review the troops. The Russian president took one step, stumbled, Karimov caught him from falling, and he and Mrs. Yeltsin led him back to a waiting limo. Later, at a signing ceremony, Yeltsin was seized by a violent fit of coughing and doctors were called. Most of this wound up on worldwide TV. Except for Russia of course. Russian evening-news viewers never saw a second of it.

Needless to say, Yeltsin cut short his trip and flew back to Moscow. His press office reported the president was confined to Gorky-9 with a bad cold.

A month ago, I'd have never believed that anything in Moscow could eclipse the Russian economic crash, but I should have known that, as so often before, Boris Yeltsin's health would once again become topic A. Lately, it's not only his physical health, but his mental health that's of concern. The Moscow press has been full of blind quotes from unnamed "Kremlin doctors" that Yeltsin has become forgetful, is prone to confuse the identities of his advisors, and is suffering the early stages of Alzheimer's disease, allegedly because one of the arterial tubes that were implanted during his heart bypass operation has come undone, and he's not getting an adequate supply of blood to his brain.

The only one of these armchair diagnosticians who's been brave enough to publicly identify himself is an eminent psychiatrist, Dr. Mikhail Vinogradov, who has been treating Kremlin bigwigs since Soviet days. He told me he is convinced the president is suffering not only from Alzheimer's disease, but also is afflicted with "senile dementia," and on the evidence of Yeltsin's fragile appearance when he's seen in public, from Parkinson's disease, too. Dr. Vinogradov has called upon Yeltsin to undergo a thorough mental examination to be supervised by Russia's Constitutional Court. The Kremlin has apparently decided not to dignify Dr. Vinogradov's comments with a response.

But Yeltsin's recent actions have spoken louder than words. He's just had to cancel a trip to the European Union Conference in Vienna. Instead, he's been moved back to Gorky-9, his personal cardiac sanatorium, for treatment of "unstable blood pressure and undue fatigue," according to his office. Politically, the president seems just as anemic. In the latest national poll, only 5 percent, one in twenty of those Russians asked, approved of the job he's doing. Ninety-three percent think he's doing a lousy job. That's not exactly what you'd call a mandate. At the same time he has lost his hold on the Russian people, Boris Yeltsin has lost most of his clout with the Russian parliament. For the first time, the legislators have stood up to the president and forced him to withdraw his choice for prime minister, and forced him to accept Yevgeny Primakov instead.

And now, finally, circumstances have forced Yeltsin to effectively turn over the whole Russian government to Primakov. The Kremlin quietly announced the other day that henceforth, the prime minister will conduct Russia's day-to-day affairs, while the president will serve out the last two years of his term performing ceremonial functions and serving as the "guarantor" of Russia's territorial integrity and civil liberties.

And the drumbeat of resignation talk we heard all this summer and autumn has suddenly ceased. It's apparently occurred to the Russian political establishment that a Yeltsin resignation now, in the midst of an economic crisis, would plunge the country into political chaos, too. Better to keep even an incapacitated president around, if only as a sort of national hood ornament, at least until the country can decide in an orderly fashion on a successor.

And Boris Yeltsin? What must he be thinking as he lies in his hospital bed in Gorky-9? I don't imagine he's ever read the words Shakespeare put into the mouth of King Lear:

> You see me here, you gods. A poor old man, as full of grief as age.
> Wretched in both.

As for that infamous resignation letter we're told Yeltsin signed, well, of course, he never sent it in. In any event, he never got his choice for prime minister, so I suppose it's null and void now. Maybe the letter's still sitting around in his desk somewhere, though I doubt it. And on Wall Street, stocks are slowly recovering. Whew!

(Postscript: Little more than two years later, the landscape of Russian politics, at least at the top, had completely changed. Most of the names and faces that the Russian people and Western reporters had come to

know in the 1990s, the Primakovs and Lebeds and Kiriyenkos, had left the scene. They'd gone into retirement, or into business, or into think tanks (they have those in Moscow as well as in Washington), or into safe seats in the Russian parliament, which was behaving more and more like the Kremlin's rubber stamp. Vladimir Putin, Boris Yeltsin's hand-picked successor, was the new president of Russia, and behaving more and more like an autocrat, more like the old Tsar Boris, every day. As for Yeltsin, he'd become a semi-invalid confined to his compound near Moscow, under the care of his ever-watchful daughter Tatyana. He'd been busy nonetheless, finishing his memoirs.)

chapter 42

Time of
Troubles

(November 1998)

The "Time of Troubles" familiar to **Russians,**
when they recall their history, was back in the early seventeenth century. For ten years, nobody was in charge. Famine and pestilence walked the land, and the only certainty was that tomorrow would
be worse than yesterday.

This Russian autumn can't compare with that old Time of Troubles, but it's been troubling enough here. There's a very real threat
of famine and pestilence to come, as the first snows begin to fly. And
in Moscow, nobody seems to be in charge. President Yeltsin is in
seclusion. His prime minister, Yevgeny Primakov, is still struggling
to form a full cabinet, and in the Duma, the legislators are occupied
with trying to sue the finance minister because he can't find them
any money to buy copy paper or soap for the restrooms. Plus they're
cold. There's no money for heating oil, either.

Whenever there's a Russian crisis of one sort or another, and these
past few months certainly qualifies, I always try to go out and find
myself a *babushka* to sort things out. A *babushka* is one of those
women, stooped from age and hard work, you see everywhere on the
streets, usually dressed in black with a dark shawl drawn up against the
cold. She may be somebody's mother or grandmother, or somebody's
widow, and she's usually managed to store up an uncommon amount
of folk wisdom and good sense in her long life, which she will happily
share with strangers, often without being asked. So I like to talk to
babushki in times of trouble here. They have a certain perspective.

My *babushka* in this case was Ludmila M., whom I found picking out a couple of cold cuts from the meat case in the corner market near where we live. The cold cuts had to last the week, she told me. She's a pensioner who is lucky to be getting her pension. Millions of Russian pensioners are still waiting for a whole summer's worth of back pension checks. But because of Russia's runaway inflation, her monthly pension, which was worth sixty-eight dollars last week, is now worth only thirty-four dollars.

I was impertinent enough to ask Ludmila her age. She's ninety-two. Did she mind if I asked her a couple of questions in front of my TV camera? She did not. What did she think about what's been happening in Russia lately?

Ludmila considered the question. "Frankly, things were a lot better under the tsar," she replied. But, with a slight smile and a twinkle in her eye, she added, "But you know, we Russians, we'll survive. We'll survive the way we always have. Selling and stealing. Selling and stealing."

When we took Ludmila's *"babushka* on the street" interview back to the office and played it in the editing room, it caused quite a stir among my Russian friends on the staff. There was a lot of hushed conversation and finally one of the editors said to me, "You know, you really have to use that part where the woman talked about us Russians surviving by selling and stealing."

"Why?" I asked.

"Because," she blushed. "That's what we Russians always say about ourselves!"

From the looks of it, Russians are going to need all their survival skills in the months to come. Since the arrival of capitalism, Russian per capita income has decreased by more than 40 percent. Because of this summer's economic collapse and the inflation that has attended it, fully a third of the population is living in poverty. That's defined here as the equivalent of $118 a month for a family of four. Most of those poor, forty-four million of them, are working poor. They have jobs of one sort or another. But the average wage now is just $70 a month.

Russia was never able to feed itself, even in the Soviet era, without food imports. But the gulf between production and consumption is now wider than ever. A drought in the Russian grain belt this summer has cut the grain harvest by 60 percent from a decade ago. And there's only half as much milk and meat being produced now as then. Russia will have to import a lot of food this winter, but it doesn't have the money to pay for it.

And it's not just food that's going to be in short supply. The country's already running out of medicines, 60 percent of which are imported. The government says there's now only a three-month supply on hand. Russians have to buy their own medicines, and prices for what drugs are still available are rising out of reach for most patients. Doctors and nurses have gone unpaid for months. That's true of most everybody who draws a government wage.

The other day, a hundred nuclear scientists began picketing the Nuclear Ministry building in a protest over back pay. Most of the one million men in the Russian military haven't been paid lately, either. In some units, mobile bakeries are being put to work to make sure there's enough bread for officers' families. Apparently, the families of enlisted men will have to fend for themselves.

The International Red Cross is busy trying to raise $15 million to feed the poorest Russians in the poorest regions.

In another eerie echo of that old Time of Troubles, Russia's center is showing signs of disintegration, as the desperate hinterlands begin to shift for themselves. Prime Minister Primakov conceded as much a few days ago when he announced he's giving local officials a bigger role in decision making. In fact, local officials, who these days are freely elected and constrained to keep their constituents fed, are way ahead of the prime minister. Many are already going it alone. For example:

- Kaliningrad, an enclave on the Baltic, has announced a state of emergency and is refusing to send tax payments to Moscow, while appealing for help to Poland and Germany.
- St. Petersburg says it will fend for itself and organize food supplies for schools and hospitals.
- In Murmansk, the governor is appealing to Norway, Sweden, and Finland for humanitarian aid.
- In Vladivostok, where the provincial governor has been going his own way for some years now, water, electricity, and heat have been cut off and the Russian Far Eastern fleet is running short of food.
- In Keremovo, the coal-mining province of Siberia, the governor has told protesting miners to disregard the Moscow bureaucrats, or as he put it, "What are they to us?"

Russia is not the monolith it appears on the map. In fact it's composed of eighty-nine provinces and regions, and before this crisis is all over, a number of them may be half-way to independence.

Moscow is suffering its own peculiar depression. It was the center of the prosperity bubble, and now it has become the first casualty. Russia's experiment with capitalism attracted hundreds of Western businesses: investment houses, factories, fast-food chains, tax and law offices, import-export firms. Some of the new business-immigrants came here simply to try to make a fast buck. Some of them, like the McDonald's restaurant chain, have invested for the long haul. And some entrepreneurs came here not only to make a profit, but also because they were fond of Russia and the Russians, and wanted to help them become truly free and prosperous someday.

They built stores and offices and peopled them with the best and brightest of the young Russians; the smart, energetic, and ambitious Russians I'd watched at work in the financial houses, in the computer stores, and at the new advertising agencies and television stations. They are the beginnings of the middle class that Russia has never really had, sixteen million people, and they'd just begun to enjoy life. Now there's a serious question about the future of Western investment here. And the future of Russia's nascent middle class seems grim indeed.

A good many of those Western business firms have gone broke. A good many more are closing up, afraid they will go broke. Thousands of professionals from New York and London and Paris and Berlin who came here with some dreams and the best of intentions are quietly going home, including a young American couple we know. They've been working in the Moscow business community for years. They're fluent in the language and most of their friends are Russian. They didn't make a fortune here and never expected to. They wanted to help Russia develop a world-class economy. But they've got a child now and they've decided to move back to New York. "We've got our son to think of," said the woman. "I suppose it's time for the two of us to grow up. There's a future here, I guess, but I've realized now that it's a very long way off. Too long for us."

The foreigners at least have someplace to go and start over. Russia's new middle class is stuck. And it's suffering something it never experienced: unemployment. By government estimate, three hundred thousand young Russian professionals have lost their jobs in Moscow alone, most of them fired by Western firms that have cut back or cut out altogether. At one office, workers said that when they returned from summer vacation they found voice-mail messages informing them they'd been terminated. Those who still have jobs often aren't getting paid anymore. An estimated one-third of American companies report they've simply deferred salary payments to their employees, indefinitely.

And the suddenly jobless can't expect much help from the government. Unemployment benefits, when they're available, amount to about $40 a month.

Some of those American companies that came to Moscow to help feed and water the new Russian middle class are also facing some uncertainties. The Dunkin' Donuts shop down the boulevard from our office is still doing business, with a much-reduced clientele. Nonetheless, the manager, David O'Hara, considers himself lucky. He imported a four-month supply of doughnut fixings just before the crash. But he's not sure what he'll do come winter when prices for importing food will be much higher. And he's most worried about his Russian employees. "They all work so hard," he says. "They save 80 percent of their salaries to help their families. And many of them put it in the Russian banks and now they've lost everything."

Montana Coffee, which has a store down by the Kremlin, has been selling high-quality coffee products here since 1991. But with inflation, things are getting complicated for the manager, Alexander Malchik. "Our biggest problem is we don't know how to price our product," he told me. "And we can't rely on the local banks. So we don't know if we will ever get paid by our customers."

There are two Starlight Diners in Moscow, replicas of real old-fashioned diners that you might have seen a half-century ago along U.S. Highway 1 in New Jersey. For several years they've been a favorite hangout for American expats and Russians alike. Jo Jo Massimiani came over here from Miami a couple of years ago to get the Starlights started, train the staff, and decorate the walls with Elvis Presley photos and Route 66 signs. She presides over things like a combination Pearl Mesta and Mother Superior. And until this summer, she and her partners were making a pretty good living. But business is down. Some of her best customers have flown west, and the others can't afford even the "budget-burger" meals she's advertising. "We're prepared to ride out this storm," she says bravely. I wonder whether she'll be back in Miami this time next year. *[Editor's Note: The Starlight Diners managed to weather the hard times, and at this writing, are both still in business and turning a profit, as is Montana Coffee. Dunkin' Donuts finally folded, to the chagrin of Moscow's new coffee-and-donuts addicts.]*

Two questions have perplexed me as I've followed this grim tapestry of current events in Russia. How do Russians manage to endure one calamity after another? And why don't they do something about it?

I'm still not certain I know the answer to the first question, but I do know Russians have a lot of experience in enduring calamities; two world wars, a famine, and a totalitarian terror being only the most recent. Part of the answer is in the language. When Russians talk about buying something, they use a word that really means "to get or obtain," in other words, "trade" or "barter." There are estimates that fully three-fourths of the entire Russian economy consists of barter. A carpenter will do some work on his neighbor's house if his neighbor, a mechanic, will fix up his car. The shoe factory will trade some shoes to the butcher for some meat to distribute to the shoe workers. The Russians call this *beznalichniie denghi,* or noncash money. No rubles involved. No taxes, either. It's part of the *tyenevikii,* or gray economy, a shadow economy that operates side by side with the "real" ruble economy. The ruble economy, of course, is the only one the government can tax, so the government never collects much in the way of taxes, and thus is always running in the red. The ruble economy is also the one the government economists must use to take the economic pulse of the nation and draw up the budgets. As a result, the economists are always about 75 percent wrong.

Part of the answer you'll find late every summer at the edge of the cities or in the countryside all over Russia. The land is alive with families out harvesting their *"dacha* plots." You don't even have to have a *dacha,* a country shack, usually, to have a *"dacha* plot." It's a little piece of land, much less than an acre, where Russians spend the warm months growing their vegetable crop for the cold months to come, like so many million squirrels storing up a nut supply. The Russians have been doing this home gardening for half a millennium, when the potato first arrived from the Western Hemisphere. Ever since, the potato has been Russia's survival food.

Not far outside Moscow one weekend afternoon, we found Aleksander Dalkin and his family—Mom and the two boys—harvesting their little potato patch. The Dalkins live in Moscow, but they drive out here every weekend from April to October to tend the potatoes and the other crops that they'll put up in the root cellar. This has been a bad year for potatoes. First it was too dry, and then too rainy. Even so, there's enough for the four of them to make do until spring. "We'll be okay," says Mr. Dalkin. "Potato soup, potato pancakes, some squash pies. And you can still buy *kasha* [crushed grain kernels] pretty cheap. Or pick wild mushrooms. Some of our neighbors gave up their plots and put their faith in the supermarkets. That'll teach them."

Not everybody's as confident as the Dalkin family about the months to come. Half of those Russians questioned in a recent opinion poll said the economic crisis has now made their own situation "So much worse that it is not clear how we will live."

The answer to the second question, Why on earth do Russians placidly put up with this state of affairs, is more difficult. Why don't they ever say, "I'm mad as hell and I'm not going to take it anymore!?" Instead, they take it. Why? These, after all, are the great-

A face of rural poverty. (© Jonathan Sanders)

grandchildren of the Kronstadt sailors and the Red Guards who occupied the Winter Palace in Petrograd in 1917. Russian history is the story of one bloody peasant uprising after another. Alexander Pushkin, Russia's beloved eighteenth-century poet, best described it: "A Russian revolt. Senseless. And Merciless."

It's not as if Russians aren't angry at what's happened to them, and furious at their politicians . . . and the West . . . and Washington

. . . and NATO . . . and the Jews . . . and anybody else they can think to blame. They've protested. They've struck. They've marched. But not once have they gone to the barricades. No shots have been fired. Everyone always goes home before any blood is shed.

It was no different on this October 7, when the Communist Party and labor leaders called for a nationwide one-day strike and protest to demand back pay and pensions, among other things. The organizers hoped to get ten million people out on the streets, across Russia's eleven time zones. They got little more than a million. In Moscow about one hundred thousand people demonstrated for a couple of hours in front of the Kremlin, a protest which had been carefully choreographed with the authorities, as always. It was picturesque enough, with hundreds of red Communist banners and portraits of Lenin, and the customary harangues from the fellows with the bullhorns. It was noisy and very peaceful. By evening, the streets were empty, and the city workers were picking up the empty vodka bottles. The next day everybody was back at work.

Perhaps it's the vodka. If you drink enough of it, you won't care that you're broke and hungry, and as the mortality figures indicate, millions of Russian men literally drink themselves to death. Maybe it's vodka, not religion, that's really the opiate of the people.

Maybe it's the herd instinct developed by almost a century of totalitarian repression; if you keep your head down, it won't get chopped off. But the Russians I've come to know are anything but sheeplike. Yet there is a very human habit, in times of trouble, to just go on as if nothing had happened. The Russians say, "Sow rye, even if you are going to die." We might say, "Keep on truckin'." You do the best you can.

But Grigory Yavlinksy, who is the head of the Yabloko Party, the Democratic faction, in the Duma, has the best explanation that I've heard, if there is an explanation. Simply put, Russians are afraid—of themselves.

"Russian history the past eighty years is drenched in blood," he explained to me. "Such an enormous amount of blood was shed that it has made the Russian people reluctant to repeat this history. That is the root of their patience. When I talk to my voters, they say, 'Our grandparents and parents and we ourselves know the meaning of this bloodshed, and what it means to be oppressed. We don't want to repeat it. We will be patient enough to find a peaceful way out of this. We will never forget what the politicians have done to us, but we will be patient while we seek a solution, because we all understand what terrible things have gone before.'"

Which, I suppose, is why they didn't join that nationwide protest in the village of Sokolniki. It's three hours' drive from Moscow, in a mining area, and virtually everybody's out of work since the mine closed down. They don't need Sokolniki's kind of coal anymore. The people we visited on Pushkin Street are living in some old unheated shacks that belong to the mining company. They're squatters. But the mining company looks the other way. And they're getting by on some potatoes they manage to steal from the collective farm down the road.

They're angry, almost desperate on Pushkin Street. Lena Filatova, an unemployed nurse, took us into her kitchen, one room of a two-room shack she shares with her daughter and six other people. She opened the little icebox. "You ask if I have savings?" she asked in disbelief. "Here are my savings. Some pickles and mushrooms. We're living like animals here. No! Even animals live better!"

So why not protest? "You don't understand," they told us on Pushkin Street. "What's the use? It never does any good. The leaders won't listen."

And there were no demonstrations that day in the little town of Donskoi, just down the road. We went over to School Number 12. It's always a good thing to go to a school when you pull into a strange town to talk to people. Schools are full of kids and parents and teachers, so you can always count on lots of opinions and lots of pictures. But there were no kids this day at School Number 12. No parents. No teachers. The teachers stopped teaching last week. They're on strike. Nobody's paid their $30-a-month salaries since last spring.

We did find one teacher. Miss Potapova was tidying up her classroom for the day when, she hopes, school resumes. She said she was ashamed of herself. She's been teaching history to the children of Donskoi for twenty years and she never missed a day of class.

"But we had to strike," Miss Potapova said. "For the sake of the children. Somebody has to notice. The children are hungry and cold now when they come to school. They are shivering. They don't have enough clothes." She was weeping now. "Don't they understand in Moscow? Will you tell them? Tell them they are killing our children. They're killing our Russia. They are killing the future."

And it shows in the numbers. The State Statistics Committee has just announced that in the first half of this year, Russia's population dropped by 245,800. It's now 146.5 million and falling. Russians are dying, or leaving, faster than they are being born.

That's the saddest silent protest of them all.

chapter 43

Pieces
of the Bell
(December 1998)

Not the least of all the crises that Russians have
had to face since the fall of Communism is an identity
crisis.

In the simplest sense, they know who they are, of course. They
inhabit a certain space on the planet, they speak a common language, and they share a common history. In fact, today's Russia is
more "Russian" than at any time in the past two hundred years. In
the old Soviet Union, ethnic Russians comprised barely half the population. In today's Russia, shorn of so many of its former Soviet
republics, four out of five people are ethnic Russian.

But where does Russia belong in today's world? And what does
being "Russian" mean? It's a question that doesn't seem to trouble
the other parts of what once was the so-called Evil Empire. Cubans
and Poles and Czechs and Azeris and Uzbeks and Latvians all seem
to have a firm fix on themselves, now that they're no longer required
to pay heed to Moscow. They've enjoyed cleansing the Russian-ness
out of their systems. Even Bosnians can now celebrate who they are.
They are not Croats, and they are not Serbs.

But Russians are understandably perplexed. Their nation has
now been reduced to the size it was three centuries ago. The population has been reduced by more than a third. They're no longer subjects of the tsars. They're no longer subjects of the Soviet Union. How
can they be citizens of a real democracy when, as one Russian soci-
ologist has observed, most Russians take the attitude that, "Things

don't depend on you. Even though you vote, people in power will do what they want."

How can they be capitalists when the means of production are run by robber barons, criminals, corrupt bureaucrats, and politicians? Karl Marx seems oddly prescient these days. His *Communist Manifesto* of a century ago reads as if he were describing Russia today: "All fixed, fast-frozen relationships, with their train of venerable ideas and opinions, are swept away. All new-formed ones become obsolete before they can ossify. All that is solid melts into air."

Russians are yearning for some kind of raison d'etre that doesn't melt into thin air. Boris Yeltsin noticed it during his presidential campaign two years ago. He said Russia needed a national idea, a "Russian Idea." So last year he set up a commission to come up with a "Russian Idea."

The commission, the object of a great deal of editorial ridicule here, solemnly studied the matter and this year published the results of its labors. But it didn't produce a "Russian Idea." Which isn't surprising, I suppose. Americans have been arguing over exactly what constitutes the "American Dream" for a couple of hundred years.

I'd like to offer a suggestion. How about a "Civil Society"? Building a civil society in Russia would be a good place to start. Nowadays, "civil society" is one of those terms that gets tossed around quite a bit. Building a "civil society" has become the rationale for everything from gun control, to antistrike legislation, to a single-payer national health plan.

John Locke, the philosopher, defined it as a society with "a standing rule to live by." He noted that the civil laws of ancient Rome were engraved on stone tablets and erected in the middle of the city. They were laws laid down by the people of Rome, agreed upon, and therefore respected by all. As Locke foresaw, democracies simply don't work unless there is a basic practical agreement among most of the citizenry about how things are supposed to work. Democracies require a book of directions that everyone understands and has agreed to follow, and a willingness to compromise when parts of the book need to be rewritten from time to time. That's what's been missing in Russia the past few years, along with some other things like peace and prosperity and justice. How do you go about building a civil society? In fact, there are some places in Russia where construction is already underway.

Not in Moscow, though, nor in St. Petersburg. Not in the big cities, either. To build a civil society here, you have to start small, and preferably in a place with some experience in civil societies. Someplace like Novgorod, an overnight train ride northwest of Moscow.

It's a city of 240,000, about the size of Raleigh, North Carolina. But Novgorod can boast of a lot more history than Raleigh. Next year will be its 1,140th birthday.

Russians regard Kiev, even though today it's in the Ukraine, as the Mother of Rus, the Russian people. In the early part of this millennium, Kiev's government was medieval, centralized, and authoritarian. Things were run by its princes. Novgorodans regard their city as the Father of Rus. In a recent visit, President Yeltsin promised to officially restore its ancient name, *Veliky Novgorod*, Novgorod the Great. "Who can stand against God and Lord Novgorod the Great?" was its proud and ancient motto. And great Novgorod was, in those times. It was Russia's window to the West, centuries before Peter the Great founded St. Petersburg. Novgorod traded with the Germans of the Hanseatic League, the Poles, the Swedes, the Venetians, everywhere from the Baltic to the Urals. Its currency was German gold coins. The door to its beautiful St. Sophia Cathedral was imported from Byzantium, and Novgorod's architects invented the onion-shaped gold dome to crown it. Its merchants kept careful records on birchbark paper. St. Nicholas, that patron saint of commerce, was Novgorod's patron saint. Novgorod's streets were paved by the eleventh century, long before those in Paris.

Kiev was an oligarchy, but Novgorod was a republic for four centuries. And not just a republic, but about as democratic as you could get in those years. Neighborhoods elected representatives to the *veche*, or town council, something on the order of a big Vermont town meeting. The *veche* was called to order by the ringing of a huge bronze bell in the city center. And any citizen could ring it if he had a good reason. There was always a prince of Novgorod, who ran day-to-day affairs. But it wasn't a hereditary job. And the prince could be hired and fired at the pleasure of the *veche*, as Novgorod princes routinely were. Talk about a civil society.

It didn't last. In Moscow, the tsars were jealous of Novgorod. In the late fifteenth and early sixteenth centuries, Tsar Ivan III and later his son, Ivan the Terrible, got up an army and terminated Novgorod. The Ivans burned much of the old city, sparing the Kremlin and the cathedrals. They slaughtered sixty thousand people, it was said, mostly the poor people. The rich merchant families, about forty thousand in all, they took back to Moscow. And to make sure there would be no more nonsense about a *veche*, they put the bell on a cart to wheel that back to Moscow, too. Legend has it that the bell fell off the cart during the trip and shattered into a thousand pieces, which the Novgorod survivors retrieved and kept in their homes. However, some modern-day scholars insist that's an old wives' tale, and that the bell actually wound up in the Uspennsky Cathedral in Moscow's Kremlin. I went to the Uspennsky Cathedral once to try to find Novgorod's bell. There are lots of bells in the Uspennsky Cathedral. Bells from Kiev. Bells from Pskov. Bells from Kazan. But no bell from Novgorod. I found the curator. "Where's the Novgorod Bell?" I asked. "What Novgorod Bell?" said she. "The one they used to call the *veche*." "What's a *veche*?" she asked.

Novgorod eventually rebuilt and became a provincial backwater, paying reluctant homage to Moscow. The Nazis savaged Novgorod during World War II, but after the war, even Moscow realized Novgorod's importance to Russian history and financed another reconstruction. All those centuries, Novgorod never completely lost its personality. Even in the latter years of the Soviet Union, Novgorod remained the least repressive and most tolerant city in the country.

The authorities have tried to keep the old center of Novgorod looking as it did before the Ivans, rather like Colonial Williamsburg in need of a remodeling. There is the old Kremlin, with its red-brick walls set along the Volkhov River, and acres of lovely parks. The gilt domes of St. Sophia and the other cathedrals flash in the late-afternoon sun. And inside, the icons on the walls are quite unlike those in Moscow. There's a fluid sensuality about them that's much more West than East. If you have a few minutes, you can go and see where Fyodor Dostoyevsky lived.

Outside Novgorod's center, the scene has more in common with the rest of Russia. There are blocks and blocks of those hideous Soviet-style apartments in various states of disrepair. But the public streets are cleaner than in most Russian cities, and there's a new fleet of German buses to get people where they're going. Novgorod's poor but proud.

What makes Novgorod unique, and what makes its future so promising, isn't so evident. But if you look carefully, you'll see signs of it. There are several industrial parks around town. Over here, there's a German fiberglass plant. Over there, a factory making truck trailers. Nearby, a franchise subsidiary of Kodak has just hired one hundred new workers. And not far away, Cadbury Schweppes has built a $120 million facility to start making chocolate. IBM is here. And Sprint is working on the phone system. There are now 180 foreign companies doing business here. They've invested more than $500 million in the Novgorod region, the highest per capita foreign investment in all of Russia.

What's made Novgorod, of all places, so attractive to Western money? In a word, security. If you've got a couple of hours, Prof. Valery N. Zelenin, of Novgorod State University, will tell you why.

Novgorod State has sixteen thousand students and has founded one of the first schools of business administration in the country. Zelenin, a gregarious sort with a neatly trimmed white beard and wearing a bright-plaid sport jacket, looks as if he belongs at an Elks Club luncheon. In fact, he has been one of the pioneers in helping to make Novgorod safe for other people's money.

"Western investors feel comfortable here," he says. "People in Novgorod know the language of investment, and what it takes to make Western businessmen and bankers feel at home." It helps that Zelenin literally speaks that language. His English and German have just the trace of a Russian accent.

Any Westerner who's tried to do business in the rest of Russia the past few years would find Novgorod a kind of Valhalla. And just like home.

There's not much in the way of red tape. A dozen different local and regional taxes have been replaced by one real-estate tax. And there's a tax-holiday program for new investors. Cadbury Schweppes, for example, doesn't have to pay any taxes here until 2001.

And there's actually a real-estate market now. New regulations allow people to hold title to land, to buy it and sell it. That includes foreigners. It's a real revolution in a region which had a thousand-year tradition of murky land titles, all of which eventually wound up in the hands of the old Soviet government. The result is that more than three-fourths of the old state-owned enterprises have been privatized, even the big production center for military electronics.

So if you're a foreigner, and you want to do business here, you can come in and buy your land, get title to it, take your tax break, and start making money, all by yourself. There are no requisite Russian middle-men to take a cut of your profits or, as so often happens, to simply take over once you've made a success of things.

And you can depend on honest bookkeeping. Novgorod's brought in Arthur Anderson & Co. to set up a system of international accounting standards. It's working with law firms in the United States and elsewhere in the West to set up a new legal system for business contracts, to be adjudicated by honest courts.

Moreover, Novgorod now has a plan to decide where everything belongs: factories and offices over here, residential neighborhoods over there, commercial districts in that part. With the help of the Urban Institute in America, Novgorod has created the first set of zoning laws anywhere in Russia. That gives investors confidence in knowing exactly where they can set up shop, without worrying about some future changes by capricious local bureaucrats.

You have to have lived in the rest of Russia for awhile to realize the novelty of something like a zoning law. In Soviet times, cities grew with shopping, residential, and industrial areas and schools and food stores thrown together, often obliterating historical districts, with no particular logic and at the whim of authorities. In Novgorod nowadays, local folks can come to zoning hearings and complain "not in my back yard," and oftentimes the bureaucrats will actually listen to them. In Novgorod, you're now allowed to be a "Nimby," just like folks in Columbus and Spokane.

There's crime and official corruption here, as elsewhere in Russia, but it's nowhere near as pervasive as in Moscow or other cities. Most businesses still have to pay somebody off for protection, but it's usually a manageable amount. The new legal and tax systems are making it more difficult for local officials to make arbitrary decisions, so bureaucrats who are tempted to take a bribe have less to sell. And, of course, Novgorod is small pickings for the really big crime lords. The financial rewards in the larger cities are much greater.

Finally, Novgorod has valuable human capital that works cheaply. It has thousands of well-educated, well-trained workers who either lost their jobs or have been waiting years for their paychecks since their state-owned enterprises folded up. And since it's still almost impossible to move somewhere else in Russia in search of a better job, they're available.

But it's not just the economy that's changing in Novgorod. They're trying to change the political system, too, or rather, resurrect it. A set of new laws have created neighborhood associations with a lot of local autonomy. Condominium regulations allow Novgorodans to buy their old Soviet apartments cheaply. And they're responsible for the upkeep, and the neighborhood's upkeep, too. It's a sort of great big co-op board, and it is gradually changing attitudes about taking care of things. If you want to clean up your vestibule or fix the elevator, you get a bunch of people together and do it yourselves. Don't wait for the government maintenance fellow to show up some day. He won't. He doesn't exist anymore. In short, it's the beginning of bottom-up government in Novgorod, instead of top-down. Not unlike the old *veche* of half a millennium ago. Except for the bell, of course.

Novgorod has managed to accomplish all this with a lot of help from the West, and the United States in particular. There's a constant stream of American advisers doing short-term duty in Novgorod, courtesy of the Agency for International Development, or one nongovernmental organization or another. This may turn out to be the kind of place those American economic advisers of a decade ago hoped that Russia itself would become by now: a fully democratic, market-oriented, prosperous member of the newly globalized world community.

Novgorod's done this despite Moscow, or at least because Moscow has decided to look the other way. The region's turned itself into the equivalent of a free economic zone, something that's anathema to the old Soviet bosses who still run the bureaucracy and the parliament in Moscow. Perhaps like the Moscow crime lords, the Moscow bureaucrats figure Novgorod is small potatoes. At any rate, in the case of the Novgorod experiment, the Kremlin has decided to practice laissez-faire, and Novgorod, for now, will settle for that.

If Novgorod is the Father of Rus, the father of today's Novgorod experiment is Mikhail Prussak, governor of the Novgorod region. He's a short, fastidious man of thirty-eight who dresses in conservative suits and sports a tidy mustache. You have the feeling he's one of those fellows who dress for bed in pressed pajamas with a handkerchief in their breast pocket. There's an eager intensity about him, and when he speaks, ideas tumble from his lips, expressed with the enthusiasm of a Baptist preacher. Except that Mikhail Prussak grew up a Communist, with an important job in the local Communist youth organization.

He was running a collective farm when Boris Yeltsin reached down and plucked him out of nowhere to run Novgorod. That was in 1991, right after Yeltsin took charge in Moscow. In 1995, when Novgorod held its first regional election, Mikhail Prussak was elected governor with 85 percent of the vote. Yeltsin is Prussak's patron, which may explain why the Novgorod experiment has been allowed to develop. But it works both ways. Prussak's office allows him a seat in Russia's upper house of parliament, where he spends most of his time lobbying for more regional autonomy.

Most days, you'll find Governor Prussak at his office in the House of Government here. It's another one of those Soviet leftovers: a five-story Stalinist structure with an ornate hammer-and-sickle facade, flanked by a large park leading to the old Kremlin. The sculptured face of Lenin still stares down upon visitors from a plaque above the main entrance.

Prussak's office is on the second floor, in a huge meeting room with a ceiling that's almost out of sight. The only furnishings are a vast conference table in the center and a desk at the far end flanked by a Russian flag. The only wall decoration is a plaque from the U.S. Chamber of Commerce.

"Unlike a lot of Russians, I have wonderful memories of the Soviet days," he says. "I remember honoring Yuri Gagarin, our first cosmonaut. I was five or six then. I remember the first TV sets. That was in the late sixties, and the Soviet Union was a superpower. The world listened to us. Life seemed good. But there was too much censorship. If the authorities then had conducted a dialogue with the society they would have realized that though the people lived well, they wanted to live better. Even the average person knew that what wealth we had was coming from trading our country's natural resources away, and second, that this money was only going to benefit a privileged few. A talented, creative person could only receive the money the state allowed him. So nobody had an incentive for a better life."

I asked Prussak how he'd been put in charge of Novgorod. "I still don't know," he said. "I couldn't believe it when Yeltsin picked me out. I suppose they were in a hurry in the Kremlin and there wasn't an obvious choice. I'd met Gaidar [Yuri Gaidar, Yeltsin's first economic reformer] once or twice, and maybe that was it. I only knew about tractors and fertilizer and production quotas. I didn't know anything about government or politics or economics, so I went back to school part-time and got a Ph.D. in economics. Everything else I learned on the job."

One of the advantages Prussak has in Novgorod that Boris Yeltsin does not have in Moscow is a legislature that will do his bidding. "There are no Reds or Whites in the Novgorod council," Prussak is fond of saying. "There are only Novgorodans."

"We work together," he explained in an interview with me. "We try to settle our differences here in my office and in the council before the battles become public. We've made mistakes, but we all share responsibility for them. No finger-pointing. In Moscow, all the parties care about is politics. They have no ideas for the economy, they don't care. Historically in Russia, there has always been only one party, the party of power. In our region, therefore, we have only one party, the party of power. But we practice a constructive dialogue with our citizens, and that is why we do not have a formal opposition. I personally go live on TV to explain the city budget every year and people can ask me questions directly. They can see what is being done and start to understand that the authorities will not change the rules of the game. On the other hand, if we hear that the people have other opinions or suggestions, we can make changes. But it's necessary to understand that the rules are the same for every citizen, including the governor."

Most people in Novgorod are of the opinion that what success Novgorod has had is mostly due to its governor's Moscow connection. I wondered what will happen here when Mikhail Prussak goes on to bigger and better things. What if some future leaders of Novgorod's "party of power" decide to *not* have a constructive dialogue with the people? And how did Governor Prussak's benevolent authoritarianism square with my romantic notions of the people power of the old *veche*? I wondered silently, because the governor was still talking.

"I believe the principle of private property will change everything here," he said. "There is a difference in the way people start to think; one attitude if this is your apartment and another if it belongs to the state. Private property is in my blood. My father went to prison for ten years under the Soviet regime for owning land. When I ran the collective farm, I always wondered, 'How can you get people to work if they don't own anything?' They kept breaking things. They'd build a road in the village and then drive heavy tractors down it and smash the concrete. A new tractor lasted less than a year because no one kept it up. So now, today, in Novgorod, the state doesn't own much of anything."

Is there a "Novgorod Model" for the rest of Russia, I wondered? "Not if Moscow has anything to say about it," Prussak replied icily. "It is a paradox, but the world learned about the Novgorod region with the help of the Americans, not from the Russian authorities. We have awards from the Council of Europe, from the Kennan Institute, but not a single honor from the government of Russia! I want enough time until the day I can go on TV and tell my people that from now on the Novgorod region is completely independent from the center and we are self-sufficient. For that moment I would give anything!"

That moment, if it ever comes, is sometime off. Novgorod suffered the same economic pains as the rest of Russia when the crash came this summer, although its effects were not as pronounced here as elsewhere. Novgorod still needs its rubles from the Kremlin, and is only getting about one-fifth of its due. The city finances are so shaky that if Novgorod ever tried to sell municipal bonds, Moody's would turn up its nose. The Cadbury Schweppes plant is in trouble because, it turns out, Russians prefer the local Russian chocolate to the kind they're making. Didn't anybody back there do a market survey?

Yet Novgorod appears to be doing all the right things to transform itself. Today it may still look like a caterpillar. Tomorrow it might well become a butterfly. I thought back to that day Betsy and I visited Governor Nazdratenko in Vladivostok, now so long ago. Since then, the Primorsky Krai region has become even more of a festering sore in Russia's Far East. Water shortages. Power blackouts. Foreign investment has all but dried up. Governor Nazdratenko's even richer and more powerful than ever. I prefer the way Governor Prussak's doing things.

Before I left the governor's office, I had one last question. "Whatever happened to the Novgorod Bell?" Prussak looked absolutely mystified. "What bell?" he asked. Mikhail Prussak is patently a man of tomorrow, not yesterday.

I made one more stop on my way out of town, at Professor Zelenin's suggestion. There's a new little shopping gallery inside the Beresta Palace Best Western, Novgorod's newest hotel. At the far end of the gallery, I found Vera Kylebyakina, her sister Tanya, and their friend Alexei Godov putting the finishing touches on Novgorod's newest business, the Alpha Graphics shop. It's due to open this month.

Vera is an attractive, bubbly blonde in her thirties, a divorcee with a three-year-old daughter. She came here from Siberia with her former husband, and decided to stay. "I had a job in the mayor's office providing investment opportunities for foreigners, and I always wanted to be my own boss," she said. "So one day I thought, Why don't I provide an investment opportunity for myself? There isn't a decent light printing and graphic firm in the whole region. I could fulfill a need. Now I'm my own boss. I do the books, I do the deliveries, and I sweep the floor," she laughed.

Vera went off to Moscow and St. Petersburg for two weeks of training at the Alpha Graphics franchises there. Then they flew her to Tucson, Arizona, where she spent another month learning business management and planning at the Alpha Graphics home office. The company gave her the start-up money, and she'll pay that back, eventually, out of her profits.

With the Russian economy in shambles, it's a terrible time to start a business. But the fact that Alpha Graphics is footing the bill at the outset, and has deeper pockets than Vera does, gives her a fighting chance. And this, after all, is Novgorod. If she'd been living almost anywhere else in Russia, Vera Kylebyakina would still be working for the government.

On the long overnight train ride back to Moscow, I tried to make sense of what I'd seen and heard in Novgorod, and in this remarkable place called Russia the past few years. My time here was almost over, and I was still ignorant and confused about so much. Not least about the future. But I recalled what a couple of Russians I'd met had told me, Russians who are far wiser than I about these things.

Vladimir Posner, the prodigal son with the New York City accent who came back to Moscow to become a TV talk-show host:

"The real problem today in Russia is that this is a society that doesn't know what to do with its freedom. It really doesn't. And I think it will take at least another thirty years for that to change. Our grandchildren don't know what it is to be afraid. They don't know what it is to have to bow and scrape to the powers-that-be, because you are totally at their mercy. It's the young people in Russia who are not part of this legacy. They are the ones who will truly change this country."

Grigory Yavlinksy, the Democrat in the Duma:

"In Russia we are coming to the end of the end. That is perhaps a good thing. It clears the decks, so to speak, for a new beginning. We have been living in a Potemkin Village for the past several years, a bubble. Despite the corruption, the lying, the dishonesty, the lawlessness, Western investors still came here with their money. Now our bubble has burst. The trick is undone. We have been playing Russian roulette, and we have finally lost. So now we must start again at the beginning and find a new way, a democratic way, with laws that people respect and that are uniformly and justly enforced, with private ownership of property, with a society where people are as good as their word. We must find our way to this civil society. It will be long and it will be difficult. But we must find our way."

As for me, I never did find out what really happened to Novgorod's bell.

Epilogue

T he French have a phrase for it. *Plus ça change, plus c'est la même chose.* The more things change, the more they remain the same. And that's a fairly accurate description of affairs in Russia, not to mention much of the former Evil Empire, in the two years since Betsy and I decamped for home.

Some of the changes have been for the good. The Russian economy, which crashed and burned in 1998, has now begun to rise, Phoenix-like, from the ashes. It has reduced its dependence on foreign imports, mostly out of necessity. Russians are once again spending their rubles on things Russian, from cookies to cars. So the economy could grow by as much as 7 percent this year. If so, this will be Russia's most prosperous year, if I can use that term, since the end of the Soviet era.

Boris Yeltsin's successor, President Vladimir Putin, has turned out to be anything but the weak cipher his critics expected. He's moved quickly and energetically to recover the political power and authority that Yeltsin had lost to Russia's regions. Unlike Yeltsin, Putin can now have his way with the once-recalcitrant Duma. And he's made some attempts to move against at least a few of those boyar-barons who wielded so much influence in the Yeltsin years.

Putin's decided to go his own way in foreign affairs. He's put more distance between Russia and the West, including the United States, while rebuilding old relationships with former client countries like North Korea. He's cozied up to neighbors like China and India, who are as wary as Moscow of the influence of the world's remaining superpower: Us.

And yet, in most respects, the timepiece of history has moved hardly at all for Russia in the interim. In some respects it may be moving backward. Life is not materially better for the vast majority of Russians. The catalog of horrors we remembered remains: a health system falling apart, rampant alcohol and drug abuse, a population that's still shrinking, a persistant crime problem, and a swiftly deteriorating infrastructure. By all accounts, the Russian military is falling apart almost as fast as its roads and railways and factories. And the guerrilla war in Chechnya continues to bleed both nations.

Putin claims he wants to preserve Russia's fledgling democracy, but his actions belie his words. He has moved against several of the media conglomerates, authored new state secrecy policies, and surrounded himself with colleagues from his days as a secret policeman. The security services are enjoying a renaissance. He has shown a fondness for the top-down sort of government that has ruled Russia, in one form or another, for the past ten centuries. Will Tsar Vladimir replace Tsar Boris? The dream that someday in Russia a true civil society will come to be seems more distant now than ever, something that the democratic nations of the globe will ignore at their peril.

Now that Betsy and I have put some time and distance between us and our years in Moscow, these things no longer command our attention. For us, as it is for other Americans, the former Evil Empire is just one more place in a big, untidy world. We have our perspective back. And happily, we still have our memories. Snow falling on birches. The Moscow riverbank dressed in red and green lights for Christmas. The faces of all the people we came to know: grim and gay, gruff and friendly, fearful and resolute. They are Russia's history, and its hope.

Tucson, Arizona
December 2000

Index

ATLANTIC OCEAN

Arctic Circle

Svalbard (Norway)

Zemlya Frantsa Io
(Franz Joseph Land)

NORWAY

North Sea

DENMARK

SWEDEN

FINLAND

Novaya
Zemlya

Barents
Sea

Murmansk

KOLA
PENINSULA

White
Sea

R

Vorkuta

GERMANY

Baltic Sea

Kaliningrad

POLAND

Tallinn

ESTONIA

Riga

Vilnius

LATVIA

LITHUANIA

Novgorod

St. Petersburg

Volga
River

Kirov

U

Ob'
River

MOLDOVA

Minsk

BELARUS

Moscow

Zaraisk

Perm

U
R
A
L

M
O
U
N
T
A
I
N
S

Irtysh
River

Kiev

UKRAINE

Chisinau

Odesa

Sea of
Azov

Volga
River

Ural
River

Omsk

Black Sea

Volgograd

GEORGIA

Tbilisi

Grozny

ARMENIA

Yerevan

Baku

Caspian
Sea

KAZAKHSTAN

Aral
Sea

Baikonur
Cosmodrome

TURKEY

SYRIA

IRAQ

AZERBAIJAN

Astara

TURKMENISTAN

UZBEKISTAN

Tashkent

Almaty

Bishkek

KYRGYZSTAN

IRAN

Ashgabat

Dushanbe

TAJIKISTAN

Persian
Gulf

AFGHANISTAN